**Conversations with
Jerry W. Ward Jr.**

Literary Conversations Series
Monika Gehlawat
General Editor

Conversations with Jerry W. Ward Jr.

Edited by John Zheng

University Press of Mississippi / Jackson

Publication of this book was supported in part by a generous donation from the Community Foundation for Mississippi, in honor of Seetha Srinivasan for her many contributions to CFM and the University Press of Mississippi.

The University Press of Mississippi is the scholarly publishing agency of the Mississippi Institutions of Higher Learning: Alcorn State University, Delta State University, Jackson State University, Mississippi State University, Mississippi University for Women, Mississippi Valley State University, University of Mississippi, and University of Southern Mississippi.

www.upress.state.ms.us

The University Press of Mississippi is a member of the Association of University Presses.

Any discriminatory or derogatory language or hate speech regarding race, ethnicity, religion, sex, gender, class, national origin, age, or disability that has been retained or appears in elided form is in no way an endorsement of the use of such language outside a scholarly context.

Copyright © 2023 by University Press of Mississippi
All rights reserved

First printing 2023
∞

Library of Congress Cataloging-in-Publication Data available

LCCN 2022052911
ISBN 9781496845436 (hardcover)
ISBN 9781496845443 (trade paperback)
ISBN 9781496845450 (epub single)
ISBN 9781496845467 (epub institutional)
ISBN 9781496845474 (PDF single)
ISBN 9781496845481 (PDF institutional)

British Library Cataloging-in-Publication Data available

Works by Jerry W. Ward Jr.

Criticism

Redefining American Literary History (coedited with A. LaVonne Brown Ruoff). New York: Modern Language Association, 1990.

The Cambridge History of African American Literature (coedited with Maryemma Graham). Cambridge: Cambridge University Press, 2011.

The China Lectures: African American Literary and Critical Issues. Wuhan: Central China Normal University Press, 2014.

The Richard Wright Encyclopedia (coedited with Robert Butler). Westport, CT: Greenwood, 2008.

Blogs and other writing, 2011–18. Project on the History of Black Writing, University of Kansas, https://hbw.ku.edu/.

Poetry

Fractal Song: Poems. Boston: Black Widow Press, 2016.

Nonfiction

The Katrina Papers: A Journal of Trauma and Recovery. New Orleans: University of New Orleans Press, 2008.

Anthologies

Black Southern Voices. New York: Meridian, 1992.

Trouble the Water: 250 Years of African American Poetry. New York: Dutton Signet, 1997.

Contents

Introduction   ix

Chronology   xvii

"Reading Race, Reading America": An Interview with Jerry Ward Jr.   3
   Eugene B. Redmond / 1995

"Resonance and Relevance Are Key Terms Here": An Interview with Jerry W. Ward Jr.   16
   Howard Rambsy II / 1999

Interview with Jerry W. Ward Jr.   21
   Kyle G. Dargan / 2006

Interview with Jerry W. Ward Jr.   27
   Joshua Guild / 2006

Jerry W. Ward Jr. Talks about Richard Wright   51
   Eugene B. Redmond / 2007

A Conversation with Jerry W. Ward Jr. on Richard Wright   65
   Diane Williams / 2008

Redefining and Canonizing African American Literature: An Interview with Professor Jerry Ward   76
   Hong Fang / 2010

Black Cultural Defender and Cross-Cultural Advocate: An Interview with Professor Jerry W. Ward Jr.   82
   Zuyou Wang / 2013

Interview with Jerry W. Ward Jr.   92
   Cleophus Thomas Jr. / 2016

The Many Influences of Richard Wright: An Interview with
Jerry W. Ward Jr.   118
   John Zheng / 2017

An Interview with Jerry W. Ward Jr.   131
   Yukuo Wang / 2017

The Septuagenarians' Sankofa Dialogue   153
   Kalamu ya Salaam / 2018

A Scholar Born to Write Poetry: Interview with Jerry W. Ward Jr.   184
   John Zheng / 2019

Cultural Exchanges: An Interview with Jerry W. Ward Jr.   201
   Tian Zhang / 2021

Index   211

Introduction

Conversations with Jerry W. Ward Jr. spans twenty-six years, from 1995 to 2021. As a collection of literary interviews conducted by writers or scholars who are in the know about Ward's scholarship, publication, and academic career, this volume adds an indispensable source to American literature and African American studies.

A highly respected teacher, scholar, editor, and writer with a specialty in African American literature, Ward has been recognized internationally as one of the leading experts on Richard Wright. Ward has published poetry, nonfiction, literary criticism, encyclopedias, and anthologies, including *Fractal Song, The Katrina Papers, The China Lectures: African American Critical and Literary Issues, Trouble the Water: 250 Years of African American Poetry, The Richard Wright Encyclopedia* (with Robert J. Butler), *The Cambridge History of African American Literature* (with Maryemma Graham), among other titles. His many awards include the Public Humanities Scholar Award from the Mississippi Humanities Council, the Daryl Cumber Dance Award for Lifetime Achievement from the College Language Association, the Thad Cochran Humanities Achievement Award, the Richard Wright Literary Excellence Award from the Natchez Literary and Cinema Celebration, and the Reginald Martin Award for Excellence in Criticism from PEN Oakland. Ward is a distinguished professor emeritus of English and African world studies at Dillard University in New Orleans and former chair and Lawrence Durgin Professor of Literature at Tougaloo College in Jackson, Mississippi.

Ward is an independent literary scholar and critic who demonstrates unique critical thinking about African American culture, tradition, and history. He points out that scholars in African American literature confront "a *surplus of postmodern options* for dealing with an always expanding body of work." He believes that constructing literary history leads to "more powerful, thoughtful, and practical forms of knowledge" and "a much clearer understanding of continuity and change within the traditions of African American literature."[1]

Ward's thinking about literary history is significant. In our discussion of the function of literature, we can explore a broader sphere. We can dig into history, culture, tradition, and race. Ward states in his introduction to Richard Wright's autobiography, *Black Boy*, that its "continuing value" engages us "to use autobiography to think about how our lives are shaped by law and custom, by ethnic encounters and interracial negotiations, by desire and psychological defeat and intrepidity."[2] This value also engages us in a historical discussion about the South, Jim Crow laws, and the existential meaning of human beings. In 2014, Ward published *The China Lectures: African American Literary and Critical Issues*, which presents his insightful ideas about literary history, cultural literacy, and current studies in African American literature.

Conversations with Jerry W. Ward Jr. offers an account of Ward's impromptu intelligence and thoughtful responses regarding literature, literary criticism, teaching, writing, experience, civil rights, Black aesthetics, race, and culture. With this broad perspective, we encounter Ward not just as an esteemed and intelligent professor, writer, and scholar but as a dignified and modest human. His charming personality glimmers through the moveable feast of these interviews with such images as a poet, mentor, intellectual, and proud child of his parents.

The interviews are arranged chronologically, beginning with one conducted by Eugene B. Redmond, a noted poet and professor and the editor of *Drumvoices Revue*, during a visit to Jackson, Mississippi, in April 1995. Redmond asks Ward about being a purveyor and conveyor of literature, the characterization of the 1960s, contemporary literary criticism, teaching, and writing. These questions open a door for us to see Ward as a writer, thinker, civil rights activist, critic, and educator. But in the deep core of his heart, Ward regards teaching as his top priority:

> I hope that what we begin to talk about seriously in the profession is—for us, in Black studies—how do we help these undergraduates to develop a very strong sense of why you talk about ideas, whether it's literature, or you talk about what they seem to be committed to—rap, or whatever, you're going to critique—how is this a part of social responsibility, as well as showing them that you have to have some real analytical skills. You have to have some skills in handling literature [. . .] you need to look at the words [. . .] when you talk about the *soulular* nature of things, that orality, you know, making people aware of language in its multiple possibilities—*that* should be what we do.

Ward is a devoted intellectual who has challenged numerous students at home and abroad through academic learning, critical thinking, and scholarly writing.

The next interview was conducted by Howard Rambsy II in November 1999. Rambsy, one of Ward's former students at Tougaloo and now a distinguished research professor at Southern Illinois University, focuses on Ward's introduction to *Black Boy*, which serves as an important guide to understanding Wright's autobiography. Rambsy's interview offers us a window into Ward's critical mind. Ward regards his introduction not as a platform to show him as an authority on Wright but as an opportunity to introduce the text of a fellow Mississippian whose early life as an African American male, in Ward's words, is "so akin to my own at a psychological level." Ward also feels that it is his obligation as a Black scholar to remind us "that the scars of racism cannot be hidden by way of cosmetic surgery."

In 2008, Ward published *The Katrina Papers: A Journal of Trauma and Recovery*, an autobiographic record that offers insights into history, spirituality, and race issues as well as Ward's observations on life, anger, and grief prompted by the destructive hurricane. His attitude toward the aftermath of Hurricane Katrina, as expressed in a 2006 interview by Kyle G. Dargan, a professor and award-winning poet from American University, is that "I had to try to deal, in some way or other, with that frustration for myself. And the only out I had was to write." *The Katrina Papers* shows the emotional revelations that have strengthened his spiritual mind.

In another 2006 interview by Joshua Guild, a scholar in history and African American studies at Princeton University, Ward talks more about the damage to New Orleans and Dillard University, about teaching and learning experiences in the difficult times, and about the confidence he, his community, his colleagues and students, and his university regained from dealing with those difficulties. Ward also eloquently talks of the hopes and future of the community, people, music, and city. Unlike many other African American scholars, Ward has spent his entire career teaching at historically Black colleges, which he sees as his way of giving back to the community of people. In the interview, Ward asks a thought-provoking question: "Why is it we say historically Black and we never say historically white?" He thinks that there is a paradox in the identification issues, "You may always in certain ways be able to project the identity as the so-called historically Black institution because you're going back to matters of your origin, but your day-to-day practice may have a different kind of identity because it's much more a part of what is going on in the twenty-first century."

The next two interviews in this volume concern Richard Wright. Redmond conducted his second interview with Ward in 2007 when Ward spoke at Southern Illinois University. In this interview, Ward talks about his first reading of Wright while in college, Wright's fascination with films and novels, his fellow writers Langston Hughes and James Baldwin, and the Wright centennial. Ward vividly describes meeting Baldwin one afternoon on the Tougaloo campus: "I was petrified. I had seen pictures of him, but I hadn't realized what his eyes did to people. When James Baldwin looked at you, he wasn't looking *at* you; he was looking *through* you, or so I felt. So I was like transfixed across from him in this room, just hanging onto his words and afraid to say anything." The next interview is a radio talk between Ward and Diane Williams, a noted storyteller and at the time the arts industry director at the Mississippi Arts Commission, focusing on Wright's early education in Mississippi, his legacy as an African American writer, and activities organized to celebrate the Richard Wright centennial in Mississippi and at the Natchez Literary and Cinema Celebration Conference, for which Ward served avid supporter and adviser.

Four other interviews in the collection were conducted by Chinese scholars. In 2009, Ward was invited to go to China as the keynote speaker at a national conference on African American literature I organized with a US Embassy grant I received while I was a Fulbright Scholar in Wuhan. During the conference, Hong Fang, a professor of English at Nanjing University, interviewed Ward on the canon of ethnic American literature and the anthologies of African American literature used as teaching texts. Ward has subsequently returned to China many times to teach and lecture on American literature. He has been awarded the titles of distinguished overseas professor (2011–14) by the Chinese Ministry of Education and honorary professor (2015–17) by Central China Normal University. Zuyou Wang visited Ward in New Orleans in 2013 and conducted an interview that features Ward as "a bridge between Chinese and American academic circles" who "tries to promote cross-cultural discussions that are very necessary in the twenty-first century." In 2017 Yukuo Wang, a professor of English at Nanjing University of Posts and Telecommunications, conducted a lengthy interview of Ward that touched on the issues of race, Black Arts, gender, the civil rights movement, African American fiction, drama, and literary theory. The piece highlights not only Ward's scholarly knowledge but also his insightful observations regarding racial issues. Ward points out that "race is an extremely problematic idea, but race or a reasonable facsimile thereof can be located in the construction of many literatures throughout the world"; "what has changed with regard to late twentieth-century and early twenty-first-century literary criticism is the choice of seeing or not seeing the importance of race in literary analysis and interpretation." Finally, Tian Zhang, a professor of

English at Central China Normal University, spoke with Ward in 2021 about the cultural exchanges he has brought to Chinese universities and on experiences in and impressions of China. The positive responses Ward's lectures there have received demonstrate the country's strong interest in African American literature, but he found scant library resources for research and teaching. To nurture this interest and foster a positive connection between Chinese and American scholars, Ward has helped establish the African American Research Network to enable the exchange of ideas.

In 2016, Alabama attorney Cleophus Thomas interviewed Ward about his life as a man of letters; his role as an anthology editor; his views about culture as evidence of civilization; his effort to find a genuine voice as a chief purveyor, curator, and advocate of African American culture; and his dedication to the study of Wright. Ward straightforwardly declares that contemporary Americans make little investment "in trying to understand what it means to be an American": "We have a tremendous vein of anti-intellectualism that seems to be a part of the changing definition of what it is to be an American. To be an American is to not be interested in other languages. To be an American is to be suspicious of foreign cultures and of anyone who has any respect for foreign cultures." This assertion reveals an aspect of Ward's critical thinking about culture as well as his international mind.

Ward's 2018 dialogue with Kalamu ya Salaam, a poet, activist, and social critic living in New Orleans, offers compelling coverage of American politics, culture, and history, including women's liberation and the Black Arts Movement and other elements of Black culture. Ward explains political literature as creative literature: "We can make a useful distinction between literature that overtly denies its political implications and literature that is at once aesthetic and covertly political so that we know to a better degree what we're talking about. I don't even know if our history of so-called literary struggle has any popularity or credibility anymore. Contradictions abound."

Finally, this volume includes two interviews that I conducted with Ward. In 2015, we talked about Wright's many influences, with Ward expressing a genuine affinity with his predecessor: "Wright's use of literacy, of language to communicate his vision, was very attractive. The more I study Wright, the more fascinated I become with how he did things with words." Four years later, we focused on Ward's creative talent, including his 2016 poetry collection, *Fractal Song*. Ward developed a love for poetry as a student at Tougaloo College, where he received a bachelor's degree in mathematics where he published his first poem in 1964. Ward's poems have subsequently appeared in numerous journals, among them the *Mississippi Review*, *Iowa Review*,

Drumvoices Revue, Black Scholar, Georgia Review, Black Magnolias, and *Black American Literature Forum,* and have been included in anthologies such as *Mississippi Writers, The Jazz Poetry,* and *Modern American Poets.* Ward says, "I was prompted to write poetry by my fascination with words and my yearnings to develop my skills in the arena of art."

Ward frequently uses music in his poetry to express ideas about the "chaos, entanglement, and contradictions of being human." Ward's signature poem, "Jazz to Jackson to John," shows his experimentations with music, which focus on the sound of poetry and the use of allusions:

> When I perform that poem, I use vocal techniques from spirituals, blues, and jazz. In "movement one: genesis" I associate an unidentified occasion with "sheets of sound wrinkled / with riffs and scats," with the blues flying out into jazz. I refer to sounds one might have heard in Jackson, Mississippi, on Farish Street—the voice of Billie Holiday, the playing of Monk and Parker; here also are fragments of album titles, song titles, and lyrics—"these foolish things," "angel eyes," and "around midnight." Near the end of this movement are the crucial lines "who dug whether race records were / lamentations or lynchings: jazz."

Ward has been cultivating a sense of musical aesthetics from his cultural traditions. Influenced by both his father and mother, he has nurtured an interest in literature and music and maintained his racial dignity.

These interviews cover a wide range of topics that show Ward's thoughts as a contemporary scholar, professor, writer, and social critic, bringing his views to a wider audience and enriching what has been expressed in his scholarly books and articles. These "inner views" allow us to see into his mind, feel his heartbeat, and appreciate his wit.

The interviews could not have been published without the support of the interviewers and the original publishers. I am grateful to all of them. I also thank editor Mary Heath, series editor Monika Gehlawat, and all University Press of Mississippi staff for their efforts to bring this book to fruition. Dr. Jerry W. Ward Jr. has offered generous support and precious time to this book. I am also in debt to him for his selfless and longtime devotion to the *Journal of Ethnic American Literature* and *Valley Voices.*

JZ
December 2021

Notes

1. Jerry Ward, *The China Lectures: African American Literary and Critical Issues* (Wuhan: Central China Normal University Press, 2014), 4.
2. Jerry Ward, introduction to *Black Boy*, by Richard Wright (New York: Perennial Classics, 1998), xix.

Chronology

1943	Born Jerry Washington Ward Jr., on July 31 in Washington, DC, to Jerry W. Ward Sr. and Mary Theriot Ward
1949	Moves to Mississippi
1952–60	Attends St. Peter the Apostle Catholic School in Pascagoula, Mississippi; Our Mother of Sorrows High School in Biloxi, Mississippi; and Magnolia High School in Moss Point, Mississippi
1960	Enters Tougaloo College as an early admissions student
1964	Earns undergraduate degree in mathematics from Tougaloo College
1966	Earns master's degree in English from Illinois Institute of Technology; becomes teaching fellow at State University of New York at Albany
1968–70	Serves in Fourth Infantry Division, US Army
1970	Becomes English instructor at Tougaloo College
1973	Becomes involved in the Southern Black Cultural Alliance, a community theater coalition
1974	Becomes instructor in Transition Program at University of Virginia (summer)
1974–75	Receives United Negro College Fund Faculty Grant
1974–86	Serves as advisory editor of *Obsidian*
1975–76	Receives Kent Fellowship
1976–77	Serves as English lecturer at University of Virginia
1976–84	Serves as contributing editor for *Callaloo*
1977	Serves as associate professor of English at Tougaloo College
1978	Earns doctorate in English from University of Virginia
1978–80	Receives Tougaloo College Outstanding Teaching Award
1978–83	Serves on Southern Black Cultural Alliance Executive Committee
1979–86	Serves as chair of Tougaloo College English Department
1981	Receives United Negro College Fund Distinguished Scholar Award; serves as a faculty member at National Endowment for the Humanities Institute on Southern Black Culture at Spelman College
1982–85	Serves as contributing editor for *Jackson Advocate*

1983–2013	Serves on Project on the History of Black Writing Advisory Board
1984	Serves as director of National Endowment for the Humanities Summer Seminar for College Teachers at Tougaloo College
1984–88	Serves on Mississippi Humanities Council
1984–2002	Serves as professor of English at Tougaloo College
1985	Serves as program officer for National Endowment for the Humanities
1986–94	Serves as advisory editor for *Obsidian II*
1987	Serves as visiting professor of English at University of Mississippi
1987–88	Serves as United Negro College Fund scholar-in-residence at University of Mississippi
1987–97	Serves on Mississippi Advisory Committee for US Commission on Civil Rights
1988	Serves as Rosa Parks/Martin Luther King Jr. Visiting Scholar at Wayne State University (February–March)
1988–2002	Serves as Lawrence Durgin Professor of Literature at Tougaloo College
1990	Coedits *Redefining American Literary History* with A. LaVonne Brown Ruoff; cofounds the Richard Wright Circle with Maryemma Graham; coedits the *Richard Wright Newsletter* with Maryemma Graham; serves as program director of Commonwealth Center for Literary and Cultural Change at University of Virginia
1991–92	Serves as advisory editor for *Black American Literature Forum*
1991–2002	Serves as advisory editor for *New Literary History*
1991–present	Serves as advisory editor for *Drumvoices Review*
1992	Coedits *Black Southern Voices* with John Oliver Killens; receives Tougaloo College Teacher of the Year Award
1992–94	Serves on *PMLA* Editorial Board
1992–2021	Serves as advisory editor for *African American Review*
1993	Writes introduction to Richard Wright's *Black Boy*; serves as director for Faculty Resource Network Seminar at New York University
1993–2001	Serves on *Southern Cultures* Editorial Board
1995	Receives Mississippi Humanities Council Humanities Teacher Award and Tougaloo College Outstanding Research Scholar Award; serves on *Profession* Advisory Board

1995–2020	Serves on *Mississippi Quarterly* Editorial Board
1996	Serves as Moss Chair of Excellence in English at University of Memphis
1997	Receives Mississippi Humanities Council Public Humanities Award; edits *Trouble the Water: 250 Years of African American Poetry*.
1999	Receives National Humanities Center Fellowship
2000	Receives Darwin T. Turner Award of Excellence from African American Literature and Culture Society; serves as Minority Scholar-in-Residence at Grinnell College
2000–2015	Serves on Natchez Literary and Cinema Celebration Advisory Board
2001	Inducted into International Literary Hall of Fame for Writers of African Descent (Chicago State University)
2001–2	Serves as chair of English Department at Tougaloo College
2002–12	Serves as Distinguished Professor of English and African American World Studies at Dillard University
2008	Coedits *The Richard Wright Encyclopedia* with Robert Butler; publishes *The Katrina Papers: A Journal of Trauma and Recovery*
2008–13	Serves on *Valley Voices* Advisory Board
2009	Serves as visiting fellow at Tanner Humanities Center at University of Utah (April); convenes Faculty Resource Network Seminar at New York University; inducted into Tougaloo College National Alumni Hall of Fame; serves as keynote speaker at conference on African American literature in China
2009–12	Serves on Advisory Board of Engaged Writers Series, University of New Orleans Press
2010	Receives Thad Cochran Humanities Achievement Award; serves as resident scholar for National Endowment for the Humanities Institute at University of Kansas
2011	Receives the Richard Wright Literary Excellence Award from the Natchez Literary and Cinema Celebration; coedits *The Cambridge History of African American Literature* with Maryemma Graham
2011–14	Serves as Distinguished Overseas Professor at Central China Normal University
2011–21	Serves on *Journal of Ethnic American Literature* Editorial Advisory Board
2012	Retires from Dillard University

2012–13	Serves as adjunct researcher, Department of English at University of Kansas
2013	Serves as resident scholar, National Endowment for the Humanities Institute at University of Kansas
2014	Publishes *The China Lectures: African American Literary and Critical Issues*
2015–17	Serves as honorary professor at Central China Normal University
2016	Publishes *Fractal Song: Poems*
2018	Receives Daryl Cumber Dance Award for Lifetime Achievement from the College Language Association; publishes *Blogs and Other Writing*
2019–present	Serves on *Langston Hughes Review* Editorial Board
2021	Receives Reginald Martin Award for Excellence in Criticism from PEN Oakland

**Conversations with
Jerry W. Ward Jr.**

"Reading Race, Reading America": An Interview with Jerry Ward Jr.

Eugene B. Redmond / 1995

From *Drumvoices Revue* 5.1/2 (Fall–Winter 1995): 47–63. Reprinted by permission of Eugene B. Redmond.

Eugene B. Redmond: Jerry, to start off, I almost never hear you speak without making some reference to your upbringing, your folks, and the "mother base," the cultural mother base, that produced you. Can you talk a little bit about that [. . .] and how it led to your love for, promotion of, your being a purveyor and conveyor of literature?

Jerry W. Ward: Well, if you noticed in my living room, on the mantelpiece, there are family pictures, and I think family is very important for me because I certainly always honor my parents for giving me being, and also intelligence, which comes from my father; another side of me comes from my mother, which is my, I guess, sentimentality, or kindness, or whatever. These—I think the way we're shaped by our parents—and I'm an only child, unlike yourself—so, the way you're shaped by your parents if you're an only child is lasting; it's like you have a very strong imprint. So, I got a lot from my mother about Catholicism and also, you know, about how to treat people. And I lived in great fear of my dad, who was brilliant, and I thought that I would never measure up. I refer to family because that's where you get values. I realize now, as I approach my fifty-second year, Gene, that I'm not a young person anymore, and it's becoming very apparent to me in the way that my values have hardened into the ones that I think my parents gave me. I mean, before I was a young radical, a young rebellious person, all through my thirties and forties, I was pretty free about not insisting on certain kinds of things, and then, over the last ten years, I've discovered myself talking about such antiquated subjects as morality and believing that people ought to have self-respect, dignity, self-reliance, almost a sense that people have to work because it's good for them, and it's a way of preserving your dignity that you should consider your actions. I'm very upset, for example, with all the "That's what it is, that's the way it is"—the gangster rap says, "That's the way it is." I'll be *damned* if that's the way it is, if Black men have to kill Black men or Black women or Black children. I'm not going to forgive that. You know, I understand it's a part of our contemporary reality—I cannot do the ostrich trick and put my head in the sand; on the other hand, I am not going to say, "Well, that's the way it is." That's the way it should *not* be.

EBR: Mm-hmm.

JWW: So, I think that—when I refer to my family, I'm referring to my roots here in Mississippi on my father's side of the family, my Louisiana roots that I have from my mother, and a kind of sense that I am, although born in Washington, DC, which is a southern city. For a long time I never considered myself a Mississippian—I think I am now. So, the South, the people of the South, of all colors, have been very formative in my life. I think our cultural base is something that I want to do more than celebrate. I think celebrating it is one thing, but building on it is another; and so what I do, by way of being a teacher and writer, is to try to shore up the parts of that base that might be falling down and also to leave something that's a little different.

EBR: Okay. Stemming from that, Jerry, coming from that very lucid and at the same time very complex and multilayered response/overview/observation on your life, I want to ask two questions: one is, does this cycle or spiral that you just described characterize the lives of most people—this kind of departure and return in a general sense, and in a specific sense, does it characterize the lives of those of us "children" of the sixties?

JWW: I feel more—

EBR: You know, as peers and associates, as colleagues, and so on, *now*?

JWW: Given human individuality, Gene, the first question, I hesitate to say, it does; the spiral is so general—I'm thinking of a cousin of mine, and his spiral is very different from my own. So, I think we have to be very careful about making that kind of generalization. I feel much freer generalizing on the second question about those of us who came of age, in one way or another, in the 1960s. I feel that we are in a period, as a group—when we get together—of *reassessing*. We were the people who were proposing various things that were new and strange, and we didn't, in our youthful enthusiasm, know the consequences of everything that we asked for. So, now we're getting it from both sides. The integration that apparently has not worked—because it never really *was* integration, it was desegregation—and, secondly, such "integration" as did occur left two or three generations of young African American people bereft of the old-time religion, the old-time values, of a sense of self, with false ideas of human beings and world love, and, I don't know, all these things they got in the schools through association with others, some of which is good—I'm not against human love, for even, you know—throughout the world; what bothers me is—well, that's another—that's not your answer. Let me cut this and get back. Yes, we are reassessing. The generation of the sixties may indeed be spiraling in ways that are quite similar to my own spiraling, where people are saying, "Now let's stand back." Because we are now in our fifties, sixties, we have to really figure out how to deal with young people, how to deal with these problems in America that seem not to allow those who should be carrying on some struggle to focus on what the problem *is*. Because it's so multifaceted. You know, we knew what it was. It was, "We want the signs down that said 'White,' 'Black'; we want access to the schools; we want access to jobs; we want to be fully empowered Americans." It's not easy for young people to say what it is that they want anymore.

EBR: As you say, it just veers off into all kinds of directions, virtually anything you just mentioned [. . .] about, you know, race and struggle, and literature, and attitudes, human development. The second of the two questions triggered by your opening observations is—for example, I interviewed Leon Forrest a couple of years ago, and Forrest—that interview appears in the second issue of *Drumvoices Revue*—and he was awesome, awesome on himself, and on Morrison, and other things; one of the points he made was that he felt a particular, peculiar, a very stunning, if you will, kind of isolation, as a minority in the Black community because he was Catholic [. . .] and I wonder if you—without having read what he had to say—if you'd comment on that; that's the second question.

JWW: I think that may be a part of his sensibility. I was a minority in my family in Moss Point; most of my cousins were Baptists and—

EBR: In Moss Point?

JWW: Moss Point, Mississippi, where I grew up as a child.

EBR: Right, right.

JWW: Most of my cousins were Baptists and Methodists. I was Catholic; so I was *Catholic*. I mean, the Baptists throughout the South seemed to outnumber the Catholics. But, that didn't matter; I never brooded over that. So I think it's something very, uh, individual with Forrest, you know. Because now the movement is among Black Catholics—they're trying to put a little more soul into Catholicism!

EBR: Right.

JWW: But, you know, when I was growing up, we accepted Catholicism with all of its pieties, its European pieties. So I never felt that I was a minority within a so-called minority. I was just a Catholic, and other people weren't. And I was also arrogant in those days—they were going to hell, and I wasn't.

EBR: You, a Black Catholic as a minority within—

JWW: Within a minority of Catholics, yeah.

EBR: [...] When you think of the "shore-to-shore" mentality of the United States, within a minority race [...] a Black Catholic is a minority within a Black minority. [...]

JWW: Right. So we're on safe grounds as long as we're dealing with numbers. Then, when we move to other meanings of *minority* or the connotations of *minority*, [...] which I picked up when you said [Forrest] felt like a minority—what he's saying is something other than number. We're not talking about numbers. [...]

EBR: No, he did speak of numbers first: he said, "As you know, Gene, Catholics are a minority in the Black community"; then he went on to talk about the particular status of it [...] peculiar status of the Catholic ideology, belief, doctrine [...] I guess, the way it singles you out in a predominantly, I guess, Protestant [...] situation.

JWW: Probably the geography helped me. Now, most of Mississippi is not Catholic, but for reasons having to do with colonization, there are lots of pockets of Catholics on the coast—Moss Point is on the Gulf Coast. So when you think of towns like Biloxi, Pass Christian, Bay St. Louis, D'Iberville, [...] Moss Point—well, not so much Moss Point, but Pascagoula, you will find that—those places, you'll find pockets of Catholics. [...] Catholics along the coast seemed to know each other—you didn't know all the Catholics, but somebody at each Catholic parish knew somebody else or was related to someone else, so, I think that provided a kind of buffer: you didn't feel so odd because you knew there were other Catholics around and people were well received, I think. In fact, some of them were *admired*—well, that has to do with a color thing, with, you know, race, but we won't. Anyway, all those light-colored, those fair-haired, light-skinned Catholics, right? People kind of looked unsure about themselves, looked at them with admiration. I am glad I haven't read Forrest, so I can answer you without being prejudiced by his views. I would say, in my case, that I did feel so strange and so odd, because within, even within—being numerically—the minority, there was still a sense that we were *special*: we were very special.

EBR: Well, you know, I had a similar experience as a Seventh-Day Adventist. When my mother died, I was like, oh, halfway between my eighth and ninth birthdays, and [. . .] our religious, moral, spiritual instruction, if you will, was placed in the hands of my grandmother by my father (my grandmother's son). And my grandmother, Rosa A. Quinn, was a Seventh-Day Adventist. So there was a rupture, obviously, of everything from the kinds of foods you ate to the weekly schedule—because Seventh-Day Adventists went to church on Saturday—to your social life—you know, you no longer were allowed to mingle with girls and boys of the world. I mean, you didn't have any choice unless you went off to a separate school, but, I mean, nothing extra was allowed.

JWW: Mm-hmm.

EBR: And, so, at the same time, people, because they were—the neighborhood was a Christian neighborhood, and it was a largely Bible-influenced neighborhood, people admired the discipline, even though some people may have joked about it—they liked the fact that we were religious, you know, got up on Saturday morning and walked the several blocks to the Seventh-Day Adventist church, and there was a kind of camaraderie, a kind of community, and a familiar sense that seemed to be tighter, in a way, than some of the other sects at that time, because they had so many people, you know; we were freer of scandals—admittedly, there were fewer of us. But, you know, the ministers straying and the kinds of things that you could get in the community—but, anyway, I had a similar experience.

Flowing from what you just said, I'd like to move into literature per se. I think my first question also wondered about how the moral/ethical/religious frame that you came out of sent you toward literature.

JWW: Well, it didn't send me toward literature immediately. I was sent by the frame out of which I came to mathematics—that's what my undergraduate degree is in, but my choice to go into literature came out of a very early sense of the joys of reading. I always read a lot, and in my junior year, I kind of decided I didn't want to spend all my life dealing with numbers. I was good, but I wasn't committed enough, so I decided I should take what I thought was my second-best subject, English, and I decided to get my master's and PhD in English. Literature provides you with a way of satisfying a certain kind of intellectual curiosity I have, but it's also the kind of work that requires you to deal with people.

EBR: Mm-hmm.

JWW: So, earlier today, when you echoed what I told you yesterday about my knowing that I wanted to be a teacher, I didn't think of it as being an academician. I said a *teacher*. That, too, came out of something I recognized about myself. I believe if I'd have stayed in math, I'd be teaching math. Very early on, I discovered that I had a kind of talent for explaining certain things to my peers who were having difficulties with math problems or whatever, and I just kind of lived that out the rest of my life, teaching in colleges. I've never taught at high school. I've always taught at colleges. Literature, for me, has changed over the period of my teaching career, because although I began with writing—I suppose trying to write poetry, Gene, in high school, and I wrote things in college—I never seriously thought of it as a vocation. I kind of just grew into being a writer. It took forever for me to tell anybody I was a poet because I had this sense that other people were supposed to say that— I wasn't supposed to say that.

EBR: Mm-hmm.

JWW: So now whatever little recognition I have as a writer has come over a long period of just writing without having that sense. You know, that's what I primarily do. What I do is *teach*. My writing assists me to be a better *teacher*. When I'm teaching a poem, I know something of what goes into the making of a poem. [When] I'm teaching a story, I realize I would never write—well, I won't say I'll never write fiction; I will write fiction, but I know I don't have a good ear for dialogue, so I'm not going to be a fiction writer— I'm much better as a prose or nonfiction prose writer and a poet. So, I try to continue to develop those things.

EBR: I see. So, you are an academician now, obviously, and a very good one, very respected and very prolific, and you place work in an incredibly broad spectrum of—

JWW: Because I don't give a damn about being in the right places. Let me tell you this: I know very few of our colleagues who write for Black newspapers. I don't write as much now as I used to for the *Jackson Advocate*, which is the Jackson Black paper, but I'm on the editorial board, and I continue to give them reviews or articles. In fact, [. . .] the paper I gave you—the Black history issue—has my piece on *The Promised Land*, which is another long piece I did—reviewed that miniseries, which I liked.

EBR: Mm-hmm.

JWW: So, I think—yes, I publish in a Black paper; I will publish in the *ADE Bulletin*, which is an MLA publication. You will find me in little magazines, you may find me in rather sizable magazines like *African American Review* or just whatever the spirit tells me to publish because I think publishing generally with the *right* magazines is a career choice. People who are at places where they will publish and perish have to be in the right magazine for tenure. It's not just good enough to have published. You have to have pieces in *American Literature*, in refereed journals which your tenured group thinks are prestigious. The prestige of that kind never crosses my mind. I want to be *read*.

EBR: Ah-uh. The publishing world, like the academic world, continues to be dominated by men and whites, and we—you and I—are, well, we're academicians, but our reputations rest on what we do with African American materials and multicultural experiences. I'm just wondering how does all of this play out for you, working across the grid that I just described, the publishing, academic world; you being at a historically Black college, coming along at a time in which, during your formal education, there was some recognition of Black literature, but still not much attention given to it in the academy. I mean, you could probably do the work on your own, but your degree, I'm sure, was in a more conventional—a more traditional, Eurocentric or Anglocentric—

JWW: My PhD is in literary theory and criticism, but I managed to do a dissertation on Richard Wright's critics, so I got what I wanted.

EBR: Yes.

JWW: And in terms of all this being stretched out over things, I think I began to pull some things together, Gene. Maryemma Graham and I cofounded the Richard Wright Circle and publish the *Richard Wright Newsletter*, which I think is a small and very necessary service to the field that keeps me very much on top of the Richard Wright material. I'm interested, as I said earlier, in writing something about Lance Jeffers. I just finished doing study guides for the film—the documentary on Richard Wright, and I have the desire to publish this anthology of African American poetry; I'm working on a collection of essays called *Reading Race, Reading America*. And I am also doing taping with a very well-known person from the civil rights movement here in Mississippi, Hollis Watkins, because we're doing his oral autobiography; it's a very exciting project for me, so—

EBR: Is that like *Strangers*?

JWW: Yes, with some differences. I'm not going to play—it's his story. You don't tamper with people's stories in certain ways. I will do more of what Nell Irvin Painter did with Hosea Hudson. Let the man have his own voice, right? Or at least acknowledge that there were voices there.

EBR: Yes.

JWW: What this work does, Gene, is to keep me at once very much alive and physically exhausted, because you're trying to do so many things on so many fronts at once, and then people learn that you're halfway intelligent and can do things. Then they keep asking you to do more and more, and it's only recently that I have begun to say "no" in thunder to a lot of things. I have to cut back because I'm just not thirty anymore. I don't have that energy.

EBR: Speaking of shepherding time, adjudicating time, and discipline—there's a process of disciplining oneself. What is your formula for balancing the things that you do? I mean, how do you approach it?

JWW: I can't tell tales and create formulas, Gene. I don't really have a formula. I have a *method*, I think, and it's not regular. I know approximately when I have to have certain things done—there are some things I don't get done—but I'm also very good about working under pressure, so if I goof off a little bit, when it gets down to the wire, I produce it. With teaching and writing, it's rather difficult. I notice when I'm working in my "writerly mode," as I put it, I'm really feeling good about something, writing is coming well, I get very cantankerous and I really say, "Well, why do I have to be bothered with students? I want to continue working on this." I realize very quickly that that's why I'm here, I'm here for students, I didn't come here to write, you know. So, you have to hit yourself in the head and say, "Okay, Ward, go in the classroom, do a good job, you'll get back to the writing late tonight or you will do it on the weekend." But that's the way I have to do a lot of things. I don't have—except on the times when I take a leave of absence; I've only had one sabbatical since I've been teaching here. I've had several leaves, and usually when I take a leave, I'm out on a job. Some leaves give me a little more time to write. But, Gene, I am very amazed that I have a lot of stuff from, oh, ten, fifteen years ago, when I somehow managed to be more productive than I am now. I keep looking at it saying, "Oh, I ought to freshen this up," you know. So it's hard. I think the discipline I have has to do with a *sense of how* to get work done, rather than telling you that I get up at 4:30—which I do—and work at this for two hours. There's no telling what I'm working at between 4:00 and 6:30: it might be classwork, or it might be a speech I'm writing, or, you know, just thinking about ideas for some new poems or something.

EBR: Okay. Well, flowing from the issue, subject, or question of discipline and, you know, work de rigueur, challenge, balance, insight, precision, I'd like to hear your thoughts on criticism today. I notice this is a very thorny issue—but critics and criticism, theory, theorists, literature today, gender, culture—what's happening in those arenas for you, and with you?

JWW: What's happening in those arenas for me is that I am trying to do several things well. One is to promote—as we did when I coedited *Redefining American Literary History* with A. LaVonne Ruoff—to promote a sense of how multilayered, multicultured, *American* literature is—if one is going to study it properly. Secondly, and to do my scholarship with writers on writers well, I hope, as a critic, I'm coming more and more to a position of wanting to talk about the *situatedness* of the work. How do we understand it in its own historical context? How do we understand our misunderstanding of it because of our own historicity? And I want somehow to find that middle ground where I can write about that in a way that is not disappointing to my colleagues but at the same time [is] accessible to a broader audience. I'm not interested in writing exclusively for other theorists, for other critics, for other scholars. I think that is a waste of my talent. I am supposed to help people who have a little more experience perhaps than my students would have but who are really interested in some of the issues and possibilities being raised by what is happening with writing now. Writing is just bursting out all over, as we've been talking about for the past couple of days. When you raise the matter of gender, you handled very well earlier today something that I've thought about in a different way about biculturalism—that is, the new half-and-half children who are talking about a new aesthetic or a new Black aesthetic. And half the time, I don't know what they're talking about. Because, as I said, the old Black aesthetic had not been finished yet— we were still trying to deal with *it*—don't come up with a new one *yet*. I mean, there's so much—because a Black aesthetic is misunderstood. People think of it as a moment. Many of the critics have thought it out as, "Oh, that was just a period in literary history." If they had read Carolyn Fowler's book *Black Arts and Black Aesthetics*, they would understand that where Carolyn Fowler was coming from is, "Black aesthetics is indeed a study of *perceptions*, historically determined *perceptions*, ideologically informed *perceptions*." Black people are still having those: no matter how American they become, there is something that differentiates us in our love for the blues from people who love country music, and that's part of our aesthetic being, that's part of our aesthetic training. The way we move, for example, is not the same way most people in this country move. We've got a different rhythm— I don't move like a Chinese. So you see, I think what I'm doing with literature is trying to look at this field. I'm realizing that I can't stay on top of everything that's going on, Gene, because there's too much work coming out. I'm about fifty novels behind in reading. That's too many novels. I haven't read Wesley Brown's second book yet; I liked *Tragic Magic* very much. So let me try to summarize this in a way that I summarized something at the Tennessee Williams Festival two weeks ago. When I was asked about the new public intellectual, the new Black public intellectual, and whether this was going to in some way bridge the gap between writers such as Ralph Ellison and the young Turks of the Black Arts/Black Aesthetic Movement, I said, "I think the notion of public intellectuals is a capital joke, because we've had Black public intellectuals and no one knew that, so the *New York Times* thinks it's something very new. If public intellectuals are people who make such irresponsible statements as, 'Toni Morrison is the most intelligent person since Du Bois' or 'the greatest genius since Du Bois'—if that's what the public intellectual is, I want to look at the public again." I said that with reference to someone that we know because I think that it's too much a fashion—people don't know if they're talking about literature or if they're talking about culture. It is legitimate to say that literature is *inseparable* from culture—in fact, much of my own analysis operates out of that stance—but I want the criticism directed in such a way that it is not about Habermas, it is not about Marx, it is not about Derrida—Jürgen Habermas, the German thinker who is really very good. But, I mean, a lot of people are very *good*. I don't want to get caught in somebody's pigeon coop, and so I can't say anything meaningful to African American people without bowing to Foucault? I don't bow to these people. I use what ideas they have and try to make them compatible with our needs. I synthesize. I guess I do a little voodoo work there, huh? But that to me is what has to be done now, and I hope that I am raising my children, my students, in a way that they come to understand this as a very real need, okay?

EBR: Yes. Well, that was very comprehensive and very close-quartered at the same time, you know, extremely helpful to me, and I'm sure it will be helpful to anybody else who hears or reads these remarks. Then I guess a question that might be invoked by what you just said is where do we find—I don't know if you want to say a "school"—or how do we train the troops—the combat troops, if you will—because we're in a war zone—to deal with some of the really—I think what we'd both agree is glib, rather slick kinds of, I guess really combinations of fancy footwork [. . .] or fancy mouthwork, and media exploitation or playing to media.

JWW: I see the hope in trying to nurture a certain consciousness and sense of responsibility among undergraduates. At the graduate level, it's already too late. And the graduates and the people who are going on for master's degrees and doctorates already are buying into the need to be publicized and to be trendy unless the person is going into some area like medieval or Renaissance studies, and maybe they become less trendy, or more scholarly in the old sense, or like Anglo-Saxon people who are still studying the Middle Ages. As far as we're concerned—Black American literature and culture—I don't know where else to try to train anyone. You've got to work with my seniors now who are looking at the work of Virgia Brocks-Shedd and Lance Jeffers. And the students feel, they told me at midterm, so good about this because finally they are able to write criticism that they feel is *genuine*, that helps *them* to make a contribution, and they're not writing about all kinds of, you know, *abstract* things. I have them doing some old-fashioned work, such as transcribing handwriting and annotating a poem called "In the Tent" by Virgia Brocks-Shedd, which is about what it was like for her to grow up as a young Black Mississippian looking at films with only white folks in them—because the subtitle of her poem is "In Defense of Black Films," okay?

EBR: Mm-hmm.

JWW: And they learned so much because they didn't know some of these characters that she was alluding to. They found out what sawmill quarters were, they understand what a tin tub was about, you know, and the word *quarters* was used in a very interesting way, was punning on it—quarters that you paid coming from the quarters.

EBR: The Negro quarters.

JWW: Right. The hard-earned dollars and quarters that you gave to this tent. And they didn't know what the tent was initially because they thought it was a circus tent, and I said, "Well, you know, in rural areas, people didn't have movie houses; they put movies in the tent, like the medicine show."

EBR: Yeah.

JWW: So I think that's where I want to—that, to me, is a hope—I hope that what we begin to talk about seriously in the profession is—for us, in Black studies—how do we help these undergraduates to develop a very strong sense of why you talk about ideas, whether it's literature, or you talk about what they seem to be committed to—rap, or whatever, you're going to critique—how is this a part of social responsibility, as well as showing them that you have to have some real analytical skills. You have to have some skills in handling literature. It's not just—you can't always talk about it sociologically—Ellison was right, you need to look at the words, the kind of things that you do, Gene, when you talk about the *soulular* nature of things, that orality, you know, making people aware of language in its multiple possibilities. *That* should be what we do. But the antics of my friends who are theoreticians and who are making waves, I think, may in some ways, be doing—let me try something—benevolent harm.

EBR: Benevolent harm? Wordsmithery, wordsmithing. Yes, I can get to that—I think I understand that. Do we also need to call for the makers, shakers, and rollers of the peak of the Black Aesthetic Movement to do more—I mean, the actual practitioners of the Black Aesthetic as it was known, or seen, or referred to in the sixties and before that and since then?

JWW: Mm-hmm.

EBR: I mean, should the artists do more theorizing, if you will? Or more autobiographical writing? Or more clarification work? More spadework?

JWW: Right. I would prefer more autobiographical writing from many of the practitioners—I think it would do us a world of good to hear something autobiographical from Askia Muhammad Touré as it would—well, we hear a lot from Ishmael about a problem there [. . .] and Baraka. But with Ishmael Reed in particular, I think he gives a running commentary on his own production, so I have a better sense of what he is doing—whether or not I have to take with a question mark some of the reasons he gives—but I think he's pretty straightforward in his own sly way. [. . .] Now the thing we need to do, Gene, I think, is to review a lot that was said from 1968 through, like, 1980 about the Black Aesthetic, and look at it critically and say, "Okay, this seems to deal with a principle." Now of course, given the topicality of the discourse in which that is couched, what I must do is to look at what has happened in that particular area—let us say that it is dance, all right? And certain statements were made about dance: Are the statements sufficient to cover what is going on with dance? I had a marvelous experience going to the Museum for African Art in New York recently, and in the exhibit there was a leopard dance from the northern Ivory Coast. And what they were doing in the leopard dance looked just like break dancing, and I told the woman, "It looks just like a prototype." But I don't think that's what it is. I think that at very different times, people repeat ancient forms. You know, you can't say that the Black kids who came up with break dancing looked back to Africa or *knew* that it was even *there*. It was something that they felt had to be done, and it evolved, and this was the time for it. So what's attractive about what we do with dance, what's attractive about what we do with music, and now, we talk about how aesthetic responses—going back to *Art in the Mechanical Age* by Walter Benjamin—what has happened that we don't go to a club to hear the blues, we listen to it on a recording? Or a CD? As opposed to an LP. This is very important: it is part of saying, "Now the Black Aesthetic has become commodified in a certain way. Maybe there are certain other things which come up to counter some of the impacts of commercialization. Maybe there are forms of music or forms of drama which try to avoid being *dependent* on the mercy of a merciless industry." I don't know, but we need to begin to ask those kinds of questions and to look for those things in the culture, because if the culture is going to continue to be rich and always come up with something new, always out of Africa something *new*, then we have to be aware of the forms that promote the continuity and discontinuity of forms.

EBR: Well, that certainly was an eloquent dissertation on the Black Aesthetic, with a real focus on, I guess, what is central, and that's the fluidity, the constancy in change taking place and appearing simultaneously. [. . .] You mentioned your own work, and, of course we're very much concerned about your work, and appreciative of it, but what specifically are you working on right now, and what does the immediate and long-range future hold for you and your work, Jerry?

JWW: Long-range future includes a monograph, I think, on Richard Wright, a book on Ishmael Reed, and then another book which deals with the work of Alvin Aubert, Sterling Plumpp, Tom Dent, Julius Thompson, and Kalamu ya Salaam. The oral autobiography, which I think I mentioned before, that I'm doing with Hollis Watkins. The long-delayed anthology of African American poetry.

EBR: *Trouble the Water*?

JWW: *Trouble the Water*. And then the collection of my own social and literary essays, entitled *Reading Race, Reading America*. Now, LSU Press is reviewing the manuscript for my collection of poems, *Jazz South*. So, I will write another collection of poems. So I've got a long program laid out, but now I'm saying, "Let me get one thing accomplished at a time." It's like, "Knock out this, finish it, and then move on to something else."

EBR: Mm-hmm.

JWW: And, currently, what I'm closest to finishing will be *Reading Race, Reading America*, and behind that will come the book—or whatever it turns out to be, Gene—with Hollis.

"Resonance and Relevance Are Key Terms Here": An Interview with Jerry W. Ward Jr.

Howard Rambsy II / 1999

Printed by permission of Howard Rambsy II.

Jerry W. Ward Jr., Lawrence Durgin Professor of Literature at Tougaloo College in Mississippi, wrote the introduction to the HarperPerennial edition of Richard Wright's *Black Boy* (*Hunger*) as restored by the Library of America. The following is an interview done via email with Ward between November 6, 1999, and November 8, 1999.

Howard Rambsy: What were some of the terms and conditions of your involvement in the HarperPerennial edition of *Black Boy*? That is, who contacted you about the edition? And what were some of the aims, if any, of how you would help (re)introduce Wright to readers?

Jerry W. Ward Jr.: Sometime late in 1992 I received a letter from a senior editor at HarperCollins (HC), asking if I would write an introduction for the paperback edition of the Library of America restored text. I agreed to do so eagerly. Although Arnold Rampersad and I have never discussed the matter, I suspect that he recommended me for the task. HC never set the terms and conditions of my involvement explicitly as part of the aim to market Wright's work. They didn't have to do so, because Wright was enjoying new popularity on the heels of the *Native Son* film, the Library of America editions, and the founding of the Richard Wright Circle. It was tacitly understood, perhaps, that my introduction would just be a part of the discourse on Richard Wright. Perhaps someone at HC knew my 1977 review of *American Hunger*.

My contract with HarperCollins of January 28, 1993, specifies that I would grant HC permission to use the introduction in all editions of the book published worldwide, that I would deliver an introduction of approximately fifteen to twenty typewritten pages, that the piece should be "acceptable to HC in content and form," and that the copyright for the introduction would be in my name. The publishers did not ask that I present a particular point of view. I simply followed my intuition that a broader reading public should be introduced to Wright's hunger, his never-satisfied will to know, to share his observations, and to achieve meaningful status as a writer. It was important to suggest that Wright had become a writer of international significance for having written more than the most frequently discussed books, *Native Son* and *Black Boy*. It was important to proclaim that *Black Boy* was a classic example of American autobiography. Please note and ponder why I did not say it was a classic example of African American autobiography. I am certain the book belongs on the same shelf as Benjamin Franklin's autobiography. To some degree, I thought of my piece as one that introduced readers to the necessity of thinking about how another person's record of childhood and youth can be critical in thinking about our own past experiences.

HR: Since the days of Phillis Wheatley, the positioning of the person or persons who introduced the African American writer in question to the larger readership (which was almost only white) carried certain significance. Dorothy Canfield Fisher's influence/positioning with the Book of the Month Club readers and her introduction to *Native Son* were important factors for Harper & Brothers, if for nothing else than to promote sales of Wright's novel. Not only that, Fisher was in a position to even suggest editorial changes to Wright's work before it was published. Of course, things have changed in the publishing world since the days of Wheatley and the publication of *Black Boy*. For one, African American readership and Black literary scholarship have increased dramatically. Nonetheless, I think positioning, even if in different ways, still means something to how Black writers' works are introduced to readers, whoever those readers might be. What might your positioning as a Black literary scholar mean, and how did you attempt to appropriate that meaning, especially in terms of the Wright introduction?

JWW: When I wrote the introduction, I did not think very much about my position as an authority on Richard Wright. It was an opportunity to write about a fellow Mississippian and Black male whose early life history was so akin to my own at a psychological level. Both Wright and I were driven by segregation and the "crab barrel" assumptions within our Black communities to be very angry about the constraints placed upon our intellectual development. I have a literary kinship with the man. My position began with my regard for his achievement against the odds, his eternal message that if one truly has the will to do things, they can be done by sheer hard work. That was and is my internal position.

The external position of the Black scholar vis-à-vis the worlds of scholarship and diverse readerships is not stable; it drifts according to the movements of reception. In short, the reception of one's introduction to a book (whether one is Black or white) is a function of the reader's tastes and/or of books as commodities. Why do books need to be introduced? Consider that going back to Wheatley, introductions were used to control how books would be received, placing a burden for authorizing and authenticating on the person writing the introduction. Obviously, at the end of the twentieth century, I was not authenticating Wright's work except in the most indirect way: my introduction was a signal that the book, almost fifty years old, still had relevance. Resonance and relevance are key terms here, because I think in the postmodern period, Black literary scholars who introduce older books serve to remind us that the past is never absent from the present and that some books from the past do not wither in significance. We are fighting against the widespread tendency to forget as the material and social conditions of life change (sometimes for the better). In the case of Richard Wright, one tries to suggest that the scars of racism cannot be hidden by way of cosmetic surgery. The memory of them and the clear evidence of their current manifestations preclude ignoring them in the midst of glib discussions about human progress, racial progress, and the like.

Yes, the conditions of everyday life in the United States which shaped Wright are obviously not the same as they were in 1927, but we should not assume that the systemic features of life are so radically different than they were seventy-two years ago. In the United States, mass media serves the state well in maintaining a place for "Black boys." If I appropriated anything of the small power that obtains in introducing an African American text, what I appropriated was the right to say we shall not forget. *Black Boy* will not permit us to forget. It was my obligation as a Black scholar to say just that.

HR: Now that Black folk can introduce Black writers to Black (and white) audiences, does it mean that African American literature has arrived?

JWW: That Black folk can introduce Black writers to Black and white and Asian and Hispanic and Jewish and Islamic audiences is not a signal that African American literature has arrived. African American literature, like African American peoples, must never utter the blind words "I have arrived." They must stay at home, look on chaos, and survive. I equate arrival with death.

HR: The restored text of *Black Boy* (*American Hunger*) reminds readers that Richard Wright was not just a Black boy dealing with challenges—obstacles—in the South. Rather, he was a Black boy from the South dealing with American challenges. When we consider how early editions of *Black Boy* presented Wright and his autobiography as opposed to the recent editions, we learn or are reminded that publishing matters. What do you think are some of the limits and possibilities of how publishing companies decide how—and in the case of Wright when—to present an author's work?

JWW: At this stage of late capitalism, the bottom line for publishers is money—sales and money. Only in the rarest of cases is the artistic merit of the work primary. Publishers have not totally abandoned literary standards, but they promote them only if the market is right and ripe. That is one of the limits of publishing as a business. It attends to the forces of economy. On the other hand, publishers can make some clever and socially useful decisions about what works to publish. I think this was the case recently with the publication of *Push* by Sapphire. The book exposes things that do need to be known about child abuse and literacy among African Americans, but the publishers angled the book as the heir apparent to Alice Walker's *The Color Purple* and failed in the effort. I suspect that commercial publishers are not innocent when it comes to matters of racial engineering.

When Asian Americans become major consumers of books, you may notice that publicity for non–Asian American books will diminish and Maxine Hong Kingston may temporarily displace Richard Wright in the literary marketplace. Publishers respond to demands, and demands are frequently created by what is taught in the schools and colleges and by what is championed by critics and reviewers. Draw upon your experiences, Howard, from the summer of 1998 to make clever guesses about the conversations in editorial boardrooms regarding when to publish works by Wright. There is much in the Wright Collection at Yale University that should be published, but HarperCollins will not rush to publish a complete edition of Wright's works until large numbers of readers demand that they do so. The publishers will want to know if they can make a profit from such an enterprise. And do not forget that the publishers also have to deal with the wishes of the Richard Wright estate. American readers cannot be exposed to previously unpublished works by Wright until Mrs. Ellen Wright grants permission. So, Howard, I want you to remember that publishers do not make absolutely free choices about works to be published. They are themselves subject to legal considerations and the marketplace. And why do you think *The Long Dream* is out of print?

HR: Over the years, the scholarship of Wright has evolved, and thus it is understandable that there would be certain differences in Fisher's introduction of 1945, John Reilly's afterword included in the 1966 edition, and your introduction to the 1993 edition. If you had to write an introduction to Wright's *Black Boy* again today, what issues, if any, in American and African American literature and culture (and for my purposes, issues in the world and politics of how Black writers are published and promoted) might seriously affect what you would write? More specifically, what I'm asking is, What are some of the challenges and responsibilities that we—as literary people and "Black boys" ourselves—have in resituating and reintroducing the story of a Black boy named Richard Wright in the twenty-first century?

JWW: If challenged to write another introduction to *Black Boy* for the twenty-first century, I would probably not make very many changes. I would, however, give a little more attention to how psychoanalytic considerations might enhance our reading of the autobiography, and I would add a paragraph contrasting *Black Boy* with Clifton Taulbert's *Once upon a Time When We Were Colored* and Anne Moody's *Coming of Age in Mississippi*. The great change I would make regards amplifying my closing remark about the book's providing "the opportunity to remember and to be renewed." The expansion would be along the lines of a paper I will present next year on Du Bois and Wright under the title "W. E. B. Du Bois and Richard Wright: The Colorline and the Colorbind." Despite the rapid social and cultural change, discrimination on the basis of color/racial identification will continue as a major problem in the twenty-first century, and the agony that writers will have in explaining their identities in color/ethnic frames of reference will not disappear in some magic process of creolization. The post-postmodern consciousness that claims to be color-blind merely utters a grand lie. People still see color, draw lines around color, and find themselves bound by the discourse past and present about color. Race, racism, and racialization, as *Black Boy* bears witness, are permanent features of the Western mindset. I do not know how we Black boys/African American men will resituate and reintroduce Wright's autobiography. I can only hope that those who follow me will not tell lies! I hope they will say that the pain and pleasure of engaging Richard Wright's words is different for them but eternally meaningful.

Interview with Jerry W. Ward Jr.

Kyle G. Dargan / 2006

From *Callaloo* 29.4 (Fall 2006): 1395–99. Published by Johns Hopkins University Press. Reprinted by permission of Kyle G. Dargan.

Kyle G. Dargan: Were you able to evacuate New Orleans before Hurricane Katrina hit the city?

Jerry W. Ward Jr.: Yes, I was able to evacuate. I left the Sunday before the hurricane hit. I left because I got urgent messages from friends who said, "You must leave," and I was very resistant. And then I heard the reports of Mayor [Ray] Nagin's very impassioned plea for people to leave, as he issued a mandatory evacuation order. So, I said, "Well, maybe I should leave." And I did.

Dargan: Were you resistant despite knowing the magnitude of the hurricane?

Ward: Well, the hurricane was growing from a three to a four to a five, and I wasn't quite sure how accurate the reports were. I had stayed through previous hurricanes, and nothing happened. I had very mixed feelings about just leaving, but I think my better sense told me that leaving was a wise thing to do.

Dargan: What did you see as you were leaving on Sunday?

Ward: As I was leaving, I was seeing a very deserted city, at least from the part of the city I was leaving—the Gentilly area. I got onto Interstate 610 in order to connect with Interstate 10, which was the official contraflow route to go either to Baton Rouge or to Texas, or up Interstate 55 into Mississippi, and Interstate 55 was the route I chose. Traffic was bumper-to-bumper. It was hot, and some people's cars had stopped on the side of the interstate. I guess they had run out of gas or something; I don't know. The heavy lines of traffic looked like a kind of funeral procession.

Dargan: Was anyone with you in your car?

Ward: No, I was alone. I had called a friend and asked him if he wanted to evacuate with me, but he said no because he had family in New Orleans, and he wanted to stay with his family. So I got into my car and drove up to Mississippi.

Dargan: How long did it take you to step back and begin reflecting on what happened? You know, once, I guess, you got out of the city and were just kind of able to put yourself in a place where you could really think about it. How long did that take?

Ward: It took me about two weeks to have anything that I would call psychic distance. And that's when I started writing *The Katrina Papers*. I was in Vicksburg, Mississippi. I stayed at a shelter that was provided by the First Baptist Church of Vicksburg. I had originally tried to find housing in a motel, but every motel was booked. You just couldn't get space anywhere. Fortunately, I was able to get into a very nice shelter—that is in terms of facilities and people who were very much concerned about our welfare. I suppose that what I was doing for most of the two weeks—although I tried to make myself useful in terms of helping people with their FEMA applications—was living in a kind of state of disbelief that I couldn't return to my home in New Orleans. I could see all the flooding on television. I could see people trying to make their way with makeshift boats through the water. I could even see a couple of dead bodies in one shot. I kept wondering, "Did this really happen?" And I would think, "No!" "You're confused," I would say to myself. I was very confused. Then it hit me: the city had been inundated not by Hurricane Katrina alone but also by the breaks in the levees and by the retaining walls along the canals. I was not going to be able to get back to New Orleans. Because by this time, two weeks later, I was hearing that people were told not to go back to the city and that National Guard troops were going into the city. I also heard that the poor police chief was losing his rationality and so was the mayor, to some degree, because these two city officials were very frustrated. So, I had to try to deal, in some way or other, with that frustration for myself. And the only out I had was to write.

Dargan: Over the years, didn't people in New Orleans predict that there would be a major flooding of the city? How conscious were you, and other people you knew well, of the flood actually taking place one day, possibly even this very hurricane? Did you ever think about the levees breaching?

Ward: No, I didn't think about it at all. In fact, before Katrina, I knew there were levees here, but I thought they were fairly secure. I'm much more familiar with the levees in St. James Parish, where some of my relatives live. They've always been secure because they were very well made. Nothing ever happens; the river never tops them or anything of that kind. So, my knowledge of whether the levees had been certified by the Army Corps of

Engineers and would hold was minimal. It's only after the fact that you realize that the Army Corps of Engineers was trying initially to cover up what recent reports have revealed—that the levees had not been checked on a very regular basis, that in some instances inappropriate materials had been used. And as long as minimal standards seemed—and I think we have to stress the word *seemed*—to have been met, there was no need to suggest the levees might not protect New Orleans. You don't want to create any panic or much concern among the people who were being protected by levees. So, in my day-to-day talk with people in New Orleans, the condition of the levees was never part of the conversation. Of course, I am not a native of New Orleans. I didn't become a resident until 2003. One of the things that I think is very telling has to do with the book called *The Flood*, a very interesting discussion of the flood of 1927. If you read that book very carefully, you discover that some decisions had been made that were very unfortunate for some of the parishes below New Orleans, because it was decided that levees should be broken in such a way that the water would bypass New Orleans and go farther to the south. But I don't think people thought that—almost eight decades later—the government would still be willing to sacrifice human beings for business interests. And maybe that's what happened. The pre-Katrina history of the levees needs to be thoroughly investigated by a nongovernment group of American citizens.

Dargan: It is somewhat scary watching the role that natural disaster seems to play in gentrification these days. There seems to be a process: we have a natural disaster, and the builders find a silver lining. They build condos, etc. Isn't Donald Trump planning to build a lot in New Orleans?

Ward: Yes, he's planning to build a tower, according to early reports. I was talking to a friend not long ago, and he said, "Well, you know, no one's going to build, no investor is going to really start building anything here until after the next hurricane season is over, because everybody is waiting to see what happens." And when you tell me that gentrification seems to follow natural disasters, I say "amen" to that. Based on what I have been reading and on conversations I've been a part of, I've discovered that some urban planners and major architectural firms welcome the opportunity to build, as they say, "better communities." In other words, they want them to be designed not to grow as cities grow. Cities, as you know, seem to grow organically—that is, there is planning involved in the development of cities, but over the years those cities deviate from those plans and evolve as needed or desired by the collective; neighborhoods change and new things are put in place. Over the years, the city takes on a unique shape.

Dargan: Do you think that the culture of New Orleans will be vulnerable as they try to put the city back together?

Ward: I would say the culture of New Orleans is not vulnerable. But it's going to be significantly different. The first difference I notice will be the impact of immigrant populations, such as the Vietnamese and Latinos, whose presence is already evolving new cultural configurations in New Orleans.

The part of the culture of New Orleans that is threatened is music, jazz in particular, because one of the special features of the city is what I call jazz families. New Orleans has any number of extremely talented people who are all related by blood or marriage to each other. And this tradition of passing on techniques and musical concepts from one generation to another may come to an abrupt halt. And you get a lot of people coming in trying to play as if they are New Orleans musicians, and technically they might do a good job of that. But the creativity, which depended much more upon a lifestyle, will have vanished.

Dargan: Do you think there will be an effort to get the displaced musicians back? I rode through the Essence Festival this year. It was in Houston, and the festival seemed a little strange. It was not quite the same as it was in New Orleans, especially with New Orleans musicians scattered all over the country.

Ward: I think some of the musicians will try to come back. There is an effort, I believe, to bring them back. The Tipitina's Foundation initiated the effort. The Ashe Cultural Center is also involved in the effort. There is also an effort to create a musicians' village, which would be a place for many displaced musicians to come back to live in. I'm not sure what will be the outcome of this. But at least it will give them a place to live, and maybe someway they might be able to acquire homes if they had homes before the hurricane. Many of them lived in the Lower Ninth Ward. There are musicians who live north of where I live, north of Gentilly, going toward the Lake Pontchartrain. And there were a lot of musicians who lived uptown. So there was no single neighborhood that you identified with music or with musicians. And I'm not sure if that's the intention of really trying to put them all together in some kind of village. New Orleans had hundreds of musicians, and hundreds are going to need immediate housing if they return to the city. Some of them are not going to return, but others are going to remain here. One of the Nevilles said he was not ever going to return, although his niece is very much committed to staying in New Orleans. She sings every Monday night at Snug Harbor.

There're other musicians who, even if they're not actually living in the city, do come back and play, quite frequently.

Dargan: Do you notice a generational divide between the people who want to stay and the people who aren't coming back?

Ward: Not in any scientific way. It's my sense that older people who have very special health needs and family elsewhere may not come back. Now, very quickly, add a correction to that. My next-door neighbor is eighty-five. She is legally blind. But she wants to come back, and she actually is in her house now for a couple of weeks. Her daughter is encouraging her because she is aware that her mother can actually function here, and they've got people to take care of her. So you can't say that just because a person is an octogenarian, that person will not come back. I think many older people who don't have the kind of support this woman is lucky enough to have might not come back.

I'm not sure that young people are overly anxious to come back. Students miss their schools, but given what's happening with the school system here, one can understand their reluctance. The school system is virtually powerless, as a hundred or so schools are being taken over by the state because of poor performance. I guess the maximum number of schools that are actually controlled by the New Orleans School Board would be six or seven. Students want to come back, but then they're in places like Houston or other states where the school systems are so much better that they might prefer to stay there. You know, it's a very real problem for people who are sensitive to the needs of their children. You hear many stories: "Well, my granddaughter, who was not doing well in the public schools here, is thriving somewhere else." It is difficult for me to give you a yes or no answer to your question as to whether more younger than older or more older than younger people are willing to come back. I can't give you a definitive answer.

I think we are dealing—indeed, as we try to live in the city—with a very complicated situation. People may want to come back and cannot come back. And they can't come back because there is no housing. And they can't afford the housing that is here. The average rent in New Orleans now starts at $800. Four of the housing projects are scheduled for demolition. Families lived in those units. Approximately twenty thousand people lived in those units.

One of the things I found exceptionally disappointing in the mayoral election was that neither Mitch Landrieu nor Ray Nagin seriously addressed the issue of labor, of jobs. They just talked out little slogans: "We're going to rebuild and have new opportunities." But never was there any serious discussion about what happens to the workforce. Not everybody should be in the service industry. We don't have major conventions coming. The American Library Association Convention, held over a month ago, was the last one to come here.

Dargan: To conclude, I'd like you to talk a little bit more about *The Katrina Papers* and where you'd like to see the city to go in the next ten years or so.

Ward: I will tell you. *The Katrina Papers*, which I began writing in September—I'm going to continue writing (the subtitle is *A Journal of Trauma and Recovery*) the *Papers* until August 29 of this year. And then I'm going to stop wherever I stop. It has been a kind of a yearlong project for me. You know, some of the writing is, some of my readers have told me, rather interesting. I think it's going to say a lot about what was happening to my head.

Where would I like to see the city go? I would like for us to be able to restore much of the infrastructure because we're having some problems with that right now. All the water pumps are broken or unstable, and we're losing up to five million gallons of water per day. You can see fire hydrants with water leaking out of them. It's out of control. There are potholes developing in areas of the city. One of my friends who's also a writer discovered he has a sinkhole under his house. He lives in an area of the city where this is not supposed to happen.

Interview with Jerry W. Ward Jr.

Joshua Guild / 2006

Interview with Jerry W. Ward Jr. by Joshua Guild, June 2, 2006, Interview U-0261, in the Southern Oral History Program Collection #4007, Southern Historical Collection, Wilson Library, University of North Carolina at Chapel Hill. Reprinted by permission of the Southern Oral History Program Collection.

Joshua Guild: So maybe you could just start with a little background. Tell me where you're from, your people, stuff like that.

Jerry W. Ward Jr.: I was born in Washington, DC. My parents, of course, were from Mississippi and Louisiana. My father is from Mississippi. My mother is from St. James Parish, Louisiana. We moved back to Mississippi when I was six years old—to my dad's hometown, Moss Point, Mississippi—and that's where I grew up. I took my undergraduate degree not in English but in mathematics at Tougaloo College and graduated in 1964. Then I did my PhD in English at the University of Virginia and got that degree in 1978. In between, I had done graduate work elsewhere, had been in the army for two years, and I began teaching at Tougaloo in 1970.

JG: What led you to a teaching career?

JWW: Something that's buried very deeply in my childhood. I remember when I was very young, kids in the neighborhood were not quite as gifted as I was in doing certain kinds of things, so occasionally I would play schoolteacher. A number of people in my family had been schoolteachers, so I kind of fell into this by accident and a kind of desire I had to pass on information to other people, especially if I noted that they had more difficulty with mastering ideas and concepts than I had. I was really very much disposed to being a teacher, and I have discovered I have no regrets.

JG: That's good. Tell me about Tougaloo, being there as an undergraduate.

JWW: As an undergraduate, I was there between 1960 and 1964, and those were exceptionally exciting years. It's at the beginning and leading up almost to a kind of high point of what I would call the classic phase of the civil rights movement if we're going to only date that as something that started with the 1960s. Of course, the civil rights movement has to be interpreted in a much broader way and certainly over a longer period of time.

The advantage of being at Tougaloo in those years was that I received what I call a dual education. There was the academic work, what we did in the classrooms, but there was also the interaction with any number of people who are now exceptionally famous as civil rights workers, heroes of the movement, including some of my classmates. We went to—we, and I'm not speaking for every student at Tougaloo—but most of us went to forums, went to meetings because we had friends who had suffered, some of them quite seriously, from physical injuries in this effort to assert our citizenship. I learned much about a world beyond Mississippi. I learned a great deal about the difficulty that what we called integration posed for us. You could do that at Tougaloo: it was an oasis. But once you left the gates, you were in the really brutal world of the South, of Mississippi, and it was dangerous, and we knew that. Some of us were brave. Students braved danger; we were taking risks.

That part of my education, Josh, involved the resentment of what this country allowed to happen, of its hypocrisy in light of what the Constitution should have guaranteed, particularly after we had the late nineteenth-century amendments involving the rights of formerly enslaved peoples. It also taught me what balances resentment, and that is the strength to believe that things will not always be as they are. There is a possibility of something better happening, and holding that belief certainly for me—in terms of a memory that my ancestors were much stronger than I, that they had endured the most inhumane treatment, and while what I endured under the laws of segregation was inhumane, it was less inhumane. I was not branded. I did have an adequate diet. I was allowed to read and write, and I had an education. Many of the things that I've done in my teaching and in other activities all go back to the person that was formed during my undergraduate years.

JG: At what point did you return to Tougaloo on the faculty?

JWW: Six years after I graduated. As I told you, I graduated in '64, and I returned as an instructor in 1970, immediately after I was discharged from the US Army.

JG: Was that a conscious decision to return home, so to speak?

JWW: It was not a conscious decision. I had an invitation from the chair of the English department to return, and I received that invitation while I was still in Vietnam and immediately said yes. That was really going home, and I wanted to see how it would work out, and it worked out very well. I only intended to stay maybe for four years. I actually stayed on the faculty of Tougaloo College for thirty-two years.

JG: What brought you to New Orleans?

JWW: An offer that I did not wish to refuse. I had the Lawrence Durgin Chair at Tougaloo. I had been chairman of the English department for seven years, and then I served an extra two and a half years as acting chair as things changed. I felt that I didn't want to refuse this invitation because I had always liked New Orleans. I had been coming to the city since I was four years old because on my mother's side, we had relatives here; my godparents lived here. And the offer from Dillard was extremely attractive. I had the leverage to say, "If I actually decide to stay at Dillard, I'm not going through the tenure process. You will have to grant me tenure the second year." They couldn't do it legally at Dillard for the first year. And that did happen. People at Tougaloo were in a state of disbelief. They said, "You're not really leaving." I said, "Yes." And I did.

Despite what we are now having to endure [in the wake of Hurricane Katrina], I don't regret the decision because the years—my brief time at Dillard prior to last August—was very fruitful, and I was able to have a real sense of community here. I knew a lot of people in New Orleans before I came down, and I met a lot of wonderful new people at Dillard. So, if you asked me to put in a nutshell what I've kind of meandered around telling you, I came to Dillard because it was to be, as I said, a new life with old friends. I could do something that continued my personal mission as a teacher but in a very new way with a new set of students.

JG: What did it mean to teach, to come to another historically Black college?

JWW: That's part of the mission. Unlike many people in my academic peer group who decided that they wanted to teach at very large universities, Research 1 institutions, I decided that there was a sacrifice that had to be made. Not everyone should be at the so-called major institutions. If you have a sense of responsibility that I think was ingrained in me in my undergraduate years, that if you were gifted, you had to give back, my way of giving back to a larger community of people was to teach, and the site for teaching had to be either my alma mater or another historically Black institution.

JG: How would you describe the Dillard student body? What students does Dillard serve?

JWW: Dillard serves a very diverse student body both in terms of the geographic origins and the range of abilities and talents that Dillard students bring during their first year. I would think that if Dillard students were compared using various measures with students at other historically Black schools, we would find that there were not that many dissimilarities. Perhaps it would be New Orleans and their reasons for coming to Dillard, if they're in-state, as opposed to going to Southern or Grambling or UNO [the University of New Orleans] or SUNO [Southern University of New Orleans] or even some of the other schools here in New Orleans. That would have to be looked at very carefully. Also, what programs at Dillard University did they find exceptionally attractive? I've noticed that Dillard students, like students at other schools that I know of, develop a fierce attachment to the place and a fierce attachment to their classes and their classmates. What I've noticed is slightly different, and I'm not on the inside, so I say this guardedly, as an alumnus of Tougaloo College, I feel that there is an easier interaction with alumni for Tougalooians than there might be for people who graduate from Dillard, but that's just a kind of difference. My perception may be quite false.

JG: What kinds of relationships does Dillard have, in the time that you've been there, with other institutions within New Orleans? I mean other colleges and universities.

JWW: From the perspective both of the humanities division and the division of social sciences, I have things to do with both, I think the exchange with other universities was not as rich as I would have liked it to have been. I knew people at Xavier, and I would occasionally tell them about things that were happening at Dillard, but there was no real sense that we were going to have an ongoing exchange in terms of even just communicating what programs were going on at either institution between Xavier and Dillard. I really had very little sense of what was going at SUNO unless one of my friends said, "You know, there's a special program. Yanker's going to be there. Let's go to that." Prior to Katrina, I think it would be fair to say if you're only asking about the communication among the historically Black schools.

JG: Actually, any of the institutions.

JWW: Oh, okay. Well, I would say that there was, as far as I could ascertain, minimal exchange. Now at another level, in terms of administration, there might have been more things going on. I don't know. Certainly, if we talked about libraries, yes: sharing books, library loan, and that kind of thing, and having access to other libraries, which we had in a limited way with UNO, Tulane, Loyola. That kind of cooperation was there. I think the library people probably had the most formalized relationships. But if we're talking about academic units, I just felt that there was an awareness that other things were going on at other places, but whether you participated or encouraged your students to participate depended very much on who you knew at the institutions, not that you got the information, say, from a calendar of events or memos coming from administrators at Dillard.

JG: How about the relationship between Dillard and the Gentilly neighborhood?

JWW: It seemed to be a very good relationship. I didn't have a sense of that clichéd division of town and gown. Dillard, when you notice the campus, is fenced. It's like a park in the middle of residential areas and a business area, residents with business area. The students went to the stores that were nearby, going down toward Elysian Fields, and seemed to have very little difficulty. There was, as you would have in any urban area, a real need to provide a lot of security for students, especially for our women students, because it was all too easy for someone to get in under the wire despite having guards at the two major gates. There was a part of the campus that was not fenced, and that was called Gentilly Gardens. So if someone really wanted to walk in under the cover of darkness, it would have been possible.

JG: How would you describe the campus, the physical plan?

JWW: Well, I think I used the image of the park, and I would pretty much stick with that, because you have the immaculate white buildings. This has always been one of the main features of Dillard—the white buildings, lots of greenery, wonderful oaks, and the Alley of the Oaks. The grass was usually very well kept. In fact, at its best, Dillard had a very manicured look, and everyone who came was impressed with the physical plant. Many who came said that it was—and this is a hyperbole—the most beautiful historically Black campus in America. I'm not prepared to say that because I haven't been to all of them.

JG: Where in the city did you live or do you live?

JWW: I live four blocks from the university. The university's address is 2601 Gentilly, and my house is 1928 Gentilly, so I'm very close.

JG: How would you describe the Gentilly neighborhood?

JWW: I wouldn't call it upscale because it's a very mixed neighborhood involving people who obviously have blue-collar incomes, some who have less than that, and a lot of people who have upper-middle-class incomes—a nice mix. I will tell you—and this may give you an indication of how I really felt about my end of Gentilly—as you went east on Gentilly, there were in those neighborhoods, if we just talked about neighborhoods in terms of blocks, there were many much nicer houses. But what I felt about my very mixed end of that boulevard was a kind of security. I didn't worry about theft, and I have two huge glass windows, one in the front and one in the back. If anyone really wanted to rob my house, especially if they knew I was not there, it would have not been that difficult, although they would have had to deal with a security system. I mean, you don't just invite trouble. But I was pleased, I was very pleased with where I lived.

I was especially pleased because my house is two houses off of St. Bernard. I'm at that intersection of St. Bernard and Gentilly Boulevard, and at that intersection is a wonderful sculptural construction called Spirit House that was designed by John Scott, and I'm trying to remember the other fellow's name; his last name is [Martin] Payton, who had been a student of John Scott, I believe. They used some schoolchildren in conceptualizing this project, which was a city-sponsored project. It's a wonderful memorial to African American and African history. It was thought of as a kind of spiritual space. I remember there was, at least in one instance, storytelling for children under the Spirit House. So it became a great reminder of where people came from, what had happened to them, and the possibilities for the future. To be able to look at a work by perhaps the most gifted artist in New Orleans was just wonderful.

JG: Where were you when Hurricane Katrina struck?

JWW: When it actually hit, I was in Vicksburg, Mississippi, and I stayed for two weeks in a shelter—a very nice one, I must say—that was provided by the First Baptist Church of Vicksburg. That was just a matter of luck because the first night—and I left the Sunday before the hurricane—I could not find a place to stay, not in Vicksburg, not in Natchez, not in Monroe, Louisiana, and I'd been driving around for about fourteen hours. I just crashed at a rest area, and when I drove in that Monday morning, I was able to find a shelter in Vicksburg. I stayed there for two weeks, and then I was able to rent an apartment, which I still have.

JG: What communication did you have with the folks at Dillard during that time?

JWW: When I was at the shelter, obviously people were searching for other people, and through the telephone, people got to know where I was and I found out where people in Dillard's administration were. They were all in Atlanta. And after I had moved into my apartment, the communication was mainly by telephone, including a very early one, I guess it was actually October. There was a conference call involving Dillard faculty and the Dillard administration in Atlanta, which was very good because we really did need to know what we were going to do. There was a long period of great uncertainty, and various ideas were being tossed around about what

Dillard should do. Should Dillard try to use the facilities of Morris Brown in Atlanta, since that campus was no longer being used as a major part of the Clark Atlanta complex? Or should it try to set up camp elsewhere?

I think it would have been overly disruptive for us to have gone to Atlanta because finding housing for faculty and students might not have been that easy there. It wasn't easy in New Orleans either when we knew that we could not use the campus because of the devastation, but at least New Orleans had a lot of hotel rooms, and fortunately Dillard was able to make a deal with the Hilton that has worked out as well as it possibly could. And to be back in New Orleans was very important. One, because it was an announcement that Dillard and its students and faculty and administrators were very much committed to being in the city.

Secondly, I think despite our having to grapple with our various forms of trauma, the healing might have been better in place than trying to do it away from the city. I felt much better because at least I could see my house. The entire period during which we were not allowed to return because there were threats that if you came in and you weren't supposed to be here, you might be shot, and I did not wish to be shot. But I was able to come back to New Orleans in October, very early October. To see the city as it was then—absolutely unbelievable. The first thing that hit me on my return, as I'm driving in on I-10, is that the city does not sound right. There was an eerie silence here. You couldn't even hear a bird chirp. And the city had never in my memory been dry—I mean bone dry. I said, "This is like going into a frame from an old Western. The only thing that's missing is tumbleweed." It was just that dry, that dusty. Everything was covered with this gray dust.

JG: So no standing water?

JWW: Well, by the time I came back, which I think it was October 6, the water had evaporated or had been pumped, and there was probably still water in certain areas that I didn't go into, but around Dillard and certainly in Gentilly—I drove part of the way out toward the east on Gentilly, no standing water. Lots of stench from debris, trash, garbage, and the famous refrigerators that we all put on the curbs. What was most unsettling was the silence, and I was accustomed to hearing the schoolchildren at St. Leo the Great Elementary School laughing and playing, and that wasn't there. The other thing that was rather unsettling if you stayed here at night was the absence of streetlights and of traffic lights and the absence of cars, the silence and darkness, and it made it feel very much like a graveyard to me.

JG: Did you see any of your neighbors?

JWW: Not on my first trip; I saw not one neighbor. On the second trip, when I came back to participate in a poetry reading at the Gold Mine Saloon, this is the Seventeen Poets Reading Series, I did see my next-door neighbor, and I was delighted to see him. He owns a two-story house next to mine. He rents it, and for a while his daughter lived upstairs and then one of his nephews. Don comes in from Houma, Louisiana, which is not that far away, to do work on his property from time to time. It was really good to see Don. The woman who lived closest to St. Bernard—that's to the right, if we were facing Gentilly Boulevard, of my house—was elderly and partially blinded, so her family took her away. Another neighbor who was a member of St. Leo the Great, where I go to church, was in Baton Rouge, I think. Much of the neighborhood was deserted, but by December, you saw more people in the neighborhood, although not a large number, but more people were coming back, trying to attend to their property, to clean out as much mold as we could, take out rugs or just gut the walls, or whatever people were doing.

You have this visual assault or had this visual assault when you first came back. The more painful part of all of this was to walk into your house. And I was glad that I had not had nine feet of water; I had probably six inches. But when water stands in a house, and water of whatever kind we had in New Orleans, it becomes like a petri dish, and all kinds of things grow. Books that were on the lower shelves in my house, anything that I had on the floor, was destroyed. If the water didn't get to it, the mold certainly did. The water and the mold got to my collection of about four hundred LPs. I had to toss all of those. The same with books that I had in a storage area next to my garage, because water really got in there and the books were in cardboard boxes. One of the things that I lost was a rather unusual collection of African American poetry volumes, some of them I just will never see again. It was very painful to have to throw that out. I was also able to save some things.

Probably one of the things that made me feel good in the middle of all of my being upset about losses was that I had a friend named Chakula cha Jua. His real name was McNeal Cayette, but Chakula is his professional name. During August or late July and August, we were working on a celebration for the Chakula cha Jua Theater, and I served on the board and we were going to have this grand thing happening in September. We had urged him to put all of his original plays together. Well, he did gather them, and I made a copy of each. When I came back, I discovered that all of that material was sitting on the dining room table and it was in perfect condition. When I talked to him, he told me everything that he'd had had been lost. So I felt rather good about being able to send him his plays so at least he had that. He had not lost all of his years of creativity.

JG: Take me again to—I'm interested in this conference call that took place, you said, in October. Describe the call and some of what was discussed and what were some of people's questions.

JWW: Well, we knew or suspected that there would be a reduction of staff and faculty. What we were not sure about and we were assured of during that call was that all of us who were being retained would continue to receive our salaries. That was really very good news. We were told about our return to New Orleans. We were told that that was a great possibility because the notion that we would maybe move into Atlanta for a certain period until the campus was restored had not yet been abandoned. So there was a little uncertainty about that. But I think the call might have been designed also to allow us to hear one another. That was very important to have a sense that no one had died, or people you knew were living with relatives or in shelters or whatever, but they were alive. That feeling of knowing that your colleagues were physically still there led me to think, "Okay, there is life after Katrina. We will have something. We will be back together eventually."

During this conversation, we developed at least a preliminary sense of our commitment to the university, and I had been invited by a young woman who was a Dillard graduate to talk at Northern Arizona University. And I said to her before I even knew that we were having this conference call, "Well, I'm going to give my honorarium to Dillard." I was able during the conference to announce, "Well, I'll be sending you a check for $1,000." One of my colleagues in the English department said, "I think I'll try to match you." For faculty who were displaced and having their own problems, maybe even financial problems, whose property has been destroyed, to say that I want to give back to this institution because I believe in it is a very positive sign.

JG: Did you have offers or opportunities to take visiting appointments elsewhere?

JWW: Yes, and indeed we were encouraged to take visiting appointments or to take research opportunities. We were not encouraged to be seduced by these. I spent two weeks at Grinnell. One of my friends who had been with me at the National Humanities Center is associate dean there, and I had gone to Grinnell two years before Katrina. He asked me if I would come back and give some lectures and also do a two-week short-term course for students. I gladly said yes. So, I spent two weeks and I then spent a week at

Dickinson College. I had a chance to speak out in Arizona and at the University of Utah. I had an offer to speak at the Schomburg before December, but I couldn't do that. So, I actually went to the Schomburg at the end of February as a part of the Shabazz conversations.

JG: Talk to me about coming back to New Orleans and coming to the Hilton.

JWW: Well, I'd established a new pattern of life in Vicksburg, which involved many trips to my alma mater, which is only forty-some miles away, and enjoyed interacting with former students who were still around Jackson and old friends and people I knew on the faculty. I came back to New Orleans with, well, I suppose, the notion that this is going to be a real challenge. We'd been prepared for that in the conversation because President [Marvalene] Hughes had said, "This is going to be an uphill struggle for us." So I was prepared for that. I didn't know exactly what an extended period in a hotel would be like. I didn't know when I came back January 3 exactly what classrooms would be like. We're sitting in one of them now. There were just a lot of unanswered questions.

We began teaching January 10. There was a lot of adjusting that had to be done. Approximately one-half of the population of students that we had in the fall returned. That was wonderful. We had approximately 1,083 students here. Most of them were living in the hotel. Most of us on the faculty were living in the hotel and are still doing that, with a few exceptions of people who were able to get back to their homes fairly early. How do you teach under circumstances where you're in one of these partitioned classrooms and you are distracted by another class and you realize that you're distracting the class too? I didn't respond very well, Josh, to that initially because I suppose when I'm teaching my students, I like a space and I don't like to shout. I mean, I can raise my voice, I can be very loud, but I don't like that. Sometimes you had to really kind of be very forceful so students could hear you. It was hard to hear them, so the quality of the exchange was not what I desired.

I also had to think about what I could not do that I had habitually done in terms of my teaching. There were certain assignments in the courses that I was very reluctant to make, beyond reading the texts and holding them responsible for ideas and certain basic facts. One of the things that I like to do is to create assignments that really demand some work in a library. I'm rather old-fashioned about this, Josh, because especially for English majors, I think new technology—the challenges of making a good marriage between the humanities or actually any discipline and technology is fine. But what has happened is the joy of scholarship has somewhat diminished within certain disciplines. There was for me a particular joy of reading the first edition of Equiano in the British Museum. I went when it was still the British Museum. The British Library and the British Museum have now split. To just feel, oh, I mean, this is a high point. I felt the same way using Richard Wright's materials at Yale.

I want for my students a sense that it's not just going to the internet and looking at articles. There's a different discipline that you develop when you have first to go to the MLA International Bibliography, select articles, and then find some of these articles in the bound periodicals. Because despite all the wonderful things that are done on the internet, say with something like JSTOR, there are articles that have not been digitalized, and some of them are very important and much older. There are texts that you can only have in print.

There is among the late twentieth-century and early twenty-first-century generation of undergraduates that I am familiar with a real reluctance to use libraries in the old sense. They want instant information, and this is a part of a society that has socialized them, that they've been raised in. And I'm of an age where that's not what shaped me, and I realize that they've been shaped differently. I also realize that we will discover perhaps in the future that long-term exposure to electronic media will alter the way the brain processes information, and I think we have begun to see not necessary and sufficient evidence but some evidence that this is beginning to happen. Those things force me to make certain kinds of decisions about how I would teach.

Sensitivity to students also affected how I would teach. Not that I was going to become a softie or that I was going to become touchy-feely or overly sentimental about what had happened, but you had to be aware that like oneself, the students were suffering. Even if they were not aware of it, the students were suffering from this rupture, from dislocation. It affected how much they could concentrate on things. So that if I saw a student in a class nodding off, I did not become alarmed. Because many of Dillard students worked and still were working in various kinds of jobs when they came back, such as they could find.

The experience of the hotel, of the new physical conditions as well as the new intellectual conditions under which one would teach and students would learn was a very real challenge. So too was this sense that we were— let me put it this way. Good teachers try to prepare for the courses they're going to teach as many months ahead of the start date as possible. If you've been teaching for more than twenty years, obviously there are some things that are fairly easy for you. What is not always easy is being asked to teach courses that you have not taught for five years or something of that kind, courses that may not have anything to do with the projects that you're trying to deal with at the present time. So although you do what is necessary because you know this is part of your obligation to the university, I'm not sure that you always do it well, and I had not taught world literature for a very long time. So I kind of felt, "I'm learning along with my students." And the reading was wonderful, and the discussions were wonderful, but I didn't have the same mastery of that course that I would have of a course in southern literature, African American literature, or a course devoted to Richard Wright or James Baldwin and some authors that I think I know, or to some of my favorite topics such as autobiography or African American poetry.

JG: What did students get their books from? Did you do course packets?

JWW: No, we didn't do that. Extraordinary efforts were made to find book dealers who would be able to set up sites for students to acquire books, and we had to send in our book orders before we came back to New Orleans. Initially, it was thought that the books would be out at some large shopping center, which is quite a way from downtown New Orleans, but we did manage to set up a bookstore within the hotel, so the students did not have to go very far to obtain books. Sometimes the book orders didn't get here exactly on time. So for two or three days, you might be compelled to give the students an overview of what the course is, to do a little more lecturing than you would like, and to know that they had no reading material if it was not available online—and much of it was not. That was done both for term 1, which ended in April, and also for term 2, which began in April.

JG: Can you describe the teaching schedule?

JWW: Okay, the teaching schedule. As I said, what was unusual here is that many of us had more than what we thought of as our normal loads. I taught three courses, and I've taught three courses for both terms. Normally, given my privileged position here, I only do two or one, but most times I do two, especially because I was working before Katrina with our honors program, and I was teaching the sophomore colloquium, which was a real joy. So I had classes term 1 Monday, Tuesday, Wednesday, and Thursday. [Now] I'm a little more fortunate. Term 2, I only have classes on Mondays and Wednesdays. And the classes are an hour and a half, but it works out to be an hour and fifteen minutes for each, twice a week.

JG: Now I understand that the university did have to let go of some faculty and staff.

JWW: Yes. Approximately 59 percent, initially 59 percent of the faculty and staff were notified that their employment would not continue beyond November 15. A decision was made to keep senior faculty and tenured faculty and a few people who were, by virtue of their expertise, crucial. But most of the junior faculty did not receive contracts. Then when we were back here in January, there was this frantic effort to find teachers to do things because it had not been anticipated that the number of students would return, nor what would be the range of their needs given that many of the students had done a semester at a college in their hometowns or at some other university where they'd relocated. Because many of the schools in America were very good about opening their doors to Dillard, to displaced students from New Orleans, whether it was Dillard or Xavier or SUNO or whatever. So you found yourself with oddities such as a single student needing a course, so you're almost doing a tutorial with that student and then you would have, as I had, seventeen or eighteen students in a course. Then one or two people, there was a time conflict, so you had to make special provisions to meet with them separately from other students in the class. All of this did work eventually, but believe me, initially there were any number of glitches and minor frustration on top of the major frustration about "Are we going to ever get this all together?" But we did, and I think fairly credible teaching and learning occurred and is still occurring.

JG: How did you balance your professional obligations here with your kind of personal needs to look after your house and to rebuild that part of your life?

JWW: Well, given the problem of identifying a contractor, negotiating with my insurance companies to get insurance money so that I would be able to rebuild, that was very time-consuming. Then also the matter of having to deal with FEMA, which was not a major problem for me because I had initially asked for a trailer and then none seemed to be forthcoming and I said, "Well, I really don't need it if I'm going to be at the hotel." A trailer would just be taking up room in front of my house. Even people who did get trailers had problems about getting electricity connected. So I said, "Okay, that'll go by the wayside."

What I did find myself doing, Josh, was with trying to communicate and have some, as I call it, social communion with my friends who were back in the city. It became very important that one of my friends, who's an exceptionally gifted writer and all-around Renaissance person and also a teacher at an alternative program called Students at the Center, and I would be able to get together weekly for dinner. And this is very satisfying for both of us. It's not just so much the food; it's the conversation that's important.

JG: What's this person's name?

JWW: You may have heard his name—Kalamu ya Salaam.

JG: Yes, absolutely. I've actually been trying to get in touch with him. I'd like to talk with him.

JWW: Okay, I can take care of that. Remind me to give you his number when we end this interview.

On doing something very pleasant, I have two friends who are lawyers here, and our little ritual is to have breakfast on Saturday morning and one of the places to have it is at Le Richelieu on Charter Street. It's a hotel, and there's a very nice little eating area there, and one of the lawyers has a favorite waiter because he goes there very often, and again, that's a matter of a wonderful meal and conversation. The other ways of keeping myself very much engaged had to do with my friend Dave Brinks, who is the owner of the Gold Mine Saloon and also himself a very fine poet who had instituted, I guess maybe four or five years ago, what is called the Seventeen Poets Reading Series and he invited me back in October for the first readings that we had at his venue under the title, We're Still Standing or just Still Standing, I think, was the phrase used. I also participated in a program there that was taped by PBS in March.

Dave was the person who came and helped me get the rugs out and remove the refrigerator and do all kinds of things back in October. His yeoman efforts to reunite writers and artists in this venue certainly have to be applauded. That is an important part of our community, and it's separate from the writers that you would hear about most. I mean, it's not Tom Piazza; it's not Richard Ford; Ann Rice; [Douglas] Brinkley, who has a book, *The Great Deluge*; and some other names that kind of stand out because of their national and/or international prominence. These are very good artists, many of them emerging, some of us fully emerged or as emerged as we're going to be, I guess. The whole atmosphere is much more Bohemian. It's reminiscent almost of the 1950s in terms of openness and acceptance, and it's the most democratic reading space in the city. So that was a very important part of what I did and what I'm still doing, because next week, I'm introducing Dave for his book party. He has a new book coming out.

The other activity—I became much more active in doing things with St. Leo the Great Church, was basically through our partnership with all congregations together, so that's consumed a lot of my time. But much of my time, when I've not been teaching or doing those things or having these interactions with my friends, has been devoted to my own writing. I'm working on a manuscript that I had not intended to be a book called *The*

Katrina Papers: A Journal of Trauma and Recovery. I've been sharing some of those entries for that journal with people. One was published in *African American Review*. Bits and pieces have been published online in *ChickenBones*. I've shared it with people and gotten quite good feedback about it. Very early on, Joe Parsons at the University of Iowa contacted me and asked me what I was doing, and I told him. So he wants to look at the manuscript and so does Bill Lavender, who is a publisher here. I said, "Okay, I'll let people look at a manuscript."

However, I did not intend this to be a book, and I'm not going to stop writing whatever I'm doing until the end of August of this year. But it's been a very necessary engagement with my own feelings, my critical and sometimes sarcastic and ironical perspectives on what's happening here in the city, what's happening to me. There's a great deal of subjectivity here. It's a writing experience that precludes my grieving over much because I'm fascinated by what's coming out of my head, and very often I don't know where this stuff is coming from. It just comes. A lot of it I know has to do with something musical, as today I said, "Hmm, I need to rewrite a line from 'What did I do to be so black and blue?' I don't know what I'm going to put it with, which would go, 'What do you do to be red, white, and blue?'" So, I'm playing off music, I'm playing off literature, I'm playing off media reports. Also, the other thing I got involved with was the elections, not in terms of working for any camp, but I went through the two training periods to qualify as an election commissioner and to work on the polls. So I worked both for the primary and then the runoff elections.

JG: Was that something that you had done in the past?

JWW: No, this was my first time in New Orleans. But I said, "It's a part of civic duty." It certainly gave me a sense of further anchoring myself in the city and doing something very meaningful at that level. I found it very interesting in terms of sitting there and meeting more of my neighbors than I had met for a long time. I worked at one of the mega polling centers up at UNO, and I worked for the precinct in which I live, which is Ward 7, Precinct 17. So a lot of people from the neighborhood were coming by, and I was saying, "Hey, I'm glad you're back," and I told them where I lived, and we had these brief exchanges as I was certifying them for voting.

JG: How soon after the hurricane did you start writing?

JWW: I think about a week. The initial things are very, very brief, and then it began to grow. There are some longer entries, and there are some days I would write only three lines or whatever. That's been a very important part of my being here.

JG: Let's talk a little bit about the future. Let's start with Dillard. How does Dillard come out of this experience?

JWW: Dillard comes out of this experience with a new sense of its history—a commitment, if you listen to the words of our president, to be not the same but better than it was, a bit of surety that it can survive against the odds and will become a part of the new New Orleans. And perhaps in a rather different way because of the planning that is being done for both the restoration and expansion in some ways of the campus, a more integral part of the Gentilly community.

JG: In what ways?

JWW: Physically, mainly. I mean, it will be as much a part of the Gentilly community as any other entity there, but if Dillard happens to acquire the property or to lease it or buy it or whatever, property that belongs to the City Park Services which abuts our campus, that would give us a little bit of space to expand, and we would be more on a different street, a new border for us. To speak about a future—I will not say *the* future, I'm going to say *a* future because I think the futures of New Orleans may be quite varied, and the determinants will be whether we're talking about people or we're talking about institutions. I think all will be changed.

Dillard will continue as an institution of higher education. Reality will encourage and perhaps force Dillard to change in ways that we can only guess at. To be very specific, any institution of higher learning is very much dependent upon the number of students it must serve, the availability of scholarship money and other kinds of grants to meet basic operating expenses, as well as the always-present need to build endowment. How does that affect a curriculum? When an institution is very dependent upon X number of students who have Y number of desires in terms of what they want for an education and what major they want to focus on, you have to reshape your curriculum slightly—and sometimes in major ways. If you have a department and there are only a very small number of majors, it's not, in cold terms, economically feasible to continue that program.

Maybe what you want to do to continue your viability is to reshape the curriculum so that you have some very strong programs, and you have some other things that serve a supportive service. What that will be? I'm not prepared to tell you at this moment. I will put it this way: President Hughes uses the word *signature*. She wants Dillard to have a signature, and in a cryptic way, my chair said, "Hmm, I like this much better than having a brand name." And I think the difference between a brand name and a signature is the difference between having Walmart and Neiman Marcus. Walmart is a brand name; Neiman Marcus is a signature.

JG: How about Dillard's prospects for continuing as a historically Black college in New Orleans?

JWW: That part of its identity will remain for a while. It will not surprise me that in a few years, you might find that the percentage of students who are non-Black might rise a little bit. At present, it's very low. In fact, as we put it, we have one white student at Dillard—one identifiable white student at Dillard. I think—and Josh, you will appreciate this as a historian—that a future for Dillard is not going to be shaped in the absence of its awareness of the shaky futures for education, educational institutions in toto, and historically Black educational institutions in particular. We've noticed a trend of certain public institutions being absorbed in larger systems and are no longer identifiable as historically Black because the student body is much more diverse.

I think we have to kind of open up another part of this conversation, which is rarely had, and this is—I just ask and I don't want an answer to this—but why is it we say "historically Black" and we never say "historically white"? I think we have fallen into a little trap here. I'm going to put it this way: I think colleges and universities that have chosen to serve the educational needs of all people but who see a special need and can form a rationale for providing a space for students who have a particular kind of ethnic history, if you can make a case for that, you will continue. That also depends very much on whether people from that ethnicity make a major effort to ensure your longevity. The argument of reparations, guilt offerings, and all of this is not working in the twenty-first century. The bottom line is: What can you deliver? There's no magic about the delivery. If you prove that a Dillard, Xavier, or UNO is in some way excellent, you have to be prepared for the fact that people who are seeking excellence are not exclusively African American. You may always in certain ways be able to project the identity as the so-called historically Black institution because you're going back to matters of your origin, but your day-to-day practice may have a different kind of identity because it's much more a part of what is going on in the twenty-first century.

JG: How about a future or futures for New Orleans? What kind of city should New Orleans be in the future?

JWW: Please do not ask me what it should be. I will tell you that New Orleans—

JG: What would you like it to be?

JWW: You know, in my worst nostalgic moments, I would like for New Orleans to be what it was in the year 2000.

JG: Which was what for you?

JWW: Simply the wonderful crazy place that it had always been, the place that had rhythm, that had great people and great music, and that is not at all to minimize the fact that it had tremendous problems, particularly in terms of the education of young people, particularly in terms of class tensions, and not such a good track record as far as labor was concerned, because this city became far too dependent on tourism. I'm not putting tourism down, but if you're going to be a tourist city, you should also have a vision that maybe other kinds of work have to be possible for the young people who are born and who grow up and are educated in the city. You don't leave them all at the mercy of the service industry.

I would hope that as far as possible, what comes out of the total recovery effort for the city is first of all building levees, floodgates, and whatever else it takes to live in this mainly below-sea-level place, that that's done very well. We who live in this city, who have chosen to live in this city, have to also be prepared for the fact that weather is with us forever. It doesn't mean that we're not going to continue to get hurricanes. It just means that we have to be a little more prepared in terms of trying to do those things physically that can be done to preclude major flooding of the kind that we had, and we also have to be evacuation-ready because at any time, the city may have to empty out for everyone's safety. So the future involves first that kind of awareness about man and nature.

The future, as I said when I was asked to speak on a panel entitled "What Makes Community?" I said the future of this city must involve honesty. Now this is a loaded word. What am I talking about? When I say it must involve honesty, I think we have to look at our political situation and realize that if we have in the state of Louisiana and in the city of New Orleans a culture of political corruption, that citizens have been complicit in that culture. Let us not make scapegoats of the politicians who are playing the roles that have historically been designed for them. If they are cheating us, maybe we didn't want that, but we certainly helped.

So there must be in a future New Orleans as much political honesty as possible. If people are going to steal money, as Marc Morial's uncle did, I'm cynical. If you're going to do it, be good at it. The man stole pennies. He didn't steal any money; he stole pennies. That was so cheap. He's a shame to all thieves. Well, I'm not going to encourage anybody to be a thief. We don't need Enrons anymore. But honesty means that you have to become much more informed about what the political process is. You have to make more demands of those people who say they represent you. You have to make daily demands of them and ask them to be accountable as you yourself try to be accountable for where you live, your house, and the people who live in your neighborhood.

The future or a future for New Orleans has to involve honesty about the exploitation of the major contributors to a part of the culture of this city: musicians. Without any reference to their ethnicities, but if we're talking about jazz and we're talking about certain kinds of blues and varieties of funk and of the new varieties of hip-hop-inspired music, at least with the jazz, we can identify that part of the tradition here has been apprenticeship, the elders teaching younger musicians, and of course, what I call musical families. If you look at the history of music in this city, you find that an overwhelming number of musically talented people are related either by blood or marriage to a large number of other musically talented people. I don't know of any city in this country in which that has happened in terms of music. So if this is going to be what you sell to the world, ways have to be carefully thought through that you do not, in that process of commercialization, destroy the ingredients that have led to a rich evolution of music, and certainly you do not continue the practice of exploiting musicians.

The musicians here—and don't take my evidence, talk to musicians; I'm not one—but when people are surprised that many musicians said, "I'm not coming back to New Orleans," it is very much akin to what people who have said "I'm not coming back" found elsewhere: better opportunities. Particularly for people who had children, there were better opportunities for schools because the public school system in New Orleans has been an abomination for a very long time, and that too has to be addressed for a future as well as, as I put it, the possibility of having labor here that can pay decent fair wages to people and it's not all flipping hamburgers and changing sheets and driving taxicabs. A future for New Orleans involves honesty about racial resentment, and this is not a feature only of New Orleans; it's a national issue.

We have played, Josh, certain polite games post–civil rights about how wonderful it is that we are now all Americans. Even when I grant you that, and we don't have laws countenancing segregation and other forms of discrimination, whether it's on the basis of race or sex or gender identity or sexual preference—although some of that's still there, we don't have it on the books; we have it in the practice. We have it in how people live. In the city of New Orleans, class tensions may have a lot to do with one's sense of family history, wealth, and finances, but there are tensions that have to do with the notion that if you belong to a certain class, you may tend to despise people who have less than you and are seen as problematic.

That's why in the media treatment of New Orleans if you watched in the first months after the hurricane and were not well informed, you would think no one other than African Americans had to be evacuated from this city, because no one else lived here except whites who were in the Garden District and the French Quarter—very strange. It wipes out the awareness that the population of New Orleans has never been exclusively white and Black. It may have at various times involved minority/majority ratios that were racially identifiable, but there's always been a rich mix here of people, and to not be aware that in the Lower Ninth Ward, there were people who were not poverty-stricken and that in New Orleans East, there were people who had a great deal of money and that the largest Vietnamese community in this city lives in the east and they suffered a great deal. To ignore any of these facts is to do a real disservice to even thinking about planning a future for the city.

There are people in the city of New Orleans who are gleeful that an overwhelming number of people who were renters, not property owners, or people who lived in projects such as the ones that remained, have not been able to get back to the city. They think this will solve some problems because they are always transferring to those people the onus of being criminals, and there has been some very interesting work done in terms of why this stereotype is used not only for New Orleans but for urban areas period. So what I said in my closing remarks at this conference over at Tulane two days ago was we have to stop doing whiteface. This kind of minstrelsy that involves an attitude that New Orleans is a 24/7, 365 Mardi Gras has to end. It will not serve us well in terms of building a future and of healing. I really believe this very deeply because it's good for sales and attracts visitors to say, "New Orleans is just wonderful. Even now, it's just wonderful. Look at downtown. Look at all the things. Look at the number of people here. Look at all the festivals we have and the celebrations and etcetera."

That's okay, but you have to also say we have a growing crime problem, and the composition of people who perpetrate crime may be changing. Maybe some of the people who are here as guest workers are also criminals, and I'm not trying to criminalize Latinos, but MS-13 is active in this city, and it's becoming more active. We have a problem with drugs. We have a problem with a vision of what an adequate public school system for this city will be. It's very hard to say that because we don't even know how to project the demographics of young people for the next decade. We don't know that. We can guess at it, but we won't really know, and I think we had better do some very intelligent guessing so we don't wait forever to find out before you plan a system. But education is very important; something must be done there.

Something must be done to have adequate facilities for health care in this city, and not only adequate facilities for health care, but someone had better be bright enough to figure out that it's not about New Orleans when you're talking about health. You're talking about the entire southeast region of this country that continues to be affected by all kinds of weather conditions and changes in the soil and I don't know what else. And that we need some kind of long-term monitoring of what is happening to the health of the population. We have such things that we call a "Katrina cough" and people having viruses and skin rashes here. And I don't know what's actually happening with health in Alabama, Mississippi, Florida, and parts of Texas, but I think people may be experiencing a little more illness than is normal, and that seems not to be factored in sufficiently as a part of this major equation that we're going to be trying to solve for the next fifty years.

So when you ask me about a future, without trying to hedge overmuch, I will say that we believe—and I want to put that in bold italics—*we believe* that New Orleans will have a future as one of the unique cities of the United States, as a city from which other cities that in the future as a result of global warming may be threatened, but we don't know really what that future is going to be like. It's going to be exciting and painful simultaneously. It's going to involve a lot of bonding, making of new alliances and what-have-you, but it's also going to involve memory, which must not be erased. I think that twenty-first-century America plays at history when it's convenient to remember events that become legends, that become myths. When you deal with real historical facts and the impact of historical events on human beings and the descendants of those human beings, there is a tendency to want to back away from that and say, "Oh, why don't we just forget the past and try to get along and to coexist? Why don't we forgive and forget?" Well, you know, I suppose in some ways I will forgive you, but I will never forget, and the remembering sometimes brings back the temptation to not forgive.

JG: How does that apply specifically to Hurricane Katrina when you say memory, history?

JWW: Well, I'm thinking in terms of how people responded to you if you were trapped in the city. How did authorities respond to you? Who were those authorities who responded to you negatively or positively? Who were the people who came if you were on your roof and helped you to get out? There was a kind of immediate gratitude there for that help, but as you struggle more to come back if you make that choice, and you realize that there is bureaucratic red tape and a lot of planning. I mean, the number of people who are planning the city for the future is enormous, and the variety of plans—which I don't know how they're going to all become unified. They have to become unified in one way or another. That's mind-boggling, because it is really good for any urban planner or any architectural firm to have on its résumé, its track record, "We worked in New Orleans." That's very sexy at the moment. I think people are going to respond to that. They're going to respond, to say, "Yeah, so-and-so helped me, but you know, these other people were doing things and they were making plans while we were absent and they didn't want us to vote and they tried to disenfranchise us and make us feel that we were no longer a part of the city and they welcomed our exile and they would like to keep us in exile and they would encourage us not to come back."

A certain reality is that if you're going to the city of the new New Orleans of the future, Josh, you're going to have to be able to earn money. The motto for the new New Orleans is three M: money, money, money. That is all that's going to be important in terms of actually being able to afford to live here. In addition to that, culture will continue to shape itself and become revitalized. But let's get down to the reality of being able to live in a place. Living in a place means having a shelter, paying for utilities and services, paying taxes, and having transportation because the city is large enough that the existing transit system can't handle your being able to get to various sites that easily. So it means you need to have transportation, and you're going to be paying five dollars a gallon for gas. And you know, what does that leave for food? The food costs are going to go up as they will go up nationally, in proportion to national rates. If your ability to earn much more than you did prior to Katrina is not there, your future in this city is very uncertain.

So I think we are involved in an interesting kind of drama, an interesting kind of theater here. We're all acting and some of us are writing our own scripts, and others are following scripts that they didn't even know were written, and others are just following instincts and habits. All of this is happening simultaneously, and that's why it's very difficult to talk about. Because no one, no single person, and indeed maybe no group of people have the big picture. The big picture is like an impressionist painting, especially if you were using pointillism. You stand away from it and you think you've got it, but then when you move in closer, you see all these little dots and these little pixels that are very important. How many pixels do you have to deal with if you're going really to be able to describe what you've got there? That's what I feel about New Orleans, the future: that I need to know about soil. I need to know about sewage processing. I need to know about psychological problems and how they play into crime. There's just a lot to know about the urban [area], that if you're sensitive, you feel overwhelmed. You say, "I'll never master it all, but I'll have to master enough of it to be fairly intelligent in my participation in trying to rebuild this city."

JG: Was there ever a point or might there come a point when you would not return to New Orleans? I guess those are sort of two questions. Did you ever think about not coming back?

JWW: I never thought about not coming back, no. I will put it this way: if a hurricane of magnitude 5 hits this year and my house is damaged again, I will not hesitate to make a certain decision, and that is to take such resources as I have and build a house in St. James Parish, where I have property.

JG: Last question. This will sort of maybe bring it back to your intellectual, academic interests. What would Richard Wright say about Hurricane Katrina?

JWW: I've been asked that question many times.

JG: Really?

JWW: Yes, because I am a Richard Wright scholar. I think Richard Wright would have said—and I'd hesitate because I don't know what he would have said. So I'm just making a nice guess. I think he would have written about Hurricane Katrina much in the way that he wrote about the flood of 1927 in "The Man Who Saw the Flood," which was one of his treatments of it, and "Down by the Riverside," which was the other treatment: that when a natural disaster occurs—what he would now also have to account for man-made errors which intensified the devastation—that there are victims and that in America even in the twenty-first century, victimhood has a certain color, and that has to be admitted. Not that the people you relegate to victimhood think of themselves as victims, but Wright would have dealt, as he did in that story, with a person. And I think given Wright's own bent, it would have been a male. A man will do whatever he has to do to protect his family even if what he does is criminal, and that man—who has lost his wife who dies in childbirth and who has been put in a position where he knows that he will not receive justice because of what he did, and there are witnesses—decides, "I will not allow that system of justice which I see as, in many ways, unjust because I'm dealing with natural law and not man-made law, I will not allow that system to annihilate me. I will select to do something that will force them to kill me." It's like self-imposed suicide, social death, that is involved here. I think he would have had to write about Katrina in very much that way. It's important that Wright did not write about '27 until eleven or twelve years later. So the story I'm thinking that Wright would have written would not be written, were he alive and younger, until probably 2017. Then you'll have a very different picture of what Katrina, Rita, and levee disasters and barges creating ruptures was all about.

JG: Thank you for your time.

JWW: You're quite welcome. I enjoyed this.

Jerry W. Ward Jr. Talks about Richard Wright

Eugene B. Redmond / 2007

From *Drumvoices Revue* 16.1/2 (Spring–Summer–Fall 2008): 56–68. Reprinted by permission of Eugene B. Redmond.

Eugene B. Redmond: Let's start by having you talk about your first encounter with Richard Wright.

Jerry W. Ward Jr.: My first encounter with Richard Wright was at Tougaloo College. I might have heard his name and had no reference for it when I was still in high school, but at Tougaloo the first book by Wright that I read was *Uncle Tom's Children*, which I found to be a quite fascinating series of short stories. And then I went from there, bypassing *Native Son* to read *Black Boy*. And from that time, I really valued what Richard Wright was doing, what he was writing about. I liked the toughness of his mind. And of course reading *Black Boy* was an interesting revelation for me, because I was a reader—an avid reader—as a young person, and that didn't fly very well with my peers in Moss Point, Mississippi, the small community where I lived, because that was not a community where reading was valued among young people. Everything else *except* reading was valued.

So I was an odd person, but I could get by because I also made very good grades. I was their champion, the smart guy, but they just thought it was really strange that anybody would want to do all that much reading that wasn't assigned in school. "Why would you want to do it?" So I found out that Wright was like that as a young person, that he read, that he had a rich imagination. I had exercised my imagination very early on by coordinating memories from movies with the radio programs that I really would get into, like the cowboy shows or the science fiction series on a children's program I used to listen to. And I would always imagine what was going on as the description was being uttered on the radio. So Wright had that imagination too, but his, I think, was more a matter of taking things that he saw in reality. I'm not sure about his early days with movies. I doubt that very much was there until he became an adolescent and was able to work at the Alamo, the old Alamo in Jackson. But it was his defiant attitude that really hooked me. I resented—and I think even to this day, Gene, I resent—certain aspects of growing up in Mississippi because of the trapdoor that was shut over my head. There were things that, because I was an African American male, I was not supposed to do, that it was dangerous to do. And I remember being very upset when I was twelve and Emmett Till was killed, and you know, being warned, "You better learn what the code is, you better learn the ethics of living Jim Crow." Although not in those words—those are nice words. But I don't know that people now, given all of the rapid changes and loss of memory that have happened, realize what great agony Wright is describing in *Black Boy*. But I didn't have the agony within the family; my family was structured in a very different way than Wright's family was.

EBR: How so?

JWW: I was not tossed from one relative to another during my childhood, but I understood this sense that people thought you had to observe limits, the social limits, the mores of a society. But there was another series of limits that had to do with your not wanting to be white. Wright never put that in his book, but it's like if you do certain kinds of things you're being white, you're being too proper, you're violating unwritten codes within the African American community as it was structured at that particular time. And I was feeling this, and Wright then brought it together for me. So I think that's the beginning of my having a very deep affinity with a man I never met, Richard Wright.

EBR: Okay. You mentioned movies. Wright also had a fascination with movies. Would you talk about that for a little bit?

JWW: Wright's fascination with movies. I think we have one of the fine examples of that in *Native Son*: it's the whole scene where Bigger and Gus go to the movie. Of course, they're misbehaving very badly in the original, sitting in the movie and masturbating and carrying on. But it's the very fact that Wright was attentive to film and the newsreel, which would have brought into view the rich white girl who misbehaves on the beach with her boyfriend, who is a communist.... So what Wright's really pulling together, although one may not give very much attention to that in our rush to get through to what *Native Son* is about—he is very astute in his use of film to deepen or somehow amplify the thematics of his fiction. You have the whole business about the "native" in African films of the time: What is a native, the savage, the brute? And in the film where he did the movie version and inserted film, there's the scene of the dog being fed, and that's why—

EBR: Do you mean the movie version of *Native Son*?

JWW: Yes, the 1950 movie version in which Wright himself appears, not the 1985 version. So he inserts this film clip in which the maid is waiting on the dog, and then there's the comment, "They feed their dog better, they take care of their dogs better than people." So you've got both in the print version, in the novel, and in the film made from the novel this use of cinematography, showing how film records certain kinds of things not always by way of documenting it. We think of documentary as being different from feature-length films, but certain kinds of social attitudes, certain kinds of behaviors, class-determined behaviors, are reflected in part of the film, and that what Wright is mining. He's exploiting that in the book. So Wright did like film. Now I can't tell you in great detail, not having done the proper kind of biographical research, which films he actually viewed. But that's one of the things I've been trying to figure out. I do know in his journal of 1945 he has some comments on films that were showing at the time in New York, and he didn't think very highly of certain kinds of films. And I do know he saw, probably in Paris, Jean Cocteau's *Blood of the Poet*, which is a very interesting, surreal film, and of course Wright was interested in surrealism. So while we talk about Richard Wright's use of film, there is a very obvious reference made in *Native Son*, but I think Wright might, in the techniques that he uses, have borrowed something from the techniques that are native to the medium of film. How you present narratives: he never takes it to certain extremes, but you can certainly see why some of his work could very easily be made into film because he has that sense of how you use the visual at a certain point to forward a narrative or retard it or whatever you intend to do with it. And his interest in film is certainly borne out by much of the unpublished material from the late years in his life, where if you're reading in the Wright Papers at Yale, you will find screenplays—not full screenplays but little scenarios, treatments, that he wrote about possible films associated with any number of people whose names today mean nothing to us. I suppose because they never made it as big-time folk in the cinema industry. But that was how he was kind of positioning himself to get into other—or to participate in the making of other—genres. So we certainly have to do more research on Wright in film, particularly if we're going to talk about this once-popular phrase of a decade ago, *the gaze*. In other words, not just simply looking at something, but how you look at something with a particular kind of interest or how you direct the attention of a reader or viewer or spectator to something by using jump shots or slow motion or something, and how you do that in writing so that you're constantly manipulating visual as well as ideational potential.

EBR: Thanks for those rich insights. Yes, it seems to me that *Native Son* is very cinematic. I sometimes dream about it, and sometimes in my third eye, as I'm walking or driving, I can picture certain images. I guess one of the most memorable works for me in a visual sense is *Native Son*. So we're into Wright now, and you became fascinated with Wright as a student at Tougaloo, and what years were those?

JWW: It was either my sophomore or junior year, and I suspect that it might have been my junior year. I'm really not sure about which year. A lot of this has merged in my memory of what I did then, but I also put this in a nice framework. When I became interested in Richard Wright, I was not an English major or in the humanities at all. I happened to be at the time a mathematics major who just happened to be interested in everything in the sciences and the nonsciences alike. So it's not that I came to Richard Wright by way of some formal training in literature; I came to him as an interested— more than *merely* interested—reader of works. Certainly there was also the satisfaction of knowing that we had a Black writer like this. I did know probably at that time much more about James Baldwin than I knew about Richard Wright because I had a chance to meet Baldwin on the Tougaloo campus one afternoon while he was there working with some people on matters of civil rights. And I had read Baldwin before I went to college by way of a piece he published in *Esquire* magazine on Norman Mailer.[1] I liked that piece very much, and I said, "Oh, yeah, here it is. This Black man is giving it to this white guy and, you know, not backing down." And remember I'm very much accustomed to the discourses of deference in having grown up in the South, where, you know, the Black man is supposed to—if he's going to be critical of the white man, he has to do it with extreme care. And there is James Baldwin bare-knuckling it with Norman Mailer, and that was really great for me.

EBR: That had to be exciting.

JWW: Yes. It was probably like the great enthusiasm that people had as they listened to radio before I was born and just had a jubilee because Joe Louis was the champ. He was the champ for America, but he was the champion of Black people, right? So, there was a slight analogy, I would say, in my own jubilation in reading Baldwin. And then when I met him I was petrified. I had seen pictures of him, but I hadn't realized what his eyes did to people. When James Baldwin looked at you, he wasn't looking *at* you; he was looking *through* you, or so I felt. So I was like transfixed across from him in this room, just hanging onto his words and afraid to say anything.

EBR: Was it through Baldwin that you got to Wright? Or had you read Wright before?

JWW: No. See, the piece by James Baldwin on Mailer was not the kind of thing that would have taken me to Richard Wright. I came to Richard Wright by a different path.

EBR: Okay.

JWW: But I know perhaps why you're asking that, because now the very knotted conversation, Gene, is about what I call WEB. And that's not the initials for William Edward Burghardt [Du Bois]. That means Wright, Ellison, Baldwin. And that's a very interesting trinity that people wish to talk about, or to oppose fathers to sons by way of Harold Bloom's *Anxiety of Influence*, and to suggest that Baldwin had to kill his father. I don't know what Ellison did with his brother—fratricide? No, it's not that at all. I think this is all so much nonsense. It is true that Richard Wright was very helpful to Baldwin, and I think this is reflected very much in Arnold Rampersad's new biography of Ralph Ellison. And he was helpful to James Baldwin also with the Saxon Fellowship, you know, giving him, I suppose, a few francs to help him along in his worst days in Paris until the appearance of "Everybody's Protest Novel," which, I suppose, was the axe that severed the relationship, and you know, any civility that would have been there, because Wright felt betrayed, naturally. And you know, any writer's ego—yours, mine, anyone's—we can take a certain kind of criticism, but when the criticism is put "out there." . . . Remember, Wright's greatly lionized; he's *the* Black writer of the forties and we're moving into the fifties, right? And then to have this abrupt signal, "Okay, you're no longer going to be seen as *the* Black writer, *the* spokesperson, even if you believe you're that; you've got some competition. The young lions are coming, and you're going to have to fight for your space." And indeed within a period of two years—the years 1952 and 1953—all of this bursts out with the publication of *Invisible Man* and *Go Tell It on the Mountain* and *The Outsider*.

EBR: Yeah, quite a rush.

JWW: Right. You've got these three powerful books all coming at the same time, so now it's a matter of who's going to be *the* Black writer. Gene, I think this should make us very cautious about how we speak about these writers and others and also quicken our attention to the role of publishing, of publishing houses and all of the apparatus that goes along with being published, unless you're talking about self-publications or being published in venues that are totally controlled by a particular social group. And I'm thinking of socioethnic groups such as Broadside Press, the Lotus Press, Third World Press, Black Classics Press, and a few others. You know, we can be fairly sure that these are Black-owned presses and that they can have control over certain things (along with major problems in distribution and whatnot). So it is the publishers and the social critics, the literary critics, who have so much to do with projecting worth, one's worth, who have so much to do with determining worth, literary worth, social worth, why it is at a given time people ought to be reading so-and-so to the exclusion of someone else. Doing, playing very much in the larger field of publishing and reading in America the battle royal game, either as that's nicely depicted in *Invisible Man* or in a different way in the pages of *Black Boy*, where the workers try to pit Richard Wright against one of his fellow workers for their entertainment. You begin to think that you don't want to push this too much; you don't want this to become a preoccupation. But we have to ask in terms of a full literary history or full critical history just precisely how it is that certain works of literature come into being. We know about the intervention of the Book of the Month Club with *Native Son*, for example, forcing Wright to change certain things there. The same thing happens later with *Black Boy*. That's why we have this interesting history of half of the manuscript being published first and then Wright publishing little pieces and finally this being collected after his death, seventeen years after his death, as *American Hunger*. And that is because of publishing considerations at the end of the war, the closing years of World War II, and the argument, "Well, we have rationing; paper's being rationed, we can't publish all of this." But the real reason is, "We don't want to publish all of it. We want to publish the southern portion, and we have very interesting Caucasian reasons for wanting to do that, northern Caucasian reasons for wanting to do that."

EBR: Intriguing. . . . But what about infighting, fratricidal war, among Black writers? At what point did Wright participate in that? For example, I know he wrote a damaging review of Gwendolyn Brooks's work.

JWW: Well, if you wanted to talk about Richard Wright's participation, you would start with his review of Zora Neale Hurston. He did not especially fancy or take to *Their Eyes Were Watching God* because at the time he was under the influence of certain kinds of thought about the role of literature, a vision of the worth of literature that obviously means the writer must indeed not depart too far from whatever we think reality is when reporting on it. That is, the writer must produce work that we would today call social realism or maybe critical realism. So because he saw her treatment of a romance and a series of episodes in the life of a woman, which had nothing to do with racial struggle (it had to do with class struggle but not racial struggle, or the exploitation of the weak by the strong as that would be read through the lens of certain kinds of Marxism), he did not give this book such a good review. And Zora Neale Hurston, in kind, did not give *Uncle Tom's Children* such a good review when it came out. And back in November 2006, I was on a panel at the University of Missouri–Columbia put together by Julius Thompson in which I spoke about the two reviews of Hurston and Wright. And what I wanted to foreground was that it was not any kind of enmity between the two of them. Zora Neale Hurston was an established writer, while Richard Wright was still figuratively in knee pants, learning about literacy, learning about language and perception and how one should write. So you have here the young upstart writer, because when he reviews her book he's published a little bit of fiction, but he's not the big name yet because we don't have the *Story* magazine prize yet. In other words, he's not the big writer who's getting a lot of national attention, although he's getting attention from the Left. So my point and my comments there, Eugene, were that yes, you can look at the difference, and what is good about the difference is to realize that at a given moment in the history of our writing, all Black writers, African American writers, are not going to see the world the same, nor should they. And that there's going to be a clash. But I think the clash there was much more a matter of whether a writer is somewhat free, as Hurston would have very much argued for herself: "I don't have to march along with you, Richard Wright." Having been trained in anthropology and having a very good ear for language, for speech, she is accurate in her condemnation of Wright's rather youthful attempt to write dialect; she says he's got a wooden ear. And if you try to read the dialect as it is printed in some of those stories, you have to figure out, what do I do with that letter *t* as he uses it? Well, you figure out in context what it is, but it's not as smooth a way of dealing with dialect as we have from the pen, say, of Sterling A. Brown or Charles Chesnutt. There were models out there, and there were some very interesting things that Paul Laurence Dunbar did. Even though Dunbar seems to have been burying into this "strange" dialect of the later nineteenth century, he also countered in certain ways by compensating with the subject matter. You know, you get that little edge in there very often as you're reading Dunbar.

EBR: And Hughes.

JWW: And Langston Hughes, of course. Langston Hughes very much so, but Langston Hughes is using that with—How shall I put it, Gene?—I think with more of a sense of the urban than the rural. And Sterling Brown is getting folk speech, which folk for him is not yet the urban manifestation, although he's aware of that. I mean he lives in Washington, DC, after all. He's more interested in what was Toomer's project—to recover the sounds that are vanishing, the sounds that are evaporating. I think Sterling Brown was more about doing that. Wright is not worrying about anything vanishing; he's just simply using his understanding of what was southern. Hurston's also using her understanding of what was southern, about Black and southern people, and they had a different view.

Now, the main topic that we were talking about was the participation in fratricide or sororicide or some kind of murder figuratively. We cannot say that Wright was guiltless of this, although most of the reviews that he wrote after that were fairly favorable. I think he learned a little bit about reviewing writing in being reviewed himself and had to respond to some very harsh criticisms that he got in print with *Native Son*. For example, "I Bite the Hand That Feeds Me" is one of the pieces that certainly comes to mind. But what I'm really saying about the WEB business, as I discussed it earlier, is that all of this drama of which writers like or dislike each other—for whatever reasons—has to be somehow tempered by our understanding that that's part of a larger story. But let's look at what each of these individual players wrote. Meanwhile, we will never be able to erase from our interpretative consciousness what we know about real enmity or manufactured enmities, which are there because they are spectacular, and that's being done by the hype industry to sell something, to promote someone, to keep a process in motion. While that is certainly there and you can't deny that, I also think we have to reserve for ourselves another choice. And the other choice is to read *Their Eyes Were Watching God* and to decide that now since we are no longer operating within that same historical space where it was so important to have *Uncle Tom's Children* as a social critique, that now we can appreciate a rather sensitive—very much from the perspective of a woman—a sensitive treatment of a woman's problems outside and inside her racial being. Because you certainly have to deal with the grandmother's saying, "I feel that the Black woman is the mule of the world." So Zora Neale Hurston is getting Janie out of muleness. She may be in some ways used by a number of men and then find a beautiful kind of happiness with Tea Cake, and even in that relationship there's a type of using if you want to push that, but the point is that this is a story of a woman's being to a certain extent—to a human extent—in control of her destiny. And Wright is looking at various forms of the absence of control of destiny in his stories and struggles to gain agency and to be empowered.

Now when we look at this, I'm saying if we just take those two books, we may independently come to the conclusion that both are very good. Both are very informative. What both do is disabuse us of a notion that we use politically, a notion of wholeness, of singularity, of reductiveness of African American persons. Yesterday, at the EBR Writers Club session in East St. Louis, I was talking about this whole notion of the Black community and how it is a construction and how it has always been one, but at various times we—at least some of us—have believed in it more than at other times. And we had good reason for that: we knew the kind of fiction we were buying into, but we also knew why that fiction must exist. We were very vulnerable and outnumbered. Remember this: we were outnumbered, we are still outnumbered by others. So, what we have going on in this—I feel like I'm playing Wimbledon with myself when we're talking about literature, when we're talking about the publishing world—but when I look at Wright and what has happened after Richard Wright and what is happening in 2007, I'm so committed, Eugene, to the precentennial and centennial activities.

EBR: For Wright, now and in 2008?

JWW: Yes, for Richard Wright. What we learn of all of our writers from the past we must now begin to use. This is part of my commitment: I want Wright brought back into a broader consciousness because what I see in his total oeuvre, his total works, is a possibility of either considering him to be very prophetic or of seeing these works, which addressed many issues—domestic American issues, international issues—as still being crucially important for us. And what I'm noticing is there is a hurt, an angst, coming out of much of the contemporary literature which is not dealing with anxieties and woundedness in quite the way Richard Wright did. And maybe he's not the only model, but he will be a model that maybe some younger writers will say, "Okay, I buy into this. I now see the need to speak about the suffering of the African continent, of major politics, of the Third World, First, Second, Fourth—whatever worlds we have—I have to bring these topics back into the writing. Even if I'm writing about the people on the street and whether they're killing each other for Adidas or their drugs trade." Where are their drugs coming from? I don't know of a single Black person who has a drug farm in America.

EBR: Jerry, I wonder if you could talk about some of the projects, programs, and events, if you will, that are being planned or are in place for the Wright centennial?

JWW: Yes, Gene, there are many projects that we call precentennial or centennial events. I actually started back in the first part of November 2006 with the conference that Julius Thompson sponsored at the University of Missouri–Columbia at which Julia Wright, Wright's daughter, spoke, along with Colia Lafayette Clark and me. That went off very, very well indeed. And then with 2007, the entire calendar year, I go once each month to Natchez, Mississippi, as sort of an outreach program to discuss one text by Richard Wright with people in the community. We have a pretty nice mixture of people ranging from about sixty-five, which is a high number, to about twenty-five, which is low. But every month people have come and we've talked about Wright's books, and it's been a wonderful experience. I will continue this until December 2007.

EBR: Is that where you were going when I talked to you by phone the other day?

JWW: I think so. Yes, I think I was going to Natchez. Also, Julia made a number of trips to the United States from Paris, and she's given some talks here which I don't have a record of right now, but I do know that her son, Malcolm, went to the production of *Native Son* in Seattle, Washington, at the Intiman Theatre. A very interesting production, I'm told. That was also in November 2006. This year, 2007, in February, Jackson State [University in Mississippi] had a Richard Wright forum: Tara Green came from Arizona State University and gave a paper on Wright. I gave a paper on Wright and scholarship. Later that month I found myself giving an address at the naming of the Old South Hills Library in Jackson for Richard Wright. So we now have a Richard Wright Library in Jackson. That was quite an occasion also. In terms of future planning, there are things being planned in various states. For example, Deborah McDowell is trying to interest the Virginia Festival [of] the Book in doing something.

EBR: Quite a cultural-literary bill of fare. Other offerings?

JWW: I've asked my friend William Ferris, who is a former chair of the National Endowment for the Humanities and who also founded the Center for the Study of Southern Culture at the University of Mississippi, to plan something on the collaboration back in 1940 between Paul Green and Richard Wright on the stage version of *Native Son*. So he's got people organized over there, and they're planning a great event—much larger than anything I had expected—for April 2008, I think. The American University in Paris is planning a conference June 18–21, 2008, I believe, on Richard Wright. Also, the Japan Black Studies Association will devote part of its annual meeting in June 2008, in Hiroshima, to Richard Wright's centennial. I've corresponded with a professor in China whom I really don't know, but he was having a

Langston Hughes conference this year, and I told him he needs to have a Richard Wright one in 2008, and he seemed to be interested. At various schools throughout the country, people will be having readings and whatnot. At Yale University, so far what I know is they will have a special reading devoted to Richard Wright sometime in 2008. In March 2008—or maybe it's December 2007, I have to check this—the Organization of American Historians has a special panel which will be held at the Schomburg Center for Research in Black Culture, which Maryemma Graham is going to chair for them. And I understand John Edgar Wideman might be one of the people participating, along with Julia Wright and several other folks. Maybe Sonia Sanchez also.

Joyce Ann Joyce at Temple University is planning a program in which Julia Wright will be featured, maybe along with one or two other people, for October 12, 2007. And for the spring of 2008, the Annual Natchez Literary and Cinema Celebration is devoted to Richard Wright under the title, "Richard Wright, the South and the World," that will be February 21–24, 2008. And I have a role to play in that, naturally. I forget what I'm doing, but I know I'm saying something about *Native Son*, and I've got several other things to do there. Howard Rambsy will have an exhibit and an explanation of Richard Wright covers for *Black Boy* through the years, and other people will be there with scholarly papers. So that is part of what Mississippi is doing. And then in Arkansas, I've been talking to some teachers who want to have a Richard Wright literacy project. These are middle and high school teachers, and I may be meeting with them soon to get this off the ground in August 2007. In Spain, a professor there is finishing up the editing of a book of essays on *Native Son*, which we think will come out next year. I'm working with Robert Butler at Canisius College in Buffalo, New York, on the *Richard Wright Encyclopedia* for Greenwood Press. We hope that will be out before the end of 2008. And I don't know exactly, but there are some things being talked about in Washington, DC. I'm not quite sure what Chicago—a place that must have some Wright celebration—is doing. I think my friend Reginald Martin at the University of Memphis is writing a proposal for the Tennessee Humanities Council to do something there; on what date, I'm not sure. Let's see, Gene, I'm trying to remember; I'm trying to see in my head the summary I've done of all these events. But I think I've covered most of the major things that are going to be happening, so we do have a sense in which this whole centennial is going to be truly an international affair. It will have many, many parts, and there will be more things going on than I can imagine at this moment. But the main thing is that we will have people again reading Richard Wright and asking some very important questions of his work and probably about the man's life, too.

EBR: I was wondering, will there be any publications? For example, will the *Richard Wright Reader* be reissued? And is it still in print?

JWW: I don't think the *Richard Wright Reader* is still in print. Julia, who is now executrix of the Richard Wright estate, is in negotiations with Harper Collins about the reissuing of texts or maybe the publication of one or two unpublished pieces. But I imagine folks are planning books and certainly articles because I'm editing a special issue of *Mississippi Quarterly* that will focus on Richard Wright. Maybe we won't have the whole issue, but certainly a large portion of it. And I recently sent a proposal to HarperCollins myself for a book to be called *Richard Wright: 100 Writers Respond*. I don't know if they will want to do that or not. And then I'm working on my own book called *Richard Wright: A Reader's Notebook*, which will be a collection of some things I've written and aimed at in the process of writing about Richard Wright. So you can expect the usual outpouring of critical pieces in various magazines, you know, but to say that there are any other book projects that I know of at this time, I don't.

EBR: Earlier you spoke of your own introduction to Richard Wright and of some of his ideas, his techniques and styles, and his use of and interest in the cinema and employment of some cinematic techniques and crafts. I did want you to comment on Wright in an international context. You mentioned Wright's move to Paris, but there are some things that I've heard you say on various occasions and in different venues, including Tuesday night in East St. Louis and today in Edwardsville. Could you say a bit more about Wright's involvement in what we now call the Third World as both a writer and an activist?

JWW: Yes, Richard Wright was post-1947 when he actually moved to Paris, so the years of self-chosen exile were devoted mainly to an extraordinary outpouring of work on his part which we would obviously acknowledge as being involved with the politics of the Third World, the Cold War, the dying colonialism, issues of pan-Africanism and pan-everybody-else-ism. Wright's books in chronological order would be *Black Power*, which was his study of the liberation movement led by Kwame Nkrumah and others in the Gold Coast, which is today Ghana. He published *The Color Curtain*, which is an account of the Bandung Conference of 1955. He followed up shortly with another travel book, *Pagan Spain*, where he's looking at the nature of politics there, how the politics merged very nicely with Roman Catholicism, and how they had a happy relationship, which he found not necessarily baffling but very strange. And at the same time he is using *Pagan Spain* to figure out why Spain is rather unlike some other European countries: much of it has to do with the impact of Africa on that country, both in terms of its architecture and maybe some foodways and even belief systems. A book he really hoped would have a great impact—as the title indicates—was *White Man, Listen!*, published in 1958. During the same period, he published his extraordinary novel *The Outsider* in 1953; then there's another novel—the last one published in his lifetime—*The Long Dream* in 1958. He was also at the time, at the end of his life, writing haiku. The estimated number is about 4,000. We have 817 of those haiku now in print under the title *Haiku: This Other World*. And of course, since his death, we've had, well—writings that were not of the Paris period, such as *Lord Today*, but also *Eight Men*, which came out after his death and was very much a collection of stories that went back to the 1930s, particularly since he used the early story called "Slit," which he retitled "The Man Who Saw the River."

All of this is to suggest that Wright was a very, very busy person. He was in contact during these years, Eugene, with people like George Padmore. And I think his friendship with Padmore is crucial to understanding Richard Wright as the political activist, which many people would put in quotation marks because he wasn't in the streets; nevertheless, he was active at the intellectual level with matters of international politics and with making a diagnosis and a prognosis of the case. We have to look more in terms of our future investigations into just what were the relationships between Frantz Fanon and Richard Wright, given that they were both very much interested in all of the psychological fallout of colonialism. We need to know exactly what it was Wright had planned to do with going to a francophone African nation as opposed to an English-speaking African nation such as Ghana. Maybe to write much more about French colonialism rather than about British colonialism. So when we think of him as a political activist or thinker, what we should be remembering is that he was there raising a number of questions about what people were doing, why they were having these meetings, what were the topics they were addressing, or what topics they failed to address. These are all very important issues he was bringing to the foreground, and they are still, in our time, important issues for us. I have said on many occasions that we can read Richard Wright to discover questions we should be asking now.

EBR: Thank you very much, Jerry. This has been a very enlightening, very edifying discussion, as has been your three days with us. Any closing observations?

JWW: My closing observation, Gene, is to say once again to you, thanks very much for making my visit possible and secondly to say that our conversation, as an ongoing dwelling—as it were—with Richard Wright, is a very much unfinished business. There is no end; we are always in quest.

Note

1. James Baldwin, "The Black Boy Looks at the White Boy: Norman Mailer," *Esquire*, May 1961.

A Conversation with Jerry W. Ward Jr. on Richard Wright

Diane Williams / 2008

From *Valley Voices: A Literary Review* 8.2 (Fall 2008): 99–112. Reprinted by permission of *Valley Voices*.

Diane Williams: Good evening, Dr. Ward.

Jerry Ward: Good evening, and thank you for having me on the program.

Williams: You're welcome. You know I met you a few years ago at the Natchez Literary and Cinema Celebration, and I know you've been very involved in that event for a number of years.

Ward: Yes, I have. In fact, I will be giving a workshop for the 2007 Natchez Literary and Cinema Celebration on February 25 dealing with Richard Wright's very first novel, although it was not published until after his death—*Lawd Today*.

Williams: How did you get involved in focusing on the works of Richard Wright?

Ward: I began when I was a college student at Tougaloo College, I read *Uncle Tom's Children* and a bit of *Native Son* and thought Wright was really quite the person. However, I was not at that time training myself to do American literature at all. I was going to do the English Renaissance. But when I did finally decide what it was I wanted to do my dissertation on, I chose Richard Wright because I had been reading much more of him. And from reading *Black Boy*, I discovered there was a very strong affinity between the two of us and indeed a parallel in the trajectories of our lives, being that we were both Black males who came out of Mississippi, although at very different times. So I think that very often it's more—it's not only an intellectual interest—there's something psychological about why I'm connected with Richard Wright.

Williams: Tell me a little about your background. Are you a native Mississippian?

Ward: I'm an adopted Mississippian, I have to confess. I was born in Washington, DC. I moved to Mississippi when I was six years old. I did live most of my childhood and adult life here. I spent thirty-two years teaching at Tougaloo College before I went to New Orleans in 2002.

Williams: So you've been here a long time?

Ward: Yes, I have been here a long time. I'm from the Gulf Coast—Moss Point, Mississippi.

Williams: Where did you get your doctorate degree?

Ward: At the University of Virginia. I like to tell people I went to the Magnolia League, not the Ivy League.

Williams: I've seen some of your essays, and right now you're writing pretty much about current events if we go back about a little over a year and a half.

Ward: If we go back to that, then I wrote something called *The Katrina Papers*. It was a kind of therapy. There are some pieces of it that are really good. I think about where my mind was. I was in exile from New Orleans for almost five months. Before I went back, I stayed in Vicksburg for almost five months during the recovery process. But that's behind me now. I'm working on something else: I'm doing something called the Richard Wright Notebook. I've got editing chores—coediting the *Cambridge History of African American Literature* and also the *Richard Wright Encyclopedia*—and I'm trying to write some poems again.

Williams: Wonderful, wonderful. So you're into poetry writing. Do you have an opportunity to share your poems?

Ward: I do. I have been invited several times to read at the Gold Mine Saloon in the French Quarter. It has a series called Seventeen Poets, and I've been featured twice in that series. So I do have success with my work. But of course right now I'm much more concerned with my total involvement in the effort to ensure that Richard Wright is very well known in this state, in our nation, and also internationally because he is one of the great writers of the twentieth century. It doesn't limit him to Mississippi or to the States. He's a great writer, and he has been recognized as such internationally. Very often, Wright's works received much warmer welcomes abroad than they did here.

Williams: And you know that's true. He needs to be celebrated, but often when we have this realization, it's hard to get others on board with that thought process, and this is something you can't do by yourself. [. . .]

Ward: Well, as you will remember, we had an extraordinary meeting July 25, 2006, in Natchez, to talk about the Richard Wright centennial and my plans to go to Natchez once each month during 2007 to have discussions of a text by Richard Wright. Now that part is working out very, very well, and I was exceptionally pleased with the number of people, the diversity of the people who got in on that effort. You were there, people from the newspapers, radio, television, the Mississippi Humanities Council, the Department of Archives and History, and local groups, the Association for the Preservation of African American Culture in Natchez, and even someone from across the river in Vidalia. So you know there was a lot of interest there, and I think we're going to be able to help that interest to spread beyond Mississippi, beyond Natchez, throughout Mississippi, and to the other parts of the world.

Williams: That was so important to see all those people coming together like that, and it was really strategic. I felt that it was strategic because you had the newspapers there, and when people listened to what the plans were and how they had been laid out, they were able to envision how they could get involved. The media immediately knew: "Okay, here's something we can do; we can talk on this piece."

Ward: Right, we had a lot of help from Kevin Cooper and the *Natchez Democrat*, and there will be pieces appearing not only in papers here in Mississippi but in other papers as we progress toward 2008. One of the things I should say is that those of us who are working on centennial and precentennial events did not want to wait till 2008, which is the centennial year, to begin to broadcast information to really get people to examine Wright. So while I started in January, actually I was on a program at the University of Missouri in Columbia on November 3, 2007, with Colia Lafayette Clark and also with Julia Wright, Richard Wright's oldest daughter. The program was on Zora Neale Hurston and Richard Wright, but it was a wonderful way of kicking off the centennial. At the same time in Seattle, Washington, one of the theater groups there had done a new production of a stage version of *Native Son*. So Julia couldn't go to that—she was in Columbia talking about her father and her own work. I felt very good about that. It kind of fueled me and made me very enthusiastic about the work and amount of work that I'm trying to help people do in this effort.

Williams: Yes, and I think you have the buy-in of the people in the Natchez community and statewide as it relates to statewide organizations like the Arts Commission and Humanities Council. Did you say the Mississippi Museum of Archives and History? Are they involved in any way?

Ward: Yes. The Mississippi Department of Archives and History is. One of the staff members there is cochair for the Natchez Literary and Cinema Celebration: there is an automatic connection. Also, I think Governor William Winter, who is usually the master of ceremonies for all the programs we have in Natchez, has a connection. So we have all these wonderful networks of people who get involved with things there.

Williams: Now let's talk about why it's so important to talk about Richard Wright here in Mississippi. There are things going on nationally to bring to light some of his works and to talk about Richard Wright, but why is it important in Mississippi?

Ward: It's very important in Mississippi because there is the old cliché about prophets that are never listened to in their own country. You know, our people are not recognized at home. They have to make it abroad before anyone says a word about them. That has not been exactly the case for Richard Wright in Mississippi, but I'll tell you what the case is. If I walk down Capitol Street and say Eudora Welty, I think everyone recognizes something about Eudora Welty. However, if I walk down Farish Street and say Richard Wright, I am not sure everyone is going to respond with the same alacrity or degree of knowledge about who Richard Wright is. So part of my mission—my playing Johnny Appleseed or whatever mythic character I think I am—is to ensure that as many people in the state of Mississippi know something about their native son, know something about Richard Wright, and why he's important. One of these things that came out at our July meeting was the need to use books by Wright that were appreciated by young people in literacy efforts. I think this is going to be very important. It has to go beyond just simply giving them *Black Boy* or *Uncle Tom's Children* or *Native Son*. Because otherwise, you get people stuck with, "Oh, he wrote three books." He wrote many, many other books. I mean, many of them I would only want to teach in high school or colleges or to have discussions with adult readers because of the material that is contained there, and I know what community standards and religious beliefs [are], and you don't want to, you know, step on anyone's toes there, although that's exactly what Richard Wright wanted to do. He wanted to step on everyone's toes. He wanted everyone to become incensed about something so they would just not be complacent. He didn't just want to inspire anger or hatred or anything. He really wanted people, as he said in the ending of the first edition of *Black Boy*, to be able to figure out what was the meaning of their lives beneath the stars. Every human being has to find purpose (telos, if we're going to be Greek about it). What is your end? What are you supposed to be about? Consider his analysis of affairs in America, particularly racial matters and matters of social oppression, his views of international affairs, particularly of pan-Africanism, and nonaligned nations during the Cold War period. That interest came through in some of his later books such as *Black Power*, which was published in 1954 after he spent several months in Gold Coast, which is now Ghana, viewing what it was that Kwame Nkrumah was doing as he led his people into a free state from being a British colony. It was reflected in his going to the Bandung Conference in 1955 in Indonesia, where there were some very rich discussions about whether people were going to link themselves with the Soviet Union and China or the United States and other European powers or would they try to have their countries become totally interdependent without being dependent on the superpowers. He then wrote *The Color Curtain* and published that.

Williams: So he was stirring conversation and thought.

Ward: He was stirring conversations in his essays. They were published very late in his life—*White Man, Listen!* He stirred some interest in what was Spain about in *Pagan Spain*, which was published in 1957, by looking at Spain as a Catholic country that was very pagan and very comfortable with its fascism.

Williams: Do you think he had this kind of attitude as a young man when we think about his early writings? The first thing he wrote when he walked into a newspaper and talked to an editor about printing some of his works? He was pretty adamant about—he didn't know what he was doing.

Ward: No, he was only sixteen years old. You're talking about the story which we've not been able to recover, "The Voodoo of Hell's Half Acre," which was probably a kind of story a sixteen-year-old would write who thinks he had a very vivid imagination and was interested in swashbuckling adventures. But then the next story that was published, which people read very rarely, it's called "Superstition," published in *Abbott's Monthly* magazine in Chicago when he was in his twenties. That story has all kinds of echoes of Edgar Allan Poe. You began to see that Wright has a kind of southern Gothic imagination; he was interested in what was mysterious and what was horrible and what was frightening. Then he began to really deal with the material that was his. He looked into his life. He did not have to go to France to become an existentialist. He was his own kind of existentialist just as he was his own kind of communist, and I think he began to raise these really fundamental questions about why people are this way, why people do this. That was helped by his association as a young man in Chicago with other writers, his work in the W[orks] P[rogress] A[dministration] helping in the writing project. Also, he was able to learn about sociology at the University of Chicago, especially by way of his friend who was very learned, Horace Cayton.

Williams: Can we parallel any of his thinking and travels to that of James Baldwin at all?

Ward: We cannot do a good parallel, and I say that because very early in Baldwin's life, Wright was instrumental, helping him to get a writing fellowship which helped him when he went to Paris and of course the famous anxiety of influence kicked in, and Baldwin wrote "Everybody's Protest Novel," suggesting that *Native Son* was in many ways very limited because it was very like *Uncle Tom's Cabin*. You know, just making protests did not represent the real humanity of the character of Bigger Thomas and a few other things. That ruined their friendship. I would say that we can't find a parallel because Baldwin grew up in the church or some variety of the Black church and indeed was what I called a secular minister. If you read Baldwin very carefully, you're always hearing preaching. And it's not preaching that is tiring or boring; it's a very interesting kind of preaching because he is holding the world to standards of morality. I think Wright also had standards of morality, but he began from a very different vantage. He did not like the religion that was his grandmother's, which was Seventh-Day Adventist, and he grew not to like religion as something that he had to practice. He recognized, of course, the power of the church and religion in people's lives, particularly in Black culture. So although he could not be the believer and could certainly not be the preacher, I think he is more like the Old Testament prophet who doesn't preach: I mean, he condemns. *J'accuse*. He points the finger and says, "This is what you are; this is what you're like."

Williams: So does he try to lay out a standard that people should look at?

Ward: I think Wright was a little too clever to lay out a standard. As soon as you put any standards—and we do this daily—you're putting a grip on reality, and that is very necessary. If we didn't have that, we would be occupying a state of chaos or a state of nature or something. But Wright is saying, "Look, this is what we have here, but there are problems, and you can see these problems in terms of how characters respond. What are human desires? These are the things that are responsible for progress or someone being retarded in terms of advancing in civilization. What are you going to do about it?" He leaves us with something in our hands which is very problematic. He does not want us—and I really like this about Richard Wright, after he had some success with the first collection of stories, *Uncle Tom's Children*, in 1938, he recognized that people read the stories and felt very sorry for southern Blacks and very sorry about lynching and all the problems that you had, and they would cry about it and say, "How sad." And Wright said, "I don't want to write that kind of material. I don't want to just write material people can cry about. I want to write something that really assaults their intelligence and their souls, so they can't get rid of it." And the next book that comes out is *Native Son*. People say Bigger is a repulsive character. That's exactly what Wright wanted, because he wanted people to understand that environment and what comes from having a real lack of will—the kind of resilience that he himself had. If a character didn't have that, you get a Bigger Thomas. And as we all know, as people say, Bigger Thomas is still with us? Yes, and they're multiplying.

Williams: He sounds like he was very resilient, because I'm looking at him as a Black man. He is taking this look from the outside, not from the inside out, and saying, "Hey, you need to take a look at the way society is and the way things are going." Is that what you're saying?

Ward: Oh, that's very much along the lines of what I'm trying to drive at. When we think of the earlier twentieth century in Mississippi, Wright was growing up here. He was born in 1908 in the Cranfield area near Roxie. He was born into a sharecropping community, and of course then his parents moved to Natchez when he was about three or four years old to live with his maternal grandparents, who were there at the time before they moved themselves to Jackson. You go to *Black Boy*, and you look at how he writes about his early life, and you realize part of his resilience came from having a really little mean streak as a kid, as a brat. I mean, he was defiant. And it comes out of things he said to his grandmother, things he did when his father told him to shut the cat up: he killed the cat. He did these things, and in Memphis when he was six years old, he walked down the street and went into this bar; they thought he was cute, and they got him drunk. He created some of these things, and I could see why he could survive Mississippi because he got out when he was nineteen years old, went to Memphis, didn't have pleasant experiences there, went to Chicago, and then became a writer, and then went to New York. And when New York was no longer satisfactory in 1947, he decided to go into exile and spent the next thirteen years of his life until his death in 1960 in Paris.

Williams: How many children can kill a cat and grow up and become a writer? Usually you think of a child that does something like that or that kind of experience that he had, you pretty much set his destiny in your own mind.

Ward: Because the cat haunted him. His mother made him bury the cat and then she told him he really need to pray about what he had done. So the cat worried him. He was having bad dreams about what he had done. He wasn't happy about this later.

Williams: Who inspired him?

Ward: Richard Wright inspired Richard Wright. I think [. . .] we always look for role models. Who inspired you? I think of course my parents inspired me, some of my teachers did. I won't say I created myself: that's all too arrogant. Richard Wright created himself. There are some people who come into the world and have a lot of talents. They don't even know which talents they have, and by accident they develop those talents and become noteworthy people or certainly contributing members to society or positive contributors to society. I think Richard Wright then took all of the negative things in his environment, the efforts of people to say, "You can't be more than this," and the glass ceiling that American racism always places on Black females and males, and he said, "No, no, I'm not going to put up with that. I'm going to find ways of overcoming it." And the way of overcoming it was with language. He used language to defeat those people who would have kept him very small.

Williams: He went to the Smith Robertson School.

Ward: Right. He went to Smith Robertson, but before that he was at Jim Hill. He went to Jim Hill for a year, maybe one year at Lanier—I have to check on that again.

Williams: At Smith Robertson, didn't he have an experience when he was graduating when they wanted to write his—

Ward: Yeah, they wanted to write his graduation speech, and he said, "I'll have nothing of it," and he wrote his own. He wrote his own speech because he didn't think it was right that he should have to just simply become a kind of puppet for the words of someone else. He had ideas! In the documentary *Richard Wright: Black Boy*, which Mississippi ETV, the predecessor to Mississippi Public Broadcasting, did back in 1993, many of his classmates from Smith Robertson who were still alive kept saying, "Richard Wright read all the time. I'm surprised he had eyes when he died, 'cause it was like he's reading his eyeballs out." I remember one of his classmates said that. And most recently at a talk I was giving in Hattiesburg, a woman came up to me and said, "You know, my mother went to school with Richard Wright in Natchez and at Smith Robertson, and she is on that famous 1925 graduation picture from the ninth grade there with him." And I said, "Well, when we meet again you must point out who she is to me."

Williams: Can we even imagine how far along his work would have gone if times and society had been a little bit different? He was a contemporary of Eudora Welty. They both came up around the same time, not too many miles away from one another.

Ward: Well, they're born a year apart. She's 1909, he's 1908. They came from very different areas and very different classes, obviously. But I don't think things should have been different. I think that Wright teaches us something. You have to comfort history as it unfolds. You can wish for better things. Obviously the struggles that people have had since Mesopotamia have been about trying to make spaces better for themselves and other people. So instead of trying to retreat from the horror of life, you get up in its face. And that's what I think Wright is teaching us through his works. You get up in its face. So it would have been wonderful if I could have grown up and Wright could have grown up in Mississippi without all the pains of segregation and how people tried to damage my psyche. They did major damage to someone like Emmett Till and fortunately not to me or to Richard Wright. But the point is we have to live with that memory, and that's why I think I have become very exercised when people say, "Why can't we just all live together and forget the past?" If you want to forget, that's your business; but I'm not forgetting. I may partially forgive you, but I am not forgetting. Never.

Williams: I guess you know that Mississippi, through the visitor and tourism in the state, is looking at, studying, and laying out the trails for the Civil War, civil rights, and the blues. And I think that it's something that is very important right now because we don't want to forget those things.

Ward: We don't want to forget those things, but we also have an obligation. You can put up many numbers of monuments anywhere. Public artwork, this is part of where you are.

Williams: Yes, it is!

Ward: And people will pass by and say, "Uhmm, interesting." Never look to see what the inscriptions are; the plaque under there is to explain why this memorial is there. So I think we have an obligation when we are trying to remember ourselves. As our memories fade, we have to constantly nurture them and help others remember. It has to become part of a tradition, of the process of outside the institutions such as our schools. You take children to a museum, a blues museum, a civil rights museum, a permanent civil rights exhibit at the Old Capitol when it is restored. Or someplace else to see what was the Civil War about, and what happened around Vicksburg, why is this mammoth cemetery there with the Civil War dead, gray and blue? So, you have to teach these things because young people are not going to pick them up on their own. They're being assaulted by so much media and so much infotainment that real information and the ability to think critically is not being taught to them outside of schools where they can very easily forget as soon as school is over. And I'm saying it has to become a total habit of mind. Wright was trying that in 1941 when he published *12 Million Black Voices*, a folk history of the Negro in the United States. And you read the introduction, and Wright is at least honest about his little trick. He says, "I am not giving any attention to 10 percent of the Negro population"—that was Du Bois's "Talented Tenth"—"I'm not giving them any attention, I'm only going to look at the little people." And so you get this kind of skewer story, but you understand because he's been honest about saying, "I'm not looking at professionals, I'm not looking at doctors, lawyers, teachers, people who are very proud of their jobs in the post offices, maybe some people who are entrepreneurs. I'm not looking at those people; I'm looking at the masses, the overwhelming number of people who have not yet made it." That's how he tells that story using some photographs from the Farm Security Administration—which had this huge documentation project as you all know—and a few photos I think Wright shot himself. He was also very interested in photography, among other things like the blues and jazz. So we're talking about a man. I get more and more excited as I talk about him.

Williams: He liked blues, huh?

Ward: Yes, he did. He wrote "King Joe's Blues," which was recorded by Paul Robeson with the Count Basie Orchestra.

Williams: Really?

Ward: Yes.

Williams: I would love to have a copy of that.

Ward: I had a copy until Katrina took it away. I'm going to blame that woman for many things.

Williams: [. . .] Would you share some of Wright's writing? [. . .]

Ward: [. . .] "Long Black Song" [. . .] was one of the stories that he did in 1938 in his collection *Uncle Tom's Children*. It is about a woman—a wife—who lives in northern Mississippi, and her husband has gone off to sell crops in town to get some money and buy some things for the family, and he's been away from the family for many days. [. . .] I think here we sense something about Richard Wright's attention to potential symbolism in his description, his use of color. But what's most important—and this is a kind of teasing: I'm not going to tell you why the child is beating on a clock, but it's important having some child beat on time and the bang, bang, bang here is like that bling, bling, bling that you hear at the beginning of *Native Son* when the clock wakes up the family. So I think you see that Wright is trying as a young writer to use many, many ingredients that make us very sensitive to the ordinary things about life, which are so important in what someone calls the practice of everyday life that we usually ignore. Now I will give you another kind of Richard Wright, and this is Wright the poet, because he is not often credited as being a poet, although he did write a number of proletarian poems in the 1930s, which were published in magazines, and toward the end of his life he got into the habit of writing haiku and produced four thousand of them. Eight hundred seventeen of those haiku have been collected in a book called *This Other World*, which came out in 1998. I think some attention should be given to Wright as a poet. For me, the most magnificent poem that he wrote is "Between the World and Me."

Williams: You mentioned his haiku, and I think Dr. Zheng at Mississippi Valley State University has been looking at Richard Wright's haiku.

Ward: He has. He has looked at the haiku, and one of his students actually published a short piece in the *Richard Wright Newsletter* last year on Richard Wright's haiku. So, yes, Mississippi Valley State and Dr. Zheng are giving a lot of attention to this, and he has recently received funding from the National Endowment for the Humanities for a three-day workshop for teachers. [. . .]

Williams: ["Between the World and Me" is] so striking, so vivid. [. . .] What activities are taking place as is related to the works of Richard Wright?

Ward: [. . .] Next week, starting Thursday, February 22 through Sunday, February 25, there's the Natchez Literary and Cinema Celebration for 2007, and the theme is "Southern Accents: Language in the Deep South." And there are a number of really great things that are happening there with language and people talking about how southern writers use language, how other people in the South use language. As far as Wright material goes, as I've said before, I'm doing a workshop on *Lawd Today* on Sunday at Copiah-Lincoln Community College in Natchez. In April, Professor C. Liegh McInnis at Jackson State will be sponsoring a Richard Wright Forum on April 12, and I have the good fortune of being involved in that, and there will be some other scholars who will be talking about Wright's works. We do have something happening very soon here in Jackson in addition to the things that I'm doing in Natchez. I should say that this is just the beginning. People will know internationally things are beginning to take place. There is something planned for the American University in Paris in 2008. The Organization of American Historians in 2008 will be having a special panel at its conference, and of course there are some other things that maybe later I can tell you about, but let's just say that throughout the world people are beginning to think about all they can indeed celebrate and learn from Richard Wright.

Redefining and Canonizing African American Literature: An Interview with Professor Jerry Ward

Hong Fang / 2010

From *Foreign Literature Studies* 32.5 (October 2010): 1–5. Reprinted by permission of Hong Fang.

Creating and reshaping the canon of American ethnic literature by compiling anthologies or writing literary histories is an important mission of American literary scholars. Henry Louis Gates Jr. made such an effort with the compilation and publication of *The Norton Anthology of African American Literature*, which, more than institutionalizing American literary studies, claims a space for African American literature in American literary studies. Professor Jerry Ward and coeditor Maryemma Graham show their understanding of what African American literature is with *The Cambridge History of African American Literature*. This forthcoming book broadens and enriches our understanding of African American literature. Professor Ward presented a keynote address, "On the Study of African American Literature: The Obligation of Literary History," at the Symposium on African American Literature held on December 19 and 20, 2009. His speech encouraged us to think about how the compilation of anthologies and the writing of literary histories help shape different literary canons. With the intention of exploring how *The Cambridge History of African American Literature* changes our understanding of African American literature, Hong Fang, an associate professor from Nanjing University, interviewed Professor Ward on December 20, 2009.

Hong Fang: I think you began your talk by putting the writing of *The Cambridge History of African American Literature* in the context of the postmodern era. Is that right?

Jerry Ward: Yes. My coeditor, Maryemma Graham, and I are making a particular kind of intervention. That's the phrase we use: a particular kind of intervention. We are emphasizing that literature is writing because we are both involved in the Project on the History of Black Writing. If you go on the internet, you can find our website—Project on the History of Black Writing [https://hbw.ku.edu/]. We want to extend the notion of literature and to include writing by overlooked people. Toni Morrison is a superb and exceptional writer, but she is not totally representative of all the views embraced by women.

HF: Yes. I totally agree with you.

JW: I think it's very important to recognize that some ways of studying African American literature are very imitative of the traditional ways of studying American literature. That is to select out the major figures and try to forget about everybody else. And that leads to a kind of literary history which privileges a special group of people. I want *The Cambridge History of African American Literature* to be read by students as well as scholars.

HF: That relates to my next question. How do you interweave the literary theory into the writing of *The Cambridge History of African American Literature*?

JW: It is full of theory because, as I said, it has to be written by many people: we have thirty-four contributors. They try to tell us an enormous story about literature, and there will not always be agreement among contributors.

HF: That is similar to the compiling of an anthology of African American literature.

JW: Yes, you have to have a theory, or you have to have some notion of theory in order to put together an anthology. There must be grounding ideas in an anthology. I will give you an example. *The Norton Anthology of African American Literature* and *Call and Response: The Riverside Anthology of the African American Literary Tradition* are the ones that are most used now for teaching African American literature. You will find in both anthologies some of the same materials, but the way they are organized is very different. The editors of *Call and Response* use figures which come out of the Black oral tradition or musical traditions and certainly out of the Black church tradition. The title, *Call and Response*, refers to the minister giving a line and the congregation responding to that line. [. . .] The *Call and Response* editors have a certain view of literary history. Gates and [Nellie] McKay, on the other hand, are pretty conservative in their approach. So, they use a different idea of literary history.

HF: The anthologies talk to each other—

JW: The anthologies are not always talking to each other; they sometimes ignore each other.

HF: Ignoring is a kind of response too.

JW: It is a response.

HF: It's a negative response. So what you suggest is that both of these influential anthologists of African American literature have a sort of grounding theory for their work. They only make their grounding theory work through by putting what they include—

JW: And what they exclude! In a literary history which makes any attempt to be somewhat comprehensive, something is omitted. One cannot be comprehensive. It's mission impossible.

HF: The anthologists construct a canon of African American literature. I believe when you edit *The Cambridge History of African American Literature*, you also canonize African American literature.

JW: We are trying to canonize something, but I don't know if I like the notion of canonizing. All these literary terms are stolen. No, not stolen—they are borrowed from the Roman Catholic faith. We don't have a Pope for literature, but perhaps you want a Pope. When you have canonized writers into saints, I am kind of wary.

HF: Even though you don't like the term *canonized*, if we see *The Cambridge History of African American Literature* as part of the canonizing process, can you use a few sentences to suggest what are the similarities and differences between what it canonizes and what *The Norton Anthology of African American Literature* canonizes?

JW: I would suggest perhaps that when you talk about poets, we are certainly going to talk about Rita Dove. The poetry of Rita Dove will be considered, but we also think it is very important that you have someone who speaks about the work of Jayne Cortez, who is very different. And Jayne Cortez is not given as much critical attention as, say, Rita Dove, or even more recently, Elizabeth Alexander or Natasha Trethewey. Both of them are big names now. Elizabeth is a good poet, a very fine poet, and she read at the inauguration for Barack Obama, and Natasha Trethewey got the Pulitzer Prize for poetry several years ago. I think she is following the steps of somebody like Gwendolyn Brooks, who got the Pulitzer Prize for *Annie Allen*. But does she have the same kind of commitment as Gwendolyn Brooks? No, she does not. I am looking at what these people do with their poetry. Gwendolyn Brooks did one thing with her poetry, and Trethewey is doing something else. When you ask me to make the distinction, I would say that if we are going to have canons, we'd better know the reasons for having canons. The canon in the Nellie McKay and Gates's book is to preserve a certain kind of status quo and a certain notion that literature is a privileged kind of enterprise or a work of artifacts. It is supposed to be looked at in a certain way and highly regarded because of its excellence. And that is what everybody who is going to be intelligent is supposed to know.

HF: You mean that they maintain aesthetic values?

JW: I am not opposed to aesthetic values. I do not want to be misunderstood. I do want to point out that when a critic evokes aesthetic values, he must know what battle he has chosen. Gates once asked if African American literary works could stand under the weight of academic criticism. His question was legitimate. Nevertheless, I think literary values and craftsmanship can and should be measured in nonacademic ways. Much of world literature might not stand under the weight of academic Eurocentric criticism. We do well to consider another kind of criticism. What I am interested in, and what the editors of *Call and Response* seemed to be interested in, is a view of literature that accepts the grounds on which a people express their aesthetics, their social concerns, and their political concerns. People express the themes that they find in their culture and in the conflicts they have when they meet other cultures. That to me is more exciting, and that is why I said focusing on writing leads to a much more practical kind of knowledge. For example, if a Chinese critic studies the aesthetics of Chinese literature, that critic knows that what is aesthetic in a Chinese novel may not necessarily be aesthetic in a Western novel. The aesthetics are constituted by different kinds of cultural references. Likewise, the aesthetics of an African American novel may differ from the aesthetics of an Irish American novel. Novels are indices of our cultures. One may find that for certain periods of Chinese history, the novel was a product of the imperial courts or appreciated most by members of the Mandarin class. When did the novel become open to ordinary people? Why do these people now suddenly want novels? Are they really imitating the upper class? Or is there another reason that they want to have novels as opposed to stories, which had existed for a thousand years in your culture?

HF: That reminds me of what you mentioned that your book concerns a history of Black writing. It is not just literature with aesthetic value but broader.

JW: Yes. I wish we had been able to say more about the way Black men and women used essays. Essays are looked at as historical documents or part of a discourse on something, but essays are not always considered literature. So a very polemical document such as David Walker's *Appeal* (1829) should be talked about as literature.

HF: *The Cambridge History of African American Literature* includes both the oral tradition and the printed text. In that way, it is similar to *Call and Response* and also like *The Norton Anthology of African American Literature*. I wonder whether that has something to do with Gates's signified theory, which suggests that African American literary tradition has its roots in the African American oral tradition.

JW: My notion about the signifying? Suppose I come from a different kind of African culture that is not Yoruba—say, the culture of Mandingo. We don't have the same belief system; we don't have the same things as Yoruba. I am also African American, and that's my background. How does signifying with this privileging of Yoruba explain me? Yes, we have the signifying, and we have to be careful about the signifying you are talking about because not everything African American came out of the Yoruba culture. Genuinely, African Americans came from hundreds of African cultures. So the problem for me is to point out what historian Michael Gomez suggests: as a result of the slave trade, we have a mixing of African peoples, African ethnicities who were all mixed up on the same ship. They don't all speak the same language. Such a fact makes me very cautious about any embracing explanation such as you are going to get out of the universal signifying. In the making of literary history, Dr. Maryemma Graham and I offer an alternative to the position Gates took in his anthology.

One chapter in *The Cambridge History of African American Literature* is about popular literature. In America, the erotic novels, the romance novels, the street-life novels have great sales. They are selling wildly, but critics are not looking at popular literature as being literary. The literature is a part of commercialism. Candice Love Jackson, my former student who wrote this chapter, says that this is really a part of how we are writing now, of how many people are writing and how they are reading. They are not reading Toni Morrison less. They are reading Zane more. They are reading hundreds of writers who have all this salacious material. Their novels border on being sexually explicit pornography as far as I am concerned. So Candice Love Jackson wrote this really good chapter mainly exposing all of these writers. All of these books are just expanding, expanding, expanding. This expansion must be acknowledged and documented as an aspect of the history of a people's literature but more particularly a history of a people's reading. Why are people predisposed to read romances when they are not reading serious books like *A Mercy* by Toni Morrison, the most recent novel she has published, or Edward P. Jones's *The Known World*? Readers are going to tell you these books are too hard. They want easy books. Some writer is going to give them easy books.

This situation represents a particular set of circumstances in the history of literacy and the use of literature, and it is certainly going to have an impact on why writers write what they write. Those who are devoted to certain values are going to say, "I don't care what the reading public wants to read. This is my vision. This is what I am going to give them to read." Other writers may say, "I have got to make some money, and I can't live without making money. I don't have a teaching job. I have a novel, I'd better sell it, and I'd better give the public what it wants." And the writers get into collaboration with the editors.

That's why I said editors and publishers and especially the new forms of publication—e-books, the Kindle from Amazon—have influence. If you're really going to do in-depth studies of how literature functions in the world, it is crucial to deal with history and how literature functions at different times. Let's say literature functions in the world, and also there is a kind of closed system where literature is going to be self-sufficient and, therefore, what you have to deal with is an ever-growing complexity in the larger world.

Black Cultural Defender and Cross-Cultural Advocate: An Interview with Professor Jerry W. Ward Jr.

Zuyou Wang / 2013

From *Research in Contemporary American Contra-Mainstream Literary Thought*, edited by Zuyou Wang (Beijing: Science Press, 2015), 204–14. Reprinted by permission of Zuyou Wang.

Zuyou Wang: Professor Ward, your papers are housed at the Mississippi Department of Archives and History. Please talk about your archived papers.

Jerry W. Ward Jr.: [. . .] I began donating some of my correspondence and writings to the Tougaloo College Archives in the early 1970s. As an alumnus of the college, I thought it was important to provide items that would enhance the possibility of the Tougaloo College Archive to become a center for research in Mississippi. The archive already had a vast amount of material pertaining to the civil rights movement and the history of the college. It did not have much material about people who had served on its faculty or primary documents in the field of literature. My objective was to give my college a small number of such documents to complement its extraordinary collection of books (many of them first editions in the field of African American literature. My papers were housed in the L. Zenobia Coleman Library at Tougaloo College until they were transferred for processing to the Mississippi Department of Archives and History [MDAH]. I am most grateful to Mr. Clarence Hunter, the Tougaloo College archivist, for his dedication and expertise in putting my papers in order and preparing a finding aid for them.

Although it is advertised that my papers span the years 1939 to 2010, I am baffled by what is there which has anything to do with 1939. I was not born until July 31, 1943. The major focus of my papers is the years 1972–2012, and that focus will be expanded as I continue to produce and donate my works, correspondence, and other materials. To be sure, the MDAH staff will have more to catalog in the future. The collection is divided into the following series: personal matters, consisting of awards, collected items, correspondence, and programs of events; career, consisting of correspondence, documents, and other materials related to my career at Tougaloo, Dillard, and other educational institutions; works by me, consisting of the major works by me as a speaker, reviewer, newspaper columnist, and manuscript writer; anthologies, collected works, and larger works, consisting of writings that I authored or coauthored; scholar affiliation, consisting of correspondence, documents, and writings of noted scholars; organizational affiliation, consisting of correspondence, documents, and printed materials of professional organizations; collected magazines, newspapers, photographs, and audiotapes.

ZW: We know that you and Richard Wright's daughter, Julia Wright, were among the founders of the Richard Wright Circle in 1990, an organization dedicated to the study of Wright's life and work. Among your many writings on the subject, some of the most significant are the introduction to the Harper Perennial Edition of *Black Boy*; "*Black Boy (American Hunger)*: Freedom to Remember," a work you coauthored with Maryemma Graham; "Richard Wright and the Common Reader," written for *Black Magnolias*; and an entry for the *Mississippi Encyclopedia*. Will you please illustrate your main thought on the Richard Wright study?

JWW: Let me begin with a debatable claim. Among twentieth-century American writers, Richard Wright is the one who disturbs readers in a unique way. He forces readers to think. When we read his published works, we find ourselves thinking about the long history of intrusion, resistance, and conquest that pertains to the Americas, to what Europeans called the New World. It is not the case that other American writers, especially historians, have not addressed those issues. Wright, however, deals with the issues in his fiction, poetry, nonfiction, and essays by asking hard questions, by challenging us with moral imperatives. James Baldwin, Lillian Smith, William Faulkner, Herman Melville, W. E. B. Du Bois, Toni Cade Bambara, June Jordan, and Walt Whitman are other writers who entangle us with moral imperatives, but they seem to be less forceful than Wright in exposing the wounds of history that will not heal. I may be the only person in my country who holds this opinion. Wright fully understood the nature and consequences of the endless suffering human beings must endure. He understood mankind's hunger. As Wright put it, he was not concerned with making people happy, with entertaining them. He was concerned with forcing people to look directly at whatever it is we believe "Truth" to be. His works are unsettling. Wright understood that the primitive instinct of man and woman to be brutal in their interactions with other men and women is one of the major aspects of human existence on this planet. He knew what material and spiritual poverty is and how such poverty is related to dehumanization, to ethnic or racial hatred, to the psychological grip of religious beliefs and practices, to capitalism and class warfare. His perspectives were not always right, but he was brave enough to have perspectives and to share them with the world. He paid for his pursuit of truth, what Michel Fabre called his unfinished quest, with his life. We study Richard Wright in order to become more honest, to become brave and critical thinkers.

ZW: Will you please discuss the unfinished quest at some length as it is related to your readings of Wright's works?

JWW: My readings of Wright's works are determined by the special affinity I have with him and by what I find attractive in some iterations of Marxist literary theory, especially in the questions Mikhail Bakhtin posed about speech act theory and language. I read [Wright's] works as situated responses, as transactions, with the world he inhabited as an African American male. I summarized my thoughts about affinity, unfinished quest, and my regard for Wright's work from the stories in *Uncle Tom's Children* (1938) to his last novel *A Father's Law* (2008) in the remarks I made when I accepted the Richard Wright Literary Excellence Award on February 26, 2011. Those remarks answer your question.

Between Richard Wright and Me

We both spent our childhood and youth in Mississippi in the twentieth century. Like many American males, we were sensitive to how we were socialized by the values and expectations of our families. We were fully aware that law and custom set boundaries for our growth, and we discovered fairly early the peculiar feelings of accomplishment that come from defying limits. We were curious rebels, and the price we had to pay for our lack of meekness shaped and left indelible marks on our personalities.

Our curiosity about the things of this world was notably increased by our use of literacy. We were avid readers, allowing our imaginations to be much enlarged by words, language, and the lore one can acquire from books and from oral transmission. We were different from our peers. We were EXISTENTIAL before either of us could pronounce or define that word. Our difference was at once a blessing and a curse, a paradox within the matrix of Deep South society. We were blessed with inner strength and willpower, with knowing we had the option of refusing to become who and what the less than generous world desired we should become. Even if our bodies gave scant evidence of disobedience, our minds delighted in transgressive explorations; we entertained ideas that neither our immediate families nor our environments were prepared to understand or condone. As we grew into adolescence, our observations and readings prepared us to become exceptionally critical of injustice. And we discovered that the forms of language which so fascinated us could be instruments for effecting change. Literature and our experiences taught us that we did not have to be passive. We had agency; it was our entitlement under natural law to deny the possibility of our being wretched and tragic victims.

Obviously, I have sketched a few parallels between the life experiences that Richard Wright described vividly in his classic autobiography *Black Boy* and my memories of the trajectory of my own life. The epiphany I had upon reading *Black Boy* in my youth created a most powerful affinity between Richard Wright and me. It also created the recognition that we shared, despite the thirty-five years that separate us, similar values and tough-minded perspectives about the dynamics of good and evil that impact the lives of human beings. Although our paths in adulthood took quite different directions—Wright used his talents to establish himself as a writer of international importance, and I used my talents to forge a career in American higher education, we both dedicated our lives to trying in good faith to speak truth about our world, to find receptive ears for our words, and to shake people out of the dangerous habits of inattention and complacency. Richard Wright has indeed taught me through the full range of his writings about my obligations to humanity.

Thus, it is with profound humility that I accept the Richard Wright Literary Excellence Award and express my gratitude to the Natchez Literary and Cinema Celebration for deciding that I am worthy of such a distinguished honor. This honor entails an obligation to think and write in ways that pay tribute to the model of excellence that Richard Wright set for us all and to continue my commitment to ensuring that future generations of writers and thinkers never forget how essentially valuable Richard Wright's legacy to the world is.

ZW: By attacking the taboos and hypocrisy that other writers had failed to address, Wright revolutionized American literature and created a disturbing and realistic portrait of the African American experience. *The Richard Wright Encyclopedia*, coedited by you and Robert J. Butler, is a guide to his vast and influential body of works. What prompted you into undertaking such a giant project?

JWW: Robert Butler and I undertook the project because it was necessary to provide a reference book for students, teachers, and the general public. We wanted people to have a resource for discovering basic facts about Wright and his works, and we believe that good critical work on writers must start with facts rather than with theoretical speculations. Like Keneth Kinnamon's two magnificent bibliographies of critical responses to Wright, the *Richard Wright Encyclopedia* is an integral part of what the Richard Wright Circle was established to accomplish. I should mention that I have another big, ongoing project. I am writing *Richard Wright: One Reader's Responses*, a study of Wright's mind and his writings. I am not certain that I shall ever finish that project.

ZW: Your numerous works are expressions of your endless love of literature, especially African American literature. Besides Richard Wright, who are the writers that absorb your passion and devotion?

JWW: To use your words, I am passionately devoted to many writers, particularly to writers other critics may have chosen to overlook—Asili Ya Nadhiri, James E. Cherry, Sterling D. Plumpp, Harold Clark, Julius E. Thompson, Eugene Redmond, Kalamu ya Salaam, and Tom Dent come immediately to mind. Ishmael Reed and Lance Jeffers are at the top of my list. I am passionately interested in writers who share all or a significant portion of my commitment to struggling with whatever "Truth" might be.

ZW: Will you expound upon them respectively?

JWW: That is impossible for me to do in this interview. I would need to write several essays to expound. I will say a little about Reed and Jeffers to give you a preview of my thinking. I first read Reed when I was a soldier in Vietnam. I later had the privilege of serving with him on the Coordinating Council of Literary Magazines and of conducting extensive interviews with him in the early 1980s. In his own way, Ishmael Reed continues and takes to a new level the work Richard Wright did. I reject the idea which circulates like HIV/AIDS and cancer among American intellectuals that Wright and Reed are "protest writers." All American writers protest something. I value Reed for his sustained efforts since the late 1960s to promote genuine multiculturalism in our discussions of the literature and culture of the United States. His efforts as a novelist, poet, dramatist, musician, essayist, cultural critic, publisher, and editor are special and unsurpassed. He is dedicated to expanding the matrix for the delayed conversation about what it means to be an American. He does not merely give lip service to multiculturalism and diversity. He is profoundly engaged in the practice of inclusiveness. For this reason, Reginald Martin (University of Memphis) and I have begun to work on a book to be entitled *Ishmael Reed's Conversation with America*. Lance Jeffers, with whom I enjoyed a most rewarding friendship during the last decade of his life (1975–85), was an excellent poet and critical thinker. He was a man who had absorbed what Jean-Paul Sartre was talking about in *Qu'est-ce que la littérature?* (1947). He was *engagé*—engaged, committed. For him as for Reed, writing is an act of social responsibility. I learned much from him about poetry, cultural nationalism, and how to be a responsible person. I wrote the introduction for his novel *Witherspoon*, a novel that John Oliver Killens commended highly. One of my former students, Howard Rambsy II, published a most thoughtful essay on Jeffers and the Black Aesthetic in Kevin Powell's anthology *Step into a World* (2000). I intend to revise and expand a paper I wrote many years ago, titled "Racialized Morality in Lance Jeffers's *Witherspoon*." You remind me that I have so much work to do in fitting the writers for whom I have a passionate devotion into literary history.

ZW: In *The Katrina Papers: A Journal of Trauma and Recovery*, you fuse autobiography, politics, spirituality, history, and poetry in a highly inventive and unusual trip through the aftermath of Hurricane Katrina. Your house and your university campus were both flooded. It is from this trauma that you scramble to find hope and sanity in a world ruled by the fact that thousands have been abused by nature. What is the mission that you seem to try to fulfill in this memoir?

JWW: I do not think *The Katrina Papers* has a mission. The book has a purpose. The initial purpose was to examine and document my mind as I dealt with the trauma of loss. I wrote the book as a journal, but if people wish to call it a memoir, I do not object. It is a journal about what was happening in my mind. The first publisher to whom I submitted the manuscript said I needed to revise it to incorporate a narrative arc. I did not want to include a narrative arc. If my readers find one, that is an accident, a fortunate accident. The ultimate purpose of the book is to inform readers that they too can write their own stories and account to some for their historicity, their participation in the making of social history. All of us have to deal with the wounds of history that cannot be healed. What I tried to do in *The Katrina Papers* was to minimize the agony of the wounds.

ZW: I know that you also write poems. Do you think we should give special attention to your poem "Jazz to Jackson to John"?

JWW: Yes, you should. "Jazz to Jackson to John" is my signature poem. Of all the poems I have written, it represents best my interests in history, music, and state of existence. It addresses what I think the function of memory should be.

ZW: In discussing the poetry of Natasha Trethewey, you call our attention to Trethewey's strategies for recovering history in *Domestic Work*, *Bellocq's Ophelia*, and *Native Guard* and how her poems are aesthetic warnings against postracial delusions. To put Trethewey's nomination for the US poet laureate in proper perspective, one should read Honorée Fanonne Jeffers's brilliant essay "The Subjective Briar Patch: Contemporary American Poetry." What is its special use in understanding contemporary American poetry?

JWW: Honorée Fanonne Jeffers's essay is infused with honesty and integrity. It is a generous, scholarly, and civilizing statement about internal struggles within the field of contemporary American poetry. Jeffers challenges us to be logical and sober about how those struggles or negotiations among poets, critics, and readers of poetry are so frequently racist, sexist, and, to be extremely candid, bitchy. Her essay bids us to meditate on poetry and modernism as an asymmetrical affair, an affair that is saturated with conflicts, taste, and discrimination, desperate measures to protect privilege and maintain hegemony, and the mountains poets must conquer as they practice their craft. Jeffers illuminates the conflicts, and her essay can be used as a powerful guide for moving through the combat zone. Her essay helps us to discern how political the position of the poet laureate of the United States might actually be. In an indirect way, the essay also can be useful when we read Trethewey's most recent collection, *Thrall* (2012), and Brenda Marie Osbey's *History and Other Poems* (2012). Osbey's is a rare book that secures our participation in and control of the dialogic imagination.

ZW: Your commentary, "The Cambridge History of African American Literature and the Limits of Literary History," seeks to explain the inevitable absence in literary or historical narratives of writers who are of equal merit with and sometimes of greater importance than those who are discussed. Why do you believe this is true?

JWW: No literary history can account for all of a nation's writers or for all of the writers who have contributed something valuable to an ethnic tradition within a larger national tradition of literary production. A definitive accounting would be nothing more than an enormous listing of names, a literary telephone directory. The population of people who can make some legitimate claim to be writers has grown exponentially within the last thirty years. Population size is one reason for absence. Another reason has to do with how literary histories are constructed and with the choices made by people selected to write chapters of a literary history. In the United States, most of the scholars and critics who write literary history work at colleges and universities. Although some well-informed literary and historical comments might appear in blogs or in social networks, it would be indeed rare to find any of those comments in a literary history sponsored by a prestigious university press or a first-rate commercial publisher. Academic circles in the United States tend to be conservative and unwilling to take risks. Tenure and promotion depend greatly on one's publishing articles in the right peer-reviewed journals, publishing books with the leading presses in one's field, and publishing chapters in books that are deemed to have great merit. Excellent writers who are not canonized or strong candidates for canonization tend to be ignored. The tyranny of the academy is powerful.

ZW: As an overseas professor at Central China Normal University in Wuhan, you have a deep interest in exchanges between the People's Republic of China and the United States of America, in promoting the mutual destruction of stereotypes. A lecture you gave there on American literature and digital humanities involves a series of speculations on how new technologies may change the study and teaching of literature, especially African American literature.

JWW: Digital humanities is not a panacea or cure-all, but it is a crucial element in how literature and culture will be written about and evaluated in the future. There are still well-founded reservations about what digital humanities can achieve. I think for some time we will continue to combine traditional methods with those emerging in the field of digital humanities. Ultimately, our scholarly practices as well as our scholarly questions will be altered by new technologies.

ZW: You have been involved with many professional organizations, such as the College Language Association, the National Council of Teachers of English, the Modern Language Association, the Southern Conference on African American Studies, and the Southern Black Cultural Alliance. You have played a decisive role in the Mississippi Humanities Council and were recognized for your contributions with the Humanities Teacher Award, the Humanities Scholar Award, and with an executive position in the council. Aside from your academic affiliation, you also served on the Mississippi Advisory Committee to the US Commission on Civil Rights.

JWW: I have profited intellectually from my diverse professional involvements because they have enabled me to have exchanges with leading scholars, writers, and artists. Many of these people are more than names on a page. I have had long-term correspondence with some of them; others have become friends; some of the younger people have chosen me to be an informal mentor. During my career as a teacher from 1970 to 2012, working with professional organizations and such cultural organizations as the Natchez Literary and Cinema Celebration and the Zora Neale Hurston Festival in Florida has been meaningful. And I have worked with the Project on the History of Black Writing since its inception in 1983.

ZW: You received numerous honors and awards throughout your career. What are your most cherished awards?

JWW: My most cherished awards are the Darwin T. Turner Award of Excellence for Contributions in Research, Scholarship and Mentoring; the Teacher of the Year award from Tougaloo College in 1992; the Richard Wright Literary Excellence Award from the Natchez Literary and Cinema Celebration; my induction as Honored Griot and Lifetime Member of the International Hall of Fame for Writers of African Descent; and my induction into the Tougaloo Hall of Fame. In January 2013, Tougaloo College designated me professor emeritus. From 2002 to 2012, I was the distinguished eminent scholar and professor of English at Dillard University in New Orleans, Louisiana. I retired from Dillard in August 2012 and now enjoy the life of an independent scholar. I appreciate the awards, and I thank the people who thought I deserved them. I admit, however, that awards frighten me. They are reminders that what I have done in the past is less important than what I am doing in the present. Making worthwhile contributions depends on my continuing efforts to work harder and better. I do hope some of my accomplishments provide ideas and models for invested behavior for younger generations. I do remind myself daily that if I stopped to admire accomplishments, I would become either a failure or an arrogant fool.

ZW: As an expert in African American studies and as a bridge between American and Chinese academic circles, what are your suggestions for the younger generation of scholars concerning their research and publications in the realm of African American studies?

JWW: African American studies is an ally to the larger field, but it focuses more precisely on studies of work produced in the United States. All of these studies are like the threads of a spider web. They are part of a larger design. As a bridge between Chinese and American academic circles, I try to promote cross-cultural discussions that are very necessary in the twenty-first century. I am also something of an iconoclast. I like to knock down the false idols of the mind that Sir Francis Bacon identified centuries ago. I have the onus of providing viable alternatives to what I virtually destroy. Be wary of people who talk stridently about revolutions and who have no rational programs to replace what they would eradicate. They do more harm than good. I advise the younger generation of Chinese scholars who do work in African American and American literatures and cultures to arm themselves with in-depth knowledge about the history of the United States. They must know that history to prevent their being misled and miseducated by either Eurocentric or Afrocentric extremes. They should develop skills in making sharp critiques of African American studies. If they want to publish their work in the United States or other countries outside China, they have to master the rhetoric and protocols of scholarship that may be vastly different from scholarship published in Chinese. I urge these younger scholars to remember that cultural expressions and everyday life exist in symbiotic relationships, to remember that we are dealing with literary or intellectual ecology.

Interview with Jerry W. Ward Jr.

Cleophus Thomas Jr. / 2016

From Studio C, Music and Communications Complex, Loyola University New Orleans. January 21, 2016. Reprinted by permission of Cleophus Thomas Jr.

Cleophus Thomas Jr.: Let's start with *Trouble the Water*. This anthology is an important part of American literary history. The introductory essay is a classic example of American writing. It's a beautiful, poetic, lyrical, philosophical introduction to this body of work. How did the anthology come to be?

Jerry W. Ward Jr.: I had completed *Black Southern Voices*, which I coedited with John Oliver Killens, and we were at that time sharing the same literary agent, Lawrence Jordan. That was a kind of accident. Lawrence said, "Well, you need to do another book." So I had been in contact with any number of poets, particularly people here in the South and elsewhere. And looking at previous anthologies, I said, "Well, there needs to be a certain kind of updating"— which I did—not as thoroughly as I might have liked for reasons that have to do with permissions. So I put this together, and there is what I call a kind of secret design—which I'm not telling anybody about—in how those poems were selected, and which poems I selected. One of the wonderful things that happened (because you had asked me sometime earlier about Gwendolyn Brooks) is that when I asked for her poems, I said, "I'm not going to use 'We Real Cool' because it's been overanthologized." And she wrote me back and said, "You're a very wise man. I will let you publish these poems of mine without cost if you will put"—and then she specified the ones that she wanted. And I said, "Yes." So I pulled this together, compiled it, wrote the introductory essay, and then the problems began because of permissions. The publishers gave me an operating budget of—I think it was $12,000. That was hardly enough to pay for five permissions for five poets. So I was scrambling around, calling in chips with people, begging, "Please let me have this without cost because I'm not trying to make money. You know this is something I want to do so we can have an anthology that students can actually afford." And for many years, until they decided they were losing money on it, this anthology sold for $6.95. So people could not argue, "I can't afford it." Maybe they did not wish to afford it, but they could. So, we went through a number of negotiations, and I got such wonderful things as people at Thunder's Mouth Press told me, "Well, you can afford to pay all of this money for Henry Dumas's work because your publisher has money." And I said, "Oh my God, yes, I guess my publisher does have money. I don't have the money." The person who was in charge of [Countee] Cullen's material got very angry because he didn't get the money on time or something. [. . .] So we went through all of this, and I just, after a while, had it and threw my hands up and told them, "I'm not gonna do this." So Rosemary Ahern, bless her heart, [who] was an editor there, prevailed and said, "We must go through with this," and I said, "Well, I'll tell you what. I'll give you all of the addresses for all of the people in permissions, and somebody in the house has to do it because I'm too busy teaching and I don't have time." So they did it.

CT: And so they acquired the permissions.

JWW: They had to acquire the permissions because on a budget of $12,000, you can't do anything. It's like trying to make a feature-length movie for $100,000.

CT: I don't think the typical reader like me is aware of the economics and the legal side of creating an anthology.

JWW: It's quite a bit—a tremendous amount of work, particularly now. And I don't think it's going to get much better. That might be one possible explanation, Mr. Thomas, of why people look at anthologists and say, "Well, you don't have this poem," which might be a favorite poem or a very well-known poem by somebody. And the reason that you may not have it is that it costs too much.

CT: You mention in the beautiful introductory essay that the anthology meets an odd demand. You write, "This anthology honors poetry for meeting, in the early years of this century, an odd demand—proof of civilization." Talk about that.

JWW: Well, one only needs to go back to the prefaces that James Weldon Johnson wrote for *The Book of American Negro Poetry* in the 1920s. It was 1921 was the first preface, and I think 1931, if I've got my dates right, was the second. But as he introduced Negro poetry, as it was called at the time, he was very much concerned about language. And he was concerned about the language of his friend Paul Laurence Dunbar. And of course, we know that

Dunbar agonized over the fact that his dialect poetry was extremely popular, and it had been promoted by none other than William Dean Howells and other people, but that his poetry in standard American English was respected but not beloved by the larger buying audience. And Johnson, who had some very keen insights about language and language usage in America, was a little bit appalled about this notion of using dialect since many of the people who were using dialect were not trained in linguistics, nor were they trained in anthropology, which would have helped a little bit. So they were creating dialects, and if you go back and read some of the so-called plantation poems that were rather popular in the last years of the nineteenth century, you will notice that the dialect goes in every direction. Sometimes it's a way of ridiculing how Black people spoke, sometimes it was simply a matter of the person not having a very good ear and certainly not knowing anything about how to spell outside of the standard spelling system we have. So Johnson was very much concerned that people who were reading this were getting a very bad impression. And it was his notion also, which is rather classic, as I would say, almost—not late Victorian because it was something that had to be proven as early as the time of Phillis Wheatley—that you as an African person who was becoming an American and had acquired some degree of literacy, you were expected in certain places to prove that you were civilized by using your literacy well, along the lines of whatever was valued in terms of either British or American literature. Johnson did not necessarily object to this and suggested that one of the solutions was not to use dialect but to catch what he called the racial flavor, the cadence, the meter, the rhythm, I suppose even in some ways the diction, that people were using—ordinary people were using. And to present this to the larger reading public as evidence that, yes, these emancipated people who were, under the Constitution, now citizens, were indeed civilized, no matter what you thought about field hollers and the blues.

CT: Well, that brings me to the next question I ask. You also note in the essay that variety is a crucial feature around national literature, and you've just talked about culture as evidence, as evidence of our civilization, the ability to make some cultural performance. And as you note the divergent approaches or the various genres of the dialect poetry and then the more formal poetry, you remind us that there is a suggestion that there is almost, I guess, a culture that is indigenous. You'd almost, I guess, say, vertically acquired, and then culture that you got at college—all culture is acquired, but the suggestion that our dialect is not culture, but if you learn a sonnet or if you learn some more formalized Western structure, that is culture.

Talk about variety and talk about how this is parsed. Not really wanting to really accept variety, and not really wanting to value all culture as culture but making it so hierarchical.

JWW: Well, why don't we suggest, using your notion of the vertical and the horizontal, that we have a culture which can manifest itself diachronically, and we have aspects of culture which are indeed vertical, because you're taking a smaller slice, as it were, of duration that's synchronic. Those motions of culture at once complement and contradict one another, depending on who is in the position of moving or being in motion. So in our evolution of what we today call American literature, we have to remember that for a considerable portion of our country's history, American writers, colonial and postcolonial, felt that they were somehow not quite as good as the British. That's their language heritage unless they happened to be here in New Orleans and were using French or Spanish, and that's another story which is usually minimized in our accounting for American literary history. The effort of American writers was to use the experience of being in the New World, of committing genocide and enslaving another important population, to forge an American idiom, and of course by the mid-nineteenth century, you have marvelous essays by Ralph Waldo Emerson on the American scholar, the thinker, but none that overtly address social responsibility, but something akin to that, where he's trying to suggest there are ways, if you are very observant, of reaching this goal, of creating an American literature. What we have to be very aware of is that what was considered legitimate as literature excluded orature, excluded any kinds of cultural expressions that were not in print. And those cultural expressions certainly were there for Indigenous peoples in this country and for African peoples and a few probably for immigrants of other origins. That was not literature. Literature was what was printed and could be discriminated or distinguished from certain kinds of discourse like newspapers and histories that were not at the time literary. I mean, there were genres of literature, fiction, poetry, and drama that were respected, and always it was part of what the American who expatriated himself very early—T. S. Eliot—called tradition and individual talent. So where does this place the African American person who is making creative expressions, . . . many of whom had acquired literacy? Because what we need to be aware of in this total process of having variety in American literature is a disconnect in terms of literacy and ability to create in print between those Blacks who lived north of the Mason-Dixon Line and those who were in the South. And that doesn't mean that you didn't have people in both sectors of the country that were able to write and read despite the fact that it was quite illegal in certain states to allow Blacks to read or to have letters. And of course we go to Frederick Douglass's 1845 autobiography to understand exactly what that was about. But the notion of variety was always, as I began to work through this problem with the help of other scholars, a matter of who was excluded. Now, you had exclusions that were based upon ethnicity, and you had exclusions that were based upon gender. And the gender issue certainly was dramatically articulated by Nathaniel Hawthorne, who talked about those "damned women writers." There were many women writers who were selling their novels very well in the nineteenth century. After the emancipation and the Civil War, there were any number of Black women who were investing quite a bit of energy in writing novels to bring a certain kind of civilization. This is pre–Talented Tenth. When one looked at the kind of work that had been done by Robert Spiller and others in writing a literary history of the United States, with the exception—and I don't want to give you information that I don't remember too well, but I will say—of Emily Dickinson and maybe Anne Bradstreet, the women were not represented as authors.

CT: Well, that brings me to—in talking about variety and culture—the question of audience, and to the extent that, as you mentioned, this anthology meets an odd demand, proof of civilization, that we're called upon to prove that we are civilized, that we're not just locked in some lower class of people not able to acquire culture, how does audience factor into that? How does the pressure to manufacture this proof potentially distort, and even make comic—when you think about *Amos 'n' Andy*, and somebody misusing big words, that is suggestive of the need to try to show off, and show, "Look, I have culture, I have a big vocabulary." How do audience and interlocutors factor into the variety and the formation of the cultural artifact and work through finding a voice and finding a real means of some authentic expression?

JWW: Well, you have put it, as a good Marxist would, by compelling me to suggest that the total process is a matter of economy, of various kinds of economy. When you ask about audiences, how are audiences created? Audiences are created through education.

Their tastes are created through various kinds of training that people have, or their tastes may be acquired quite independent of education, by word of mouth or oral transmission. If someone says to you, "You know, you really should look at this because it's really good," or people in your community have a way of expressing themselves which is treasured. It's a very complicated matter which only now, I think, scholars are beginning to really grapple with in the most serious way by trying to supplement the myth of creativity with some very practical examination of what happened and is still happening with publishing. How important are publishing—were publishing houses—in terms of working with authors and trying to present the best possible work that they could of a particular author? And you had some very powerful and very good editors.

Today we have these kids who are fresh out of somewhere, who haven't the slightest idea of what an editor should be. They need instruction. It's going to be overwhelmingly difficult with digital material. We're now talking about printcentric and digicentric materials. We have to look at any number of factors and how that is part of a cultural economy. I'm not using cultural economy in a way that's metaphoric; however, I'm also thinking about the real matter of dollars and cents. How were certain instances of literature which are considered high-cultural items produced as pulp fiction or more popular forms bringing in the money that allowed the publishers to print and distribute books that would have smaller readerships? There's a great difference between reading books by James Michener and novels by Donna Tartt or Toni Morrison.

CT: You are a chief purveyor of African American culture, a curator of African American culture, a producer of African American high culture, a zealous and proud advocate of that culture. Yet you are also a prime example of classical American education and values, and you're almost something of an interloper, and I say that in the stereotypical way that people would receive an advocate for advanced Black culture as not the button-down fellow that you are. And what sticks in my mind is, in the writing somewhere, you mention being seized by trying to recall the pluperfect form of some verb, and that reminded me, and really encapsulates the very traditional, a very rigid, formal education that you have, and you're Catholic. And that's almost counterintuitive when people think about Black culture and Black writing, particularly modern writing. They think of an unguided, completely liberated genre, unconstructed—not just unconstrained by rules but unaware of them. And there's something mildly insulting about that when you think about it. Comment on that.

JWW: Well, I think what you're addressing is how little investment late twentieth-century and certainly early twenty-first-century Americans make in trying to understand what it means to be an American. There have been several attempts, usually by people who have been chairpersons of the National Endowment for the Humanities, to encourage a conversation on the topic of what it means to be an American, and each time the more conservative right-wing forces have prevailed and said, "You're not even going to have this conversation because we're not going to allow you to have the money that it takes to do it." So to address your question and your concern, I'm saying if we understood American life a little better, there would be absolutely nothing surprising about who I am. When you speak about my, in quotation marks, "classical education," which suggests that I'm akin to W. E. B. Du Bois—

CT: And T. S. Eliot.

JWW: And T. S. Eliot, and Henry James and his brother, William. We must not forget that I did not ever embrace a narrow definition of what education was. My entire life has been an education of one kind or another, and it continues to be. So that there were things that I learned and all of us learn outside of any box, outside of any classroom, outside of an institution that is called the school or the university or college or whatever. We learn things, and according to our individual proclivities or talents, we use them. So I'll take you out drinking with me sometime.

CT: I accept.

JWW: So you can understand the other kind of person I can be. But it's not what you said, necessarily. It's what is thought in this country that if a person tries to speak well or occasionally uses a word that has thirteen letters in it, that person is being pretentious. We have a tremendous vein of anti-intellectualism that seems to be a part of the changing definition of what it is to be an American. To be an American is to not be interested in other languages. To be an American is to be suspicious of foreign cultures and of anyone who has any respect for foreign cultures. You must not have too global a vision unless it is in matters of business, and then you are romping off to various parts of the world to make fortunes. So we have a country in which the very process of history allows you to say what you said. But when we begin to look at why it is that someone would think because I happen to be a Black male of a certain age, I am not fulfilling the norm as they would create a norm in terms of Shaq or Dennis Rodman or Jay-Z or Lil Wayne or somebody in the entertainment or sports industry. And those are the figures that are supposed to be Black. Well, I guess Drew Brees is the ideal white figure. But it's amazing to me that we're supposed to be very intelligent, advanced people in the twenty-first century—and don't get me talking about politics or I'll incriminate myself—but I think it is very fair to ask, "Have Americans descended into peculiar forms of stupidity?"

CT: Well, it seems to be the assumption about African American artists—in particular African American poetry or certain African American writing—is an assumption similar to that made by common viewers of abstract art: "My third grader could have done that." And the fact that it does not conform to a certain historic standard or meter they deny that there could be choice or artistic value to that. That it is your ability to reproduce some form to follow this standard. And in *The Katrina Papers*, you really explain yourself, and it's a charming story of your education, of teachers that teach you, first of all, of a father that teaches you that *t-e-h* is not *the*, but *t-h-e* is *the*. But then you go on into the classroom and you have teachers that teach you these words and expand your vocabulary and then clobber you and then say you're too wordy and verbose when you deploy the vocabulary they have worked zealously to give you. And you see them pushing you toward some refinement, that these are tools, but they are not just displayed, and your beautiful, lyrical writing style shows you have hewed to that directive of working toward the ultimate refinement of literature. And not just the acquisition of parts, you acquire a knowledge of structure and form and vocabulary. But with that, it's just a pile of supplies. It has to be individual if you are a writer, and I guess you have to find that out by seeing if you can do anything with those parts you've been given. And you tell us how, particularly in *The Katrina Papers*, you came to do that—to be the writer, the poet that you are.

JWW: Right. It's a very interesting development. And I would certainly want to say for the record that anything I have done since I began my life as a teacher in 1970 was always done on behalf of my students. I was raised to believe that since I had somehow accidentally got a little more intelligence than some people, I was supposed to use it wisely. And there were a number of people in my family that were interested in teaching. So it came as something that you could do. And I remember very vividly—with some kids in my neighborhood—when I was very small, I had—it wasn't a blackboard, maybe it was just black paper or something. And I said, "We're going to have school today." And so I decided on my front porch that I was going to be teaching. I was the teacher, of course. Because you need to know how to spell, you need to know how to add and subtract, because you seem not to be doing it too well.

And it was really a great deal of fun. That became a very serious matter for me when I took my first full-time teaching job back at my alma mater Tougaloo College in 1970. And I said, "Oh, I had such a wonderful four years here, I'll give four years back and then move on to something else." And my students kept saying each year, "But you can't leave until I graduate!" So I got suckered into staying there for thirty-two years with this whole excuse that I could not leave because they had not yet graduated. I'm very pleased at having invested that kind of effort in teaching and in another part of being a professional. I wasn't just simply a teacher. I thought that if I were going to be successful in teaching students something about language and literature, I had to also demonstrate my own skills. And at the same time I had to be a fairly decent role model especially for English majors in terms of "What is the profession about?" So I was a member of the College Language Association, Modern Language Association, and most importantly, the National Council of Teachers of English. And some other smaller groups. And I would write, let's say, book reviews for the *Jackson Advocate* (the local Black newspaper in Jackson) because I thought that was what one was supposed to do. I would publish book reviews and other kinds of things because I wanted my students to know, "Well, yes, I'm in the classroom and I'm doing this, but I also have to have another kind of life. And I have to develop as a teacher a certain network that will be of use to you later." Because when my students wanted to go to graduate schools and I was trying to give them advice, I would say, "Well, let's see, what do you think you want to work on?" And they would tell me, and then they'd probably give me all these schools that they thought they were going to, and I would say, "No, you're not going there. I'm going to contact Professor X, who is interested in this subject, and ask Professor X, whom I've met at several professional meetings, if she or he would be willing to direct your dissertation." You use this kind of networking and you put forth that kind of effort as a teacher because I had another goal in mind: I wanted to produce students. And I tell some of my students who were my mentees through the UNCF/Mellon Programs, time and again, that I always wanted to help to educate students so that at some point in their lives they would become my teachers. If you do not educate your students so that they can teach you something, you have failed.

CT: There is a modesty in your evaluation of yourself and education, and in a recent essay you wrote you talked about how all your students taught you something, even the dullest. And perhaps your long years in the classroom, everybody in there was a student, including you—according to you—and that everybody in there was also a teacher. [. . .] It's really a touching assessment of even the dullest student. Talk about that.

JWW: Well, one of the amusements, I suppose, I would occasionally produce in my classroom was I would walk in, and I would sit down. And people would be looking around saying, "What's wrong with him today?" And I would point to a student and say, "You're teaching today. What's our lesson?" Students were momentarily in a state of shock that they should have to teach. I would sometimes suspect that the person I chose had not done his or her homework, so that person had to stand at the front of the room, and students would create all kinds of things. I would say, "But sir, or ma'am, I came to learn," and what I'm doing is I'm giving them this lesson, but I'm playing the role of the student who is very smart and is going to ask the tough question that I, in my real role as a teacher, should be able to answer. So I think that the whole notion of modesty, which I will accept, comes out of a very deep sense of something that I find despicable about the academic world, and that is pretense. If we are teachers, and we knew—or maybe we didn't but we should have known—that we were not going to become extremely wealthy or important people because we are teachers, then we would always make sacrifices—as many of my teachers did for my sake. And I had to do that for many of my students. And I never liked the notion that still prevails in higher education that colleagues in various disciplines have to be highly competitive and backbiting and always creating some kind of animosity among themselves that goes beyond simple disagreement of positions or theories. It becomes a very personal matter.

And it's gotten me into a number of uncomfortable situations when I had acquaintanceships or friendships with people who were at odds with each other and I refused to take sides. I said, "You know, I like both of you, and I'm not going to talk about X with Y, or Y with X, and furthermore, I think our job, our mission, in terms of trying to understand something, to build, to make contributions or whatever we're doing, requires more cooperation than one-to-one competition. We're not playing certain kinds of sports. This is not a sport." So I suppose that seems to be modest from some angles, and I guess what you're calling modesty is just a part of my personality. I never wanted fame. I wanted respect, and I had to earn that from my students and from other people. But I did not want to be famous, and I did not want to become what is now called a public intellectual because all of our public intellectuals of whatever background are playing in a circus.

CT: You, in your splendid introduction to *Trouble the Water*, talked about the priestly prejudices of the academy. An appropriate topic to mention in the Loyola laboratory.

JWW: Yes, it certainly is, because we're very priestly over here as opposed to those Protestants across the way at Tulane.

CT: But you're speaking about, I take it, hoping that the anthology would make available to people a wide variety of reading that might be foreclosed, going back to what you were just talking about, about some of the narrow turf battles in the academy about who is canonical and not?

JWW: Right because there are many saints who are uncanonized, and there are some saints who are canonized that need to be cleansed from the list because they haven't produced any miracles for over a thousand years and I'm wondering what is the usefulness of them, and the archbishop will not excommunicate me for saying that. But the point is that the academy has half-seriously tried to be priestly, given that the church was a repository for learning for many years and that's why when you read Chaucer you read about the scholars.

And in Europe, of course, we have to remember that it was the church that was trying to preserve certain kinds of things and making judgments but that other kinds of things were being preserved even better including items of Greek culture by the Muslims who were in Spain on the Iberian Peninsula. And so it is through Arabic intellectual traditions that what might have been lost is now saved. Let us not forget that. There's a certain point at which the usefulness of pretending that we have canons has to confront the fact that if people have not been to university, they may also have canons. And this goes back to your question about creativity, cultural expression, and marketplaces. The best sellers—and I'm thinking of someone from Mississippi, John Grisham, who [. . .] has made millions of dollars. He is not canonized. You're not going to find [him taught] except in a course, an odd course—odd I say because it would be so infrequently awkward—on literature and the law. Or novels not about detective work but about the issue of law and how that plays out in corruption, for example. You're not going to find him taught, but he is very well read. One of the best-selling authors in this country is Stephen King. You cannot mention Stephen King in the academy in the same sentence in which you talk about Edgar Allan Poe, for example, or Nathaniel Hawthorne or Ernest Hemingway. It's like you're getting things all mixed up. Those other people are great writers. Stephen King is just a popular writer. Well, yes. Popularity has given him a fairly large audience.

So I'm saying I enjoy reading some of Stephen King and also his book on writing. People don't realize that he did invest a bit of time in trying to help other people to write and to suggest what it is that makes a good story. A number of well-placed writers do this, and there are various collections where they talk about writing and what it means and what kind of investments they have. So my work now, in going back to *Trouble the Water*, to what John Oliver Killens and I tried to do in *Black Southern Voices*, my blogs, which you are a little bit familiar with. I'm trying to always bring in works of literature that are not necessarily canonical because I think there is something of value there. This week I am very excited by the poetry of Mahmoud Darwish.

Why is his poetry, which is world-class, so important? Some of it has to do with the fact that he was a Palestinian. And that I wrote at one point a poem, "I Did Not Ask to Be a Palestinian" for a person who was from Lebanon. So I'm looking at his work and I'm getting very excited about it, and probably in a day or so I'll have a blog about one particular poem in his most recently published collection which is called "The 'Red Indian's' Penultimate Speech to the White Man," which actually echoes for me, as you might guess, something about *White Man Listen!* by Richard Wright. But it's amazing to me that this Arab writer should have sat and listened to American Indian chants and used this—and he has to say *Red Indian* because part of what he's doing in this piece is to chastise Columbus for thinking that he had the right to find India anywhere in any sea and ultimately telling him to go back home and go find the real India, you know. And then of course we have the problem of saying, "Well, Louisiana had an Indian governor." Oh yes, but he wasn't Houma. You know, he was of India, he wasn't [a Native American] kind of Indian. So I'm really very interested in how writers throughout the world are trying to deal with what has been made a very difficult subject, and that is the matter of identity, and how that matter of identity is not just simply a matter of how you construct a taxonomy. It's much more serious than that. It's really gotten into matters of economy and the military and life and death and terrorism. And international politics which is very exciting at the present time because it's in so many fragments, and you don't know exactly what you're doing when you try to talk about international politics. So what's happening in Sri Lanka? And how is that related to China? And why is it that certain aspects of the Chinese economy caused the Dow to go down on Wall Street? And why is Walmart, which I swear is headquartered in China, canceling approximately sixteen thousand American jobs, all right, as they close stores around this country? But the products, if you go to Walmart, with the exception of what is made in Japan, and that's less than 1 percent, everything's made in China.

CT: You mentioned Richard Wright. You are the leading American scholar on Richard Wright.

JWW: Let me correct you. I am one of many Richard Wright scholars in this country.

CT: No definitive work would be made on Richard Wright without your being consulted. Talk about your study and devotion to Richard Wright and his work.

JWW: I discovered Wright's work as an undergraduate. The first book was a collection of stories, *Uncle Tom's Children*. I was fascinated by that. I spent time between reading James Baldwin and other people, trying to read some Richard Wright. But when I started my graduate work I thought I was going to be an English Renaissance scholar who was going to be an expert on Edmund Spenser. But I finally decided, "No, that's not what I'm going to do." And when I was doing my degree at the University of Virginia and specializing in literary theory and criticism, I said, "Oh, this is exactly what I need to do with Richard Wright, with whom I feel this deep affinity." So I wrote my dissertation on Wright and his American critics between 1938 and 1960—that is, from his first earliest publications to the date of his death. And I felt that the kinship, as it were, between Richard Wright and me, was based on the fact that we both grew up in Mississippi. We very early on felt we were oddities; we were not like other people. And we had an unusual appetite for reading. In a documentary that Mississippi ETV did on Richard Wright called *Richard Wright: Black Boy*, one of his childhood friends said, "He was always reading. I'm surprised he didn't lose his eyesight because he was reading so much." You know, and I just smiled behind this because some of my cousins would always say, "Why are you reading?" And they'd look at what I was reading, and they would just like to turn their noses up at it. You know, I'm reading about Roman history or reading something in the sciences that I was interested in. And all of that was just too much for them, so they just dismissed me and said, "He's just one of the oddballs of the family. We'll just accommodate him, but you know you got to watch that Jerry W. Ward Jr. because something is not right there." And so, I just happily went along doing what I wanted to do, just as Richard Wright defied in many ways his family's expectations and certainly the grandmother who was a Seventh-Day Adventist, and [he was] reading all this fiction, and [she thought] that was the devil's work. And what really, I suppose, secured, as it were, my affinity with Richard Wright was the discovery of how interestingly political he was as a writer. He was not the person who wanted to be out with placards. And he didn't like community organizing work. He wanted to use words. And believe me, he used them very well. So as I have suggested, in March, when *Indonesian Notebook: Richard Wright and the Bandung Conference* comes out from Duke University Press, we're going to have a great deal of attention being given at least, I hope, to that book, which is the work of Brian Russell Roberts and Keith Foulcher. And the whole notion that the Cold War is over—so I'm kind of interested in 1955, the Bandung Conference, what happened there? Why did the United States kind of dismiss the importance of that, or did it? And what was it that

Wright recognized about this conference of nonaligned nations where people were supposed to be making a decision between, as [George] Padmore had it, pan-Africanism or communism, or pan-something-or-other-ism and communism? And it wasn't democracy necessarily. But that we may now understand something else happened and that we have a new crusade in process. Wright said nothing because he was very suspicious of the opiate of religion. He said that we should not dismiss the possibility that some of the religious fanatics from some of the countries that participated in the Bandung Conference might lead efforts or crusades or what we now call jihads. Well, the jihads had gotten out of hand because they are not strictly in accord with the dictates of the Koran. And we have many people who are just plain out and barbaric thugs operating in the name of Allah, and they're going to be justly punished for that. But not on this earth. The important thing to realize here about Wright—and that's why I make a most unusual and debatable claim about him—is that among twentieth-century writers, when we look at them very coldly, what we recognize about Richard Wright was that his mind seemed to move in concentric circles, ever-widening. So he would write early on about the South and things from Mississippi. And then later about the United States in such a book as *Native Son*, which obviously caused a great stir and was very popular. But then having chosen to remove himself and his family to Paris, he became much more interested in international affairs and his friendships with, say, C. L. R. James and Padmore, and getting a great introduction to Kwame Nkrumah that allowed him to go and spend time in the Gold Coast (now Ghana) and to write *Black Power*. To become very interested in Franco's Spain and to write *Pagan Spain* as he's trying to deal with, as best he could, the relationship, which is very obscured now, between paganism and Catholicism. Because we have to remember that Catholicism, as an heir to what we may call Judeo-Christian traditions, has to always look back to what forms of paganism got incorporated into our liturgy, our rituals. Those things, the roots are very deep, because even if we're talking about Judaism, let us not forget that there are certain aspects of Jewish belief and ritual which did not come down like manna from heaven. It was a part of the cultural process in that part of the world. And that there were some borrowings and adaptations and transformations of things from the Assyrians and Canaanites and everyone else in that region.

CT: You draw attention to one of Richard Wright's short stories concerning the flooding in Mississippi with Katrina. Do I not remember in *The*

Outsider, there is a subway or some sort of wreck that allows somebody to kind of—

JWW: There is the L. The L is wrecked. And Cross Damon can use this as an occasion to do precisely what he wants to do, and that is to change his identity and to leave because of some problems he's created with his wife and his girlfriend and whatnot, to become a new man and not to have certain kinds of responsibilities. So, you know, it's like a rebirth for him. But that's very different from a flood.

CT: It is different from a flood. But for some reason, the power that Wright has over his readers, when I think of one of the aspects of the flood, and maybe this is kind of from a reader of Grisham-mystery-type mindset, you also see it as an opportunity to escape for somebody perhaps. They just came to mind. The Wright writing that came to mind after Katrina was that—

JWW: Yes, but let us remember, there are two stories: a very short one which was called "Silt" when it was first published, and then it appeared in *Eight Men*, [where] it was called "The Man Who Saw the Flood." And then the more famous story "Down by the Riverside." In both, the flood does not present an opportunity for a new or better life. In the instance of "Down by the Riverside," Mann—and the name is highly symbolic—makes certain choices that involve the theft of a boat, and he murders the owner of the boat even though he is saving the family of this owner. And of course it leads to his death because everything's going on. You have to read the history of levees, the history of floods of the Mississippi, to understand what kind of situation he was in. So he's going to be given some kind of summary justice by these military forces that are there to keep order and to also keep these guys working. And so he runs away and is shot and dies in the river. In the shorter piece, the family comes back to what's left of their farmland in the Delta, and they have to start over. So you realize that the cycle, the flood, has not freed them from the cycle of poverty and being chained to an agricultural process—chained to the land, as it were. And that was—if you go back to *Black Boy*, and read a very hurtful comment that Wright makes about his father and his father's being "just a sharecropper." So Wright is—and I guess he had his own reasons which I will not try to explain right now—very unkind in saying, "Well, I've made some achievement, but my father is just like a part of nature." It's almost the way—he stops just short of dehumanizing his father but makes it very clear that his father is representative of those people who never escaped in the South from whatever cycles of poverty and being always enslaved to the land.

CT: Gwendolyn Brooks. Tell us about her significance to our national literature and about her significance to you personally.

JWW: Well, Gwendolyn Brooks was for me always a model of the very accomplished writer. The person who always used language with extreme precision. And when I thought of her poetry, I would think of the sculpture of Elizabeth Catlett and of the drawings of Charles White. I mean these are very accomplished artists. Following Margaret Walker's having won the Yale [Younger Poets] prize in 1942 with *For My People*, Gwendolyn Brooks won the Pulitzer for *Annie Allen*. So she was already at that time—and this is in the 1950s and 1940s—there are women writers who are very accomplished and are then going to be looked at as models in some way. Gwendolyn Brooks always had a very strong investment in writing about Chicago, urban life, and certain kinds of—how should I put it nicely—class and color distinctions that were being made.

CT: Within the Black community.

JWW: Yes. And of course, she wasn't of the right color. She wasn't Etta Moten Barnett. She wasn't Lena Horne, right? So, she had a disadvantage from that class and color-conscious angle. But that did not prevent her from writing a large number of really excellent poems and doing something quite well with sonnet and ballad. She was quite a craftsperson. Partially as a result of attending a 1967 conference of Black writers which Killens headed at Fisk University, her interests already in certain younger writers who were being nurtured by Hoyt Fuller of *Negro Digest/Black World*, she began to make some remarkable changes in her work—not in terms of the quality but how she wanted to address things. So even in what I suppose someone might recklessly call her "new militant poetry," you're going to find very fine craftsmanship. So I've always held her in very high regard and now we have at James Madison University [in Virginia] the Furious Flower Poetry Center, which is named from lines in one of her poems—that's where that title, "Furious Flower," comes from. And so her legacy, which we will obviously have to celebrate in 2017 because that will mark the one hundredth year of her birth, her legacy is still very, very important. And it's hard to take a single writer or a single poet especially and to say what that person means for a certain genre, because I'm not sure that if you just had listed out women writers and you put Gwendolyn Brooks, Elizabeth Bishop, and perhaps Muriel Rukeyser together, and Adrianne Rich, Alice Walker—I mean, how are you going to say who among those five women I've named has greater importance? No, that's not the way writing, that's not the way poetry, operates in our country. We have people who appeal—their work appeals—to various segments of a reading population, of a literate population. And a people who like the poetry of Nathaniel Mackey or Robert Hayden or Michael Harper may not necessarily like the poetry of LeRoi Jones/Amiri Baraka or of certain other poets who practice what I call the aesthetics of abrasion. So each of these people will either have a large or not-so-large audience. And this is the way it happens for fiction and for poetry. And well, drama is very hard to talk about now because that's no longer simply stage plays. We've got to deal with stage plays as they're competing with video, they're competing with television, they're competing with cinema, so you know, a certain audience still wants to go to a play, because as someone said, the distinction between a play and a film is that there is community when you go to a play. There is no community when you go to a film. You're locked in that dark cave or cavern that Baldwin talked about in *The Devil Finds Work*.

CT: A couple of other people, since we're talking about poets: Lorenzo Thomas. [. . .]

JWW: Lorenzo Thomas and I, partially as a result of an introduction that must have been made by my late friend Tom Dent, became friends. When Lorenzo left the CCLM (the Coordinating Council of Literary Magazines), he suggested that I should replace him on that council, which I did. And we had more than two decades of correspondence and wonderful times together. We both went to—what year was it? '95 I believe—a conference on the Black Aesthetic in Munich and had a wonderful time there together.

CT: I just think he's one of the greatest poets in the world, ever.

JWW: Well, yes, I suppose one could say that. I would say that with a great deal of caution, because I think we have many great poets in the world, and he is one of them.

CT: He is, but an individual gets to choose.

JWW: Well, you have made your choice, and I have made my diplomatic choice, and so that's how things are.

CT: And you're an anthologist so you have to be diplomatic.

JWW: Of course I—well, not necessarily. But I think Lorenzo is a person whose work will be reexamined. It's not been examined thoroughly enough despite the fact that the Project on the History of Black Writing had two seminars called "Don't Deny My Voice," which is a take-off on a title that Aldon Nielsen chose for a posthumous anthology of writing on Black music by Lorenzo. During those two seminars—and I participated as a faculty member in both of them—his work was mentioned, but there probably wasn't time really, given everything we were trying to accomplish, to really examine who was Lorenzo Thomas and what was he about and why was he—what does it mean that Lorenzo Thomas was really the baby in Umbra, the group that formed in New York in the sixties, that included people like Tom Dent and the Patterson Brothers and Ishmael Reed and Askia Touré who was Rolland Snellings. And other interesting people. But Lorenzo was the young guy, and you had the older character who really gave some creative direction I suppose to all of them, and that was Calvin Hernton. But Lorenzo was very curious. He told me once about going to Andy Warhol's studio and hanging out with that particular bohemian crowd as well as the people in Umbra and other people throughout. So Lorenzo was one of our earliest and most cosmopolitan poets. And I think that is maybe something that you find extremely attractive about his work, and he was fiercely independent and did not necessarily fall into certain traps that it was very easy for other people to fall into of spouting a party line. No, Lorenzo was always Lorenzo.

CT: Charles Rowell and *Callaloo*.

JWW: Yes. Well, that is also a very interesting story, and I have begun to write something on the first seven issues of *Callaloo*. *Callaloo* is an outgrowth of some very interesting discussions from the very early 1970s—mainly discussions about publishing, creativity, writing—in the Southern Black Cultural Alliance. It actually grew out of a group that was interested in community theater but involved a lot of people who were interested in other forms of writing as well. I remember in 1975 a meeting that we had in Birmingham—that was where the group met that particular year—and we had this very long and intense discussion involving Rowell, Tom Dent, a lot of other people, and me about what we might possibly do. And obviously Rowell said we need to have a publication, and of course Tom Dent and I agreed with that. So Dent, Rowell, and Ward became the earliest editors, coeditors of this. But I want to make it very clear that the great force behind this was Charles Rowell, because Tom was doing things that would lead to writing his *Southern Journey*. And he was very interested in doing this oral history work and at the same time he was thinking about trying to do a book with Andy Young. I was finishing up my PhD at the University of Virginia, and I did not have very much time to devote to *Callaloo* except to write a few things for it. So the matter of raising the funds, getting people to contribute the money that would allow for publication, all of that belongs to Charles. So the one thing that has been very intriguing to people is how it is that by the time we got to issue number 7 of *Callaloo*, Dent and I were no longer the coeditors, but we had been relegated to a lesser status. Well, it was Charles's choice, which I think he had every right to make, that we were not progressive enough for him because we believed in publishing all of these little people, and he wanted a magazine that was going to get national if not international attention. And his dream has now been fulfilled because that's precisely what *Callaloo* is. It is an international magazine.

CT: Professor Ward, I ordered a book of essays edited by Robert Boyers and published by *Salmagundi*. It says it's dedicated to Orlando Patterson and his wife. I also ordered your book *The Katrina Papers*. On the back, the long blurb is from Hank Lazer, who is a distinguished English professor and associate provost for many years at the University of Alabama. Both are interracial encounters, as a book by one leading scholar is dedicated to another scholar but an African American scholar. Also a book by the leading scholar Professor Ward is much admired by another leading scholar. Let me go back to a comment you made earlier [about] if American life was better understood. You are the great scholar of Richard Wright, who could not remain certainly not in Mississippi but hardly even in America. What is the life of the African American intellectual like now? What is the community in which you live and move and have your being?

JWW: I think if we're going to talk about the African American intellectual as a kind of category, we will find that there's a tremendous amount of diversity in that category. There are people who are not attached to universities necessarily who are doing wonderful things or maybe not-so-wonderful things. There are obviously professors, people in the professoriate. And you have to look at where they are located and what kinds of schools.

Are they at research one institutions? At community colleges or wherever they are? So I think it would be a big mistake to try to make a generalization about African American intellectuals in the twenty-first century. I just think that we are so different among ourselves and that we do so many different things so one almost has to be very specific about what it is that you think this intellectual does. Does she or he do hard sciences? Astrophysics? Microbiology or biochemistry? Or philosophy, as it might be the case with a number of people who are of interest to me? Or does this person write? Or just what is it that the person does? Or maybe it's a person who's in business can also be an intellectual, and obviously there are some people even in the entertainment industry who are very intelligent, and they express their intelligence very differently. And I would contrast, let's say, Spike Lee with Tyler Perry. Both are very successful, and of course Oprah is the ultimate success story. And these are all very smart people: whether one wants to call them intellectuals or not, that is a choice that one has to make. And in fact, I have in mind doing a piece on the crisis, which I want to call, "The Crisis of the Intellect" as opposed to the crisis of the intellectual.

CT: You have remained in Mississippi and contiguous states, Mississippi and Louisiana, and you have remained at historically Black colleges with countless encounters of visiting professorships at Grinnell and a zillion other places.

JWW: No, I didn't go to a zillion other places.

CT: Well, many other places.

JWW: Okay.

CT: Many other places. And when not in visiting professorships, certainly in appearances. But you were able to do what was impossible for Richard Wright to do, which was to remain in America. You speak of in your *Katrina Papers* experience, you speak of exile. And let me ask you this. Often or perhaps typically we characterize Richard Wright's years in France as expatriation, but in many ways wasn't he pretty much exiled?

I mean, he was certainly exiled from Mississippi; it was inhospitable. And in many ways, was America much better? The Communist Party was so hostile. Talk about exile and expatriation and Wright. Was it a bit of both? And then your triumphant continuing residence in Mississippi, and I'm going on too long because I would like to almost make the provocative assertion that in a way—we talk about Ellison, and Baldwin being killing the father—your just unsurpassed success as a scholar and a writer and an intellectual in Mississippi and Louisiana is almost a mild reproach to Wright and everybody else. [. . .] There is nothing that you have not accomplished. There is no literary feat that you have undertaken that you really have not successfully done, and as you talk about Wright's almost insulting his father, there's almost something of a reproach to everybody in that you can stay here, you can serve your community, this cost me nothing. I gained everything.

There's nothing that you haven't done, there's nothing that you haven't achieved, you've done it all from Mississippi and Louisiana, mainly from Tougaloo and Dillard, and for all of your fake modesty, it's a reproach! You are thumbing your nose at everybody because of this tremendous achievement in these—what some people might think are unlikely places!

JWW: Well, let me gently correct you. I have not achieved everything. I have not gotten a call from the MacArthur Foundation yet.

CT: Well, keep living.

JWW: Well, I don't have that much time. And my modesty is not fake, Sir, it's authentic. And I appreciate your esteem for me, but let's go back to the matter of exile, expatriation, and Richard Wright. I'm going to take it that for you, exile is an involuntary action.

Expatriation is a choice, for whatever reason or rationale one wants to provide. And I think we need to talk about Wright in terms of expatriation more than exile, although the conditions of being removed from one's homeland, whether you went away because you were forced to or whether it was your choice, might be rather similar because you're trying to negotiate now a new cultural space, a new language, a new history, you know, which may be somewhat alien—not in a necessarily bad sense, but it's going to be alien to you. And I think that's what Wright faced. I think there's a difference in what drove Baldwin into exile and why he said he had to leave because I would have killed someone. Or, a lesser-known artist, Allen Polite, who is mentioned briefly in Baraka's autobiography. Early on [Polite] was a poet, and I think he was published in some of the little magazines that LeRoi Jones and Hettie Cohen were doing. But his major work is in art, and he chose to go to Scandinavia. And there is a number, I discovered when we were doing some checking on him, that there was a rather large—well, large, not overwhelming but—a significant number of African American artists who went to Sweden or Norway or Denmark or someplace like that. Finland, even. And they would—some of them got to know each other, and they have things. So you had a Northern European expatriation as well as a few people like Ollie Harrington being in Germany and of course everyone who managed to get into Paris at one point or another. And of course Baldwin lived for some time in Turkey, which I find intriguing—that he should have chosen that place. So with Wright, I think it was a matter of being in an interracial marriage and having what I call interracial children. And his daughters—well, Rachel was born in Paris, but Julia was born in New York. So the insults that he knew even in the most liberal city of New York that she would face because of her mixed-race background were a bit much. And he had achieved a certain degree of success and was invited the year before he actually made a firm decision to go and live in Paris, to spend some time in France as a special guest. And I suppose he liked the conversations he was having with the existentialists and the chance that he had to have some communication with Gertrude Stein and other people that were living abroad. So I don't think that we can make a special case for his being abroad. Maybe you would make a different case for Baldwin, but I see Wright as being abroad more in the same sense that we speak of Ezra Pound or some other Americans who spent time in Europe—Hemingway, obviously, and Hemingway in Cuba. These people wanted certain kinds of adventures. Now the nuance that you have to bring to the case of Richard Wright is that many of these other people were not Black. So what does it mean for an African American man to move to Paris less than three years after the end of World War II, who has a kind of Marxist background which he's rejected but certainly has a very strong feeling about pan-Africanism and nationalism itself, being unable to talk about French colonialism? Fanon can do that. He was nobody's guest, you know—he wasn't a guest of the French government. Richard Wright was a guest of the French government, and also let us not forget that as a former communist, Wright was under FBI surveillance and under the surveillance of several other agencies. The State Department was quite interested in what he was doing. And Hazel Rowley, who was one of Wright's biographers, shared a State Department document with me because she wanted to know if Wright had written it. And I read it many times and told her, "No, he did not write this. This was written by the Department of State." But a certain kind of pressure was put on him, and this is in 1954 in the Gold Coast. And he had to sign it because you see, we must not be so naive as to think that the American intelligence community has not used many of the same strategies that you would expect from the KGB. And there are certain things that you do in this country, and you are given offers that you cannot refuse. Our intelligence community can be as cruel as the Mafia. And "You better sign this, or would you like to see your daughter's body floating somewhere. Or your wife's head in a box."

CT: So, Wright was an expat?

JWW: Yes. And the document they asked him to sign was one to build a case against his primary host, Kwame Nkrumah, and the Secret Seven. Well, these were Nkrumah's comrades, who really rather nonviolently, I would say, engineered the independence of the Gold Coast. Within—still within the British Commonwealth but independence, and this was a problem for the British. It was a problem for the Americans, it was a problem for everybody. And Wright was never able to. He wanted to move to Great Britain, but the Foreign Office there found excuse after excuse to deny him.

CT: Was she in Great Britain when he died?

JWW: Yes, his wife was in Great Britain. His daughter Julia had come back from Cambridge and was with him in Paris. I guess she had been there a month or so before he died, but the wife was still abroad. And you know, they were not divorced, they were kind of separated and leading rather different lives, and Wright was having a number of problems at the time, both with health and with dwindling income, so that he had to sell the magnificent apartment on rue Monsieur LePrince and get a smaller apartment. You know, so he had to be much more frugal than he had ever been in his life. This was not easy for a person who had his reputation and his fame. What is this downfall that you've suddenly faced? But it had to do with what we began with much earlier and that is how the wind is blowing in the publishing world and what is selling and what is not selling. Also remember that after 1953 there were two people competing for Wright's space in the imagination: Baldwin and Ellison. And the publishers were promoting them against each other. It was a kind of battle royale scene out of *Invisible Man*. Let's have these people fight each other. And of course, Baldwin, in his naivete, wrote a piece that was very offensive to Richard Wright, and it was published in a magazine that was backed by our CIA, so of course—

CT: *Encounter.*

JWW: Yes. And Stephen Spender was involved with all of that. It is very interesting how our nonliterary agencies somehow find it in their interest to invest some money in culture.

CT: Absolutely.

JWW: And how they do it is another matter, but it's really very interesting. And I think William J. Maxwell's book *F. B. Eyes*, which is about the surveillance of American writers, primarily of African American writers (and other books, Mary Helen Washington on the Black Left), and earlier books that deal with surveillance help us to begin to develop a sharper view of what has been happening with literature in America and in particular with African American literature. Or I would suppose increasingly Hispanic literature is—you know, you ramp up all of your concerns about who's legit or illegitimate and what difference do you make between those descendants of the Spanish in the Southwest who were always there and never lived in Mexico. And you might have a person like Rudolfo Anaya who will say, "You know, there is a real difference between me and Mexicans or Chicanos because my family is older."

CT: You've mentioned Anne Bradstreet and Emily Dickinson, and you note in your introduction about women writers that African American women writers have perhaps had a very particular sense of audience, giving rise to a voice at once modulated and unforgettable. And in thinking of the audience and you have personally developed a literary voice that is modulated and personal, what's your perspective on the audience as perceived by the African American woman writer and your own sense of audience and how, if at all, it affects your voice?

JWW: Well, I think if, and I would go back to two people: Phillis Wheatley and Frances Ellen Watkins Harper. Phillis Wheatley was one of those proof-giving people, right? The evidence that we began talking about. So she's writing very neoclassical poetry, but she also had a sense of the need to give certain instructions to American audiences, and I remarked on this in a piece I did for the *Journal of Ethnic American Literature* most recently on abrasion. So her audience was always going to be overwhelmingly white, and the better part of her audience would have been people who were interested in abolition. Obviously, Frances Ellen Watkins Harper was a champion of the abolition of the institution of slavery and wrote endlessly, lectured, and spoke and read her poetry, so she had also a really strong sense of her audience being those who would support the liberation of enslaved African American people in this country. So when we look at the commitment and interests of women writers and artists, I think you look at the women writers of the late nineteenth century, the women writers of the 1910s, the 1920s, you look at Zora Neale Hurston, you move forward to Ann Petry. Obviously the two women we've talked about, Gwendolyn Brooks and Margaret Walker, but you also have people like May Miller, who comes out of the [Harlem] Renaissance period. You had Jessie Fauset. All of these women writers were always at a little bit of a disadvantage no matter how well they wrote, no matter if they were as brilliant as Anna Julia Cooper because the industry was not going to have that. You know, they had to take second place to Edna Ferber and some other women writers who were supposed to be supported and advertised, and these were just Black women writers, but they did have their audiences and their audiences were developed through the pages of *Crisis* and *Opportunity* and even certain *Black* [*Negro*] *World* newspaper for Garvey. In the fifties more of them were able to write, and of course there was a breakthrough in the theater with Lorraine Hansberry coming out with *A Raisin in the Sun* and that had overwhelming popularity. And so you've got more things being done and the work of Ruby Dee and Ossie Davis, of course, the theater couple. Which could do something with literature or bring a certain perspective to attention, and of course what we have, happening at a certain stage of the very long civil rights movement, is a resurgence of the women's liberation movement in the early seventies, and this time you don't have in women's liberation the ignoring of Black women who had to petition—Ida B. Wells, and all these people—to even be a part of the women's movement in the nineteenth century because Susan Anthony and other folks were not necessarily lacking in racism, but in the seventies you have these—a new feminist assertion which is supposed to be multiracial.

But then when you look at a Toni Cade Bambara book, you see something different. When you look at the work of Angela Davis, you see something different. You look at some of the women who were in OBAC (the Organization of Black American Culture), which was a Chicago group, or women writers who participated in the 1973 Phillis Wheatley Conference at Jackson State, which was the brainchild of Margaret Walker. And you get a great deal of variety and of course a new kind of feminist politics coming from Sonia Sanchez, from Toni Cade Bambara, from Nikki Giovanni.

CT: And it's interesting I read a book on Junior Year Abroad, of Jacqueline Kennedy, Susan Sontag, and Angela Davis. And Angela Davis was in Paris—was in France, I don't think she quite made it to Paris—in 1963, during the [Birmingham, Alabama,] church bombing. And of course one of the little girls lived directly behind her and was a friend. But as you mentioned Wright in Paris, it's interesting to think that Angela Davis was in Paris when there was the Birmingham church bombing.

JWW: Yeah, but you have to remember Angela Davis was headed for a very special kind of academic career because she was an academic protégé [. . .] of [Herbert] Marcuse.

CT: [. . .] There was a wonderful letter of recommendation from Marcuse that [talked about how Angela Davis] spoke idiomatic French. And they loved her as no junior year abroad student had been loved before. [. . .] Her connection with France is kind of deep and real. You remind us when you give—the breadth of your response on women writers reminds us that it's hard to do anything without your anthology before us because typically we have such a narrow timeframe. In our small minds, we would start with Toni Cade Bambara's anthology, and you start, you know, two hundred years before then.

JWW: Well, I suppose it has to do with my sense of what responsible literary history is. And responsible literary history did not begin in the twentieth century. And of course there are other anthologies available. Mine [. . .] is out of print now. Well, it's not to my dismay because I refuse to be dismayed by it. But it stayed in print for ten years, which is quite a good run. But then there were new anthologies coming out and the publishers decided that if we're going to keep this at seven dollars, this is a loss—I mean, it's not making any money when the ordinary anthology of the same size is commanding anywhere between fifteen and twenty-five dollars, so you know, "Ward, you're out of the game," and I said okay.

CT: [. . .] Yours has been such a brilliant career. And what inspires is your devotion to the institutions of the community that have been in no way limiting. Because as I read *The Katrina Papers* and talk to you about your life as a reproach to anybody that would leave Mississippi or Louisiana, there is something continental about your style, about the literary flavor of your work. And I don't mean the American continent. It is so obviously cosmopolitan and European. You have achieved what your preparatory teachers taught you to achieve, which is a distinctive style without pretense. And just in your closing comment, just a word about that—about your service here, about developing that at home when so many others have not been able to, or who would use geography as an excuse for being provincial.

JWW: Well, I'm going to be very arrogant and tell you that when you belong to the aristocracy, you can do what peasants don't do. And my aristocracy has to do with my awareness that [unlike many people in this country], I belong to three continents: Asia, Europe, and Africa. And I feel that that's very special. And what has really, I suppose, hardened my commitment to not expatriate myself or seek exile or anything of the kind has to do with my service in the US Army, and being in Vietnam and reading in the *US Army Times* about [the 1970 police shootings at] Kent State and Jackson State, at which point I had to say, "What am I doing in Vietnam?" The fight is not in Vietnam. The Vietnamese had never done anything to me that I could think of. And I'm trying to be patriotic, like soldiers, uncles who were in World War I, relatives who were in World War II, Black soldiers who were very patriotic to the extent of being like Colin Powell, in a country that has no respect for you when you come home with a uniform, okay? Let us not forget the number of Black soldiers who were abused because they wore uniforms. You know, "N-----, take that uniform off," okay. Or one man being told, "You can't work here anymore 'cause your son's running around with his uniform on and he thinks he's one of these uppity people." So, you know, it's like, "Why would I want to leave this? I belong to this country, and the country belongs to me. It's my property." And that's why if a pit bull who wears Prada thinks she can become vice president, I have news for her.

The Many Influences of Richard Wright: An Interview with Jerry W. Ward Jr.

John Zheng / 2017

From *African American Review* 50.1 (Spring 2017): 17–25. Published by Johns Hopkins University Press. Reprinted by permission of John Zheng.

John Zheng: What drew you to Richard Wright? What drove you to choose him as a principal subject for research?

Jerry W. Ward Jr.: Living most of my youth in Mississippi and reading *Uncle Tom's Children* when I was an undergraduate at Tougaloo College drew me to Wright. When I did my doctoral work at the University of Virginia, I chose to write my dissertation on "Richard Wright and His American Critics, 1938–1960." My concentration was literary theory and criticism, so it seemed reasonable to apply what I learned about the hidden dimensions of literary study in examining how Wright's reputation emerged.

JZ: Which other literary influences have there been?

JWW: We are influenced by everything that we read. It is difficult for me to account for all of the influences on my thought and efforts to write over a period of more than fifty years. Some of my early writings were influenced by Carl Sandburg, T. S. Eliot, and James Baldwin. Kenneth Burke, LeRoi Jones/Amiri Baraka, Margaret Walker, Tom Dent, Bakhtin, William Faulkner, Kalamu ya Salaam, Shakespeare and English Renaissance writers, W. E. B. Du Bois and Ralph Ellison have also shaped my thinking about literature and life and purpose.

JZ: In what way did Wright's works catch your attention?

JWW: Wright's use of literacy, of language to communicate his vision, was very attractive. The more I study Wright, the more fascinated I become with how he did things with words.

JZ: Can you be more specific about Wright's use of language to communicate his vision?

JWW: Wright never earned a college degree, but his ability to write effectively is superior. He obviously made a strong investment in using the basic ability to read and write as a means of acquiring knowledge about the world and about himself. Wright used his interest in how words might trigger emotions and ideas along with his early intuition about human psychology to engage his readers. I have not yet resolved the ambiguity of the character Bigger Thomas's statement, "What I killed for, I am." Eugene E. Miller's *Voice of a Native Son* (1990) is one of the best explorations of Wright's poetics, but more research on Wright's diction and rhetorical choices in fiction and nonfiction can be done. Wright mixed narration or storytelling with polemics or cultural critiques in such works as *Native Son*, *The Outsider*, and *The Long Dream*. We must notice how his choices frustrate our assumptions about how reality should be represented. Wright certainly understood mimesis quite well, the functions of images and narrative descriptions to achieve multiple purposes. Consider his achievement in the underappreciated novel *Lawd Today!*, his borrowing of patterns from James Joyce and his use of techniques we associate with ethnography. We should be aware that in order to communicate a complex vision of how the world functions, Wright chose to combine the language of folk psychology with a range of literary tropes and modes of philosophical, economic, and sociological argument. Like the truly great writers in world literature, Richard Wright used language to make his messages clear to people who had little formal education as well as to those who had advanced or terminal degrees.

JZ: Yes, I'd agree with you that Wright possessed a superior writing ability. Is it at all possible that Wright's ability to write, his gift for storytelling, also shows the influence of the Black church?

JWW: I suspect that turns of phrase, pause and intonation, imagery, repetition, and so forth that we connect with African American preaching styles did have some indirect impact on Wright's eloquence. The Black church, however, is not exactly a monolith, and many different styles of preaching might have influenced Wright. Obviously, Wright combined and recombined elements from the whole spectrum of how Black and non-Black people spoke. Black preaching is but one point on that spectrum.

JZ: How did Wright's humanity—his presence as a human being—interest you most?

JWW: The key word is *affinity*. Wright's spirit and determination have long been of interest to me. Long ago I recognized a few parallels between our life experiences. The shock of recognition I had upon reading *Black Boy* in my youth created a powerful affinity between Richard Wright and me. I recognized that we shared—despite the thirty-five years that separated us—similar values and perspectives about the dynamics of good and evil and their impact upon the lives of human beings. We shared hunger for knowing that can never be completely satisfied. Our paths as adults took quite different directions. Wright invested much of his life in trying to speak a truth about his world, in seeking out receptive ears for his words and ideas, and in shaking people out of complacency. I have made a similar investment. I think our curiosity about a writer's job of deciding for whom he or she writes secures our kinship. Dealing with the full range of his writings for many years has enabled me to discover much about his humanity, his agony, and his humanism. And my own.

JZ: Hunger in *Black Boy* contains both literal and metaphorical meanings. One means starvation and the other yearning for knowledge. How did Wright satisfy that second hunger?

JWW: Wright satisfied the second hunger by reading extensively and by discussing ideas with people who were experts on various subjects.

JZ: Can you talk a bit about your writing on *American Hunger*?

JWW: I wrote a piece on *American Hunger* when it was first published for the *Virginia Quarterly Review* and tried to account for how pervasive hunger was throughout his life, how the hunger of the spirit is implacable. The concept of hunger enabled Wright to figuratively represent his kinship with all the hungry, suffering peoples of the world. I also gave notice to the fact that *American Hunger* wasn't a newly discovered manuscript. It was the portion of the "American Hunger" typescript that was not published in 1945 under the title *Black Boy*. Unused parts of "American Hunger" had been published in *Atlantic Monthly* (1944), the anthology *Cross Section 1945*, and the September 1945 issue of *Mademoiselle*. Only sixteen pages of *American Hunger* had not been in print prior to 1977, but its publication as a book forced us to think differently about Wright and autobiography.

JZ: As the continuation of Wright's autobiography, what's the importance of this book in comparison to *Black Boy*? Or if there's a difference between the two books, what is it?

JWW: The difference is that *Black Boy* is about the American South as a region, and *American Hunger* is mainly about Chicago as an urban environment. The importance of the book is its revealing that originally Wright wanted to portray his childhood and young adulthood in parts of the United States where the ethics of living Jim Crow had features that were not necessarily disconnected. *Black Boy* confirmed what many liberal white northerners wished to believe about the horrors of the South; *American Hunger* exposed that the Midwest possessed a different kind and degree of horror. It is important to note that in the 1991 Library of America edition of *Black Boy (American Hunger)*, *Black Boy* is retitled "Part I: Southern Night"; *American Hunger* [is] "Part II: The Horror and the Glory."

JZ: As an autobiographic novel, *Black Boy (American Hunger)* must have some parts that are creative rather than authentic. What would be your advice to readers or researchers if authenticity is a concern?

JWW: I would advise them to remember that *truth* is not an absolute but rather a tentative conclusion about the nature of things, and the conclusion is subject to those limits suggested by Heisenberg's principle of uncertainty. If all the propositions and claims in *Black Boy* cannot be verified, that condition is not a warrant for claiming the autobiography lacks authenticity. It is a warrant for recognizing that authenticity comes in as many varieties as validity. I do believe it is imprecise to call *Black Boy* an autobiographical novel. It is—if we still care as I do about the importance of genres—an autobiography that adapts many features that we associate with novels. I think the contemporary penchant for classifying all prose works that show evidence of imagination as novels is an unfortunate signal of decline in our ability to be discriminating.

JZ: Wright had a deft focus on alienation. How did he exploit outsideness in *Black Boy*?

JWW: By drawing attention again and again to how he was different from members of his family, his childhood friends and fellow students, the people with whom he worked. Wright portrays himself as the odd person with a radical will to think independently and critically.

JZ: Are there similarities, would you say, between this and his handling of the theme of alienation in his life at home and abroad?

JWW: Yes, in a fashion similar to the one depicted in *Black Boy*—in his life from birth to his choosing exile in France, Wright was adamant about being his own kind of Black person, his own kind of communist, his own kind of American writer. He didn't always succeed in remaining outside the cages of identity, but he tried hard to prevent his being identified as a number or as a subaltern locked in a prison of class, caste, and race. During the thirteen years of his life in France, Wright used his own ideas about existentialism to foreground outsideness; he also used his political beliefs as reasons to travel and write about Africa, Spain, and a small portion of Asia. Until his death in 1960, Wright tried to use the social capital of being the outsider to his best advantage.

JZ: You mentioned in your speech delivered at the 2012 Natchez Literary and Cinema Celebration that Wright's unpublished essay "Memories of My Grandmother" is as important for understanding Wright's storytelling imagination as is his essay "How 'Bigger' Was Born" for understanding the complexity of *Native Son*. I think readers would like to know more about its importance. Can you elaborate?

JWW: Reading "Memories of My Grandmother" is crucial for understanding what Wright thought about the creative operations of the human mind; why he thought surrealism was a crucial stage in creative actions; why, from keen observation of his grandmother's total immersion in the beliefs that constituted Seventh-Day Adventism, he had to create a world (the locus of his thinking) in which he could distance himself from how religion as such could be a disabling force in one's life. Wright had some very smart things to say about human psychology, especially Freud's thinking about the importance of dreams and about the blues and its ability to lift a person who knew how to listen to remarkable heights of vivid perception. "Memories of My Grandmother" is a rich, dense essay that resists an easy summary. For that reason, I recommend that people order a photocopy of it from the Beinecke Rare Book and Manuscript Library at Yale and read it again and again. Wright's meditation on cognition is perhaps the chief document we should use to ask good questions about all of his writings.

JZ: Wright's special presence in your research, then, is abundantly clear, but how has he influenced your attitudes toward race, culture, and society?

JWW: I developed attitudes about race, Black cultures, and American society well in advance of reading Wright. My attitudes were forged in lived experiences, not in reading. He has influenced me most in how I decide to shape questions about institutions and experiences. Like Wright, I refuse to live in a box marked "This is what African Americans are supposed to be interested in."

JZ: Your research on Wright has been helpful to your contemporaries and younger scholars. Can you give a detailed description of your research?

JWW: My early research was conducted between 1974 and 1978. I read all of Wright's works published up to that time, all of the early critical studies of his work. I took notes on what to look for from Constance Webb's wonderfully subjective biography of Wright. I did a considerable amount of reading of all the critical and popular responses to his works in newspapers at the Library of Congress; read the Harper & Brothers files at Princeton's Firestone Library to gain insights about his relationship with editors and publishers. In New York, I did work with Wright materials at the Butler

Library at Columbia University and the materials in the Schomburg Collection of the New York Public Library. Although Yale University acquired the Richard Wright Papers before I completed my dissertation, it was not possible for me to inspect them, despite the intervention of George Kent on my behalf. Charles T. Davis was working with Michel Fabre on the papers, and he was of the opinion that a graduate student had to prove himself (that is, earn a PhD) before he was qualified to examine Wright's papers. I had many talks with Margaret Walker about Wright, and I conducted an informal interview with Theodore Ward about his association with Wright. I read *The Crisis of the Negro Intellectual* by Harold Cruse quite carefully, and I did have a conversation with Cruse about Wright's nationalism and Marxism. After earning my doctorate at the University of Virginia in 1978, I continued to read everything I could about Wright. It was necessary to expose my students at Tougaloo College to continuing developments in critical discussions when I taught the Richard Wright course. The first International Symposium on Richard Wright at the University of Mississippi, November 21–23, 1985, was a unique opportunity; I met dozens of Wright scholars there and established some correspondence with a few of them. The symposium, which was the brainchild of Professor Maryemma Graham, led to my collaborating with her to establish the Richard Wright Circle and to coedit the *Richard Wright Newsletter*. Our efforts to promote the sustained study of Wright in universities as well as in public schools required ongoing research in many disciplines that are not strictly literary. In the 1990s, I became familiar with hypertext. I spent a week at Brown University, learning directly from George P. Landow how I might use the convergence of critical theory and technology to construct a website on selected works by Wright. Unfortunately, Tougaloo College did not have the computer hardware I needed to maintain and expand the website I created at Brown. Interdisciplinary research was very important, as I worked with Robert Butler to compile *The Richard Wright Encyclopedia*. For me, doing research on Wright and encouraging others to discover facts about his life and works is as natural as breathing. The bulk of my research has not been reduced to print, because I used it in teaching and for lectures that were a part of public humanities programming. I chose to avoid some of the limitations of academic publishing for the sake of having more freedom to broadcast my ideas to a nonacademic audience. And most of my work was done the old-fashioned way, without the benefit of computers.

At present, my research on Wright moves very slowly. Since my retirement in 2012, I have limited access to online academic databases. I am not always up-to-date about new work in Wright studies. And my research for the book I want to write about Wright is very, very slow. The book I have in mind requires my reading much of what Wright read as preparation for writing.

JZ: Yes, the interdisciplinary thread is crucial to understanding Richard Wright. Can you talk about your most unforgettable experience during your studies?

JWW: My most unforgettable experience was spending two weeks in 2004 at the Beinecke Library at Yale and reading Wright's typescripts and learning to decipher his penmanship. Touching pages that had once been touched by Wright was an absolutely unforgettable emotional experience.

JZ: I had the same feeling when I was examining Wright's haiku manuscript at Yale. Can you talk a little more about your research on Wright?

JWW: My research on Wright is concentrated on matters of American and African American social history. I am interested in how literature might be a situated reaction to both literary forms and nonliterary events. My work pertains mainly to African American literary history. I am interested in Wright's thesis-driven narratives or stories as instances of continuity in a Black tradition of fiction-making, one that is indebted to what Wright called the forms of things unknown. Wright was certainly aware of modernist techniques, but I feel he was more concerned with themes than with narrative innovations. I try to discover why Wright remained relatively faithful to the propositions in his "Blueprint for Negro Writing" in his novels rather than investing great energy in experimenting with a different range of aesthetic possibilities. My research is related to problems associated with literary and cultural interpretation.

JZ: What kind of distinctive voice did Wright bring to fiction or broadly speaking to world literature?

JWW: Angry, bold, critical, hard-boiled, hurtful, uncompromising, violent—I think of adjectives that might be used or were used by reviewers to characterize what distinguished Wright's voice in fiction and nonfiction from the voices employed by many of his contemporaries. Wright was measured racially. The mistake was to give insufficient attention to his art, to how he did things with words. How he depicted situations and made arguments brought sharp perspectives on race relations, victimization, and oppression into view. He upset expectations that a Negro writer ought to conform to the ethics of Jim Crow. He did not engage in minstrelsy. He did not wear the mask in most instances. The sound of his voice was iconoclastic. Had people known in the early twentieth century what we know

now about the history of African American creative expressions, they might have been less surprised that Wright sounded angry and combative. He was measuring aspects of essential disharmony in the United States in language that was at once symbolic and unflattering. How Wright passed judgment on the nation of his birth was less a matter of protest than it was a matter of indictment, a matter of providing a mirror that forced our nation to behold its vulgarity in conversation with its nobility.

JZ: Wright did not wear the mask in most instances, so he was not invisible. Could you give an example of his work or speech?

JWW: The examples are distributed throughout his works, particularly in such essays as "Blueprint for Negro Writing," "How 'Bigger' Was Born" and "Memories of My Grandmother" as well as in his introductions to *12 Million Black Voices*, *Black Power*, *The Color Curtain*, and *White Man, Listen!* Wright was self-consciously visible in explaining his sources and his objectives.

JZ: Would you say something about the recent literary criticism on Richard Wright?

JWW: Criticism and general commentary regarding Wright continue to appear, and that is a good sign. We do need to have a broader or more diverse distribution in the criticism. We have a surplus of articles on *Native Son*, for example, and too few examinations of *Pagan Spain*, *The Color Curtain*, *Eight Men*, *The Outsider*, *Savage Holiday*, and *The Long Dream*. William J. Maxwell's *F. B. Eyes: How J. Edgar Hoover's Ghostreaders Framed African American Literature* (2015) does compel us to take a fresh look at how surveillance had a great impact on Wright. Jeff Allred's chapter on *12 Million Black Voices* in his study *American Modernism and Depression Documentary* (2010) whets our appetite for examining Wright's photography in greater depth. Ayesha K. Hardison's excellent discussion of the unpublished novel "Black Hope" in *Writing through Jane Crow: Race and Gender Politics in African American Literature* (2014) demonstrates why we ought to spend more time in the Wright Papers at Yale and discover more about Wright's interest in film and in writing plays. Trying to keep up with books, journal articles, and casual references to Wright is virtually a mission impossible. In March 2016, we saw the publication of *Indonesian Notebook: A Sourcebook on Richard Wright and the Bandung Conference* by Brian Russell Roberts and Keith Foulcher. This important new book invites us to reconsider *The Color Curtain* and the 1955 Bandung Conference, Wright's presence in cross-cultural settings, the Cold War, and its political aftermath. And *Richard Wright Writing America at Home and from Abroad*, edited by Virginia

Whatley Smith, urges us to give attention to some of Wright's underappreciated works. The recent criticism assures me that Wright's legacy has lost none of its contemporary relevance.

JZ: Any suggestions about reading or researching the unfinished *A Father's Law*?

JWW: In my review of the novel,[1] I suggested Wright focused heavily on how ancient prejudices, biological anxieties, and social mores complicate efforts to act morally. I think reading John Rawls's *A Theory of Justice* can help us to bring the unfinished aspects of the novel to aesthetic closure. What demands research is Wright's interest in Roman Catholicism, disease as metaphor, and ideas that may be derived from the Old Testament and Nietzsche's notion that morality is a disease. What did Wright read in preparation for writing this novel? What were Wright's motives for staking out new territory for his fiction as he recycled the primal theme of father and son?

JZ: What do you think a contemporary reader should know or learn in reading Wright?

JWW: Contemporary readers should learn from the study of Wright's works how to ask questions that are not trivial. What we ultimately arrive at knowing from Wright and from all writers who strive to be honest is that the human mind does have the possibility of using reason and imagination to expand and refine perceptions of a world that is constantly changing.

JZ: What do you think young scholars should focus on in the study of Wright?

JWW: I urge young scholars to focus on Wright's mind, his innate intelligence, his defiance and willpower, his always-expanding interest in mankind's existence, his analyses of phenomena and experiments in many genres. Many of Wright's observations, of course, are time-bound and have more historical than topical importance; his primal questions are timeless. Thus, I urge them to scrutinize primary sources—the published works and the unpublished materials in the Wright Papers at Yale. The archival scholarship is ultimately of greater importance than reading commentary on Wright. Secondary sources and theories do have to be used as guides for asking questions, identifying references in Wright's works, and contextualizing whatever we find in his works. But the main focus ought to be on what Wright wrote.

JZ: With the main focus on what Wright wrote, young scholars can produce genuine analytical essays that present their own critical thinking or that avoid echoing the views of others.

JWW: Yes. Young scholars should generate their own ideas first, do some research about the historical moment during which Wright and his peers wrote, and then measure their ideas against the thinking of previous critics.

JZ: In your *China Lectures* book, you point out that theories "tend to be arbitrary, quite expressive of taste and private interests, and comfortable with the playing of games" and they "resemble ideological costumes" (1). Since you have been teaching in China for six years now, what have you done to help the scholars and students there to understand the use of theory in their study of Wright or of African American literature?

JWW: I have done two things to readjust thinking among Chinese students and some colleagues, especially those at Central China Normal University. During three of the six years, I have conducted an intensive seminar on research and writing for MA and PhD students which focuses on methodology and preparing manuscripts that use MLA documentation. I have individual and often lengthy conferences with the students about their proposed theses and dissertations, and one of the first things we have to discuss is whether they really understand the theory they have chosen. All the CCNU students are obligated to use one theory or another that their supervisors believe is trendy or dominant in American and European literary studies. I anticipate that when I teach in China this year or in 2017, students might be raving about the crisis of deconstruction. It is often the case that the students have vague, misleading notions about how theory is used in the West and why they should use it with caution. For example, a student wanted to use Foucault's heterotopia (*Des espaces autres*) to discuss some works by William Faulkner. When I asked if the student could explain how Foucault's ideas were related to Henri Lefebvre's theorizing about urban space and Michel de Certeau's *Practice of Everyday Life* as well as Faulkner's ideas about history, the student was totally baffled. He had minimal knowledge of the history of the American South. We agreed to read Foucault together so that I could explain why it was no easy matter to just grab a theory and make a writer's works fit the theory. I had similar conversations with all the seminar students. The conversations with students who wanted to use feminist or postcolonial theory to examine an African American author required me to make long explanations about significant differences among American ethnic cultures, about why television and Internet images of the United States are not reliable guides for understanding cultural nuances that theory minimizes. Eventually, they began to understand that as far as theory was concerned, they should not be machines without thought. They must read

Wright or any other writer within historical contexts first and then decide which theory might be appropriate.

My second effort addressed our colleagues. In November 2014, I persuaded those who had profound interests in Black literature and culture to work together under the umbrella of what I called the African American Research Network (AARN) to exchange ideas about research topics, pedagogy, methods, and theory. As you know, I frequently send information to AARN members, and I do have productive email exchanges with some of the scholars. I think the idea that Chinese scholars need not be enslaved to the winds and whims of theory is very slowly beginning to take root. Nevertheless, I know that many years of work will be required to convince our Chinese colleagues that Western theories should be looked at with some skepticism.

JZ: How does what you say in this instance comport with reading and researching Wright in the twenty-first century? What would mark itself as a continuing value?

JWW: I locate the continuing value in our continuing to ask questions about world events, people in many parts of the world, and ourselves. Michel Fabre aptly entitled his biography of Wright *The Unfinished Quest of Richard Wright*. Wright is exemplary in showing us why our quest for knowledge, for strategies of offense and defense, for wisdom is always unfinished.

JZ: Were you aware that Wright wrote haiku when you started studying him?

JWW: Yes. I read the ones published in *New Letters* in the early 1970s and thought of them as returns to the brief catalogs of images in *Black Boy* and experiments in reshaping the images which are threaded in Wright's short stories and novels.

JZ: Do you think Wright's haiku deserve equal attention in comparison to his novels?

JWW: His haiku deserve the attention you have brought to them in *The Other World of Richard Wright: Perspectives on His Haiku*, that Yoshinobu Hakutani brought to them in *Richard Wright and Racial Discourse* and more recently in *Richard Wright and Haiku*. The attention to his poetry ought to be conducted with the same rigor we accord to his novels, but we should entertain the possibility that the aims of interpretation might be different. We might study the haiku to discover more about Wright's poetics, his creative imagination, and his fidelity to or transgression of Japanese aesthetics. On the other hand, we analyze and interpret the novels with the objective of discovering more about his social vision and critiques of history and politics.

JZ: Yes, I agree that there might be different, even conflicting issues of interpretation across genres—indeed, there might be a thousand Wrights in a thousand people's eyes. What is your current project?

JWW: Reginald Martin of the University of Memphis and I are coauthoring *Words and Being*, a modest effort to deal with some of the frustrations that beset academic discussions of African American and other American combat/contact zones in the chaos of American culture. We are proposing that common sense rather than obtuse philosophy is our most powerful tool in efforts to account for the changing order of things, to minimize unavoidable confusion in studies or everyday conversations involving cultures and cultural expressions. This is our primary thesis.

JZ: I remember you were the one who helped establish the *Richard Wright Newsletter*. How was it established, who were the editors, and is it still in publication? If it continues publication, don't you think it will attract more audiences and contributions if the name is changed to the *Richard Wright Review*?

JWW: The entire run of the *Richard Wright Newsletter*, Vol. 1.1– Vol. 13.1–2, along with the bibliographical supplements Keneth Kinnamon prepared, is archived at http://wrightconnection.ku.edu. Maryemma Graham and I established the newsletter in 1991 as the organ for the Richard Wright Circle; we served as coeditors until we passed the editorship to the late James A. Miller in either 2001 or 2002. Unlike a review or journal, the newsletter was a forum for information about new or forthcoming publications, ideas about teaching Wright's works, announcements, brief commentaries by teachers and students, notes on research projects, some short reviews, and miscellaneous items. It was a print network for members of the Richard Wright Circle.

The Richard Wright Circle is in a kind of permanent hibernation, and it is rather painful for me to know that it will sleep forever. There is no future for the newsletter. It will remain as an archived resource for literary studies. If any scholars wanted to establish a *Richard Wright Review*, I would applaud their efforts. At present, there are so many societies devoted to single African American authors that they attract minimal attention. Only the Toni Morrison Society and the Langston Hughes Society continue to have high visibility and great success.

JZ: Thank you for your time, Dr. Ward. Is there anything else you'd like to say about Richard Wright?

JWW: There are many other things I want to say about Wright, but they will only materialize if I live long enough to write a book entitled *Richard Wright: One Reader's Responses*.

Note

1. Jerry W. Ward Jr., review of *A Father's Law*, by Richard Wright, *African American Review* 43.2–3 (Summer/Fall 2009): 519–21.

An Interview with Jerry W. Ward Jr.

Yukuo Wang / 2017

Printed by permission of Yukuo Wang.

Yukuo Wang: In the new century, heated debates between African American poet Rita Dove and Professor Helen Vendler and between Professor Kenneth Warren and those who disagree with him about *What Was African American Literature?* have aroused various interests and attention about African American literature, so my first question is: What distinguishes African American literature from other minority literatures in the United States—for instance, Asian American literature or Chicano/Chicana American literature or Native American literature?

Jerry W. Ward Jr.: Your large question warrants a careful answer. To begin with your implied interrogative *what distinguishes*, I must suggest the words *heated debate* and *minority* can mislead us. What occurred between Helen Vendler and Rita Dove in the pages of the *New York Review of Books* was not a debate. It was an exchange that began with Vendler's review, "Are These the Poems to Remember?," of *The Penguin Anthology of Twentieth-Century American Poetry* edited by Dove. In the December 22, 2011, issue, Dove published "Defending an Anthology," and Vendler's reply in the same issue precluded any debate: "I have written the review and I stand by it." Other poets and scholars did make comments about the exchange online and by way of private correspondence.

Minority is a word to be used with caution in American conversations. It normally refers to a numerically smaller and different portion of a mixed population. In American social and literary discussions, the word can have offensive connotations. That is to say, the heritage of many twentieth-century stereotypes of minorities, the sneaky rhetorical coding, also makes the wording *people of color* insulting for those of us who do not suffer fools lightly. I bring attention to words in order to mark or highlight my difference from many of my peers.

In the United States, our ethnic literatures—Native American, African American, Asian American, and Chicano/Chicana—are conceptual groupings of work produced by writers and thinkers who are fewer in number than some imagined "majority" in our total population. It is unacceptable, to me at least, to call what they write *minority literature*. And the phrase *literature of minorities* would be painfully awkward.

What distinguishes one body of ethnic literature from another is primarily a matter of how we write American literary histories. Our stories of literary enfolding; of reception, reading, and criticism; of exclusion and inclusion in the loosely coordinated listings called *canon*—these narratives are predicated on some ideas about time or epistemes, power, and cultural hegemony. Circumstances or situations that pertain to creation and publishing are major discriminating factors. Language is a major distinguishing factor, a sign of difference. All of the literatures are written in or translated into some variety of American English, but they may have grammatical and syntactic features, in-group slang and nuances, and allusions which seem strange to readers of Standard American English. Worldviews are often implicit in the use of language. These differ among the American ethnic literatures. All of them may share themes, traditional literary devices, and narrative gestures, but close reading and dialogism reveal distinctions.

Confluences and cross-fertilizations do occur among the American ethnic literatures, but theorizing about primal cultural values embedded in the creation of literature exposes differences. In his remarkable essay "Ethnic Import in American Literature (Reflections on a Course)," George E. Kent identified ten "key values that seem frequently to be reflected by Negro folk literature and by outstanding Negro writers."[1] I imagine a different set of key values might be identified for Chinese American or Cuban American literature.

You framed your question by referring to Kenneth Warren and his book *What Was African American Literature?* Reactions to this book remind me how passionate is my investment in African American literature. It is alleged that Abraham Lincoln said to Harriet Beecher Stowe, "So, you are the little lady who started the Civil War." My own hyperbolic statement to Warren is, "So, you are the scholar who encouraged the academic world to believe African American literature only existed between the nineteenth-century slave narratives and the publication of *The Autobiography of Malcolm X*." Calculated rage may be yet another special feature of African American literature.

Wang: W. E. B. Du Bois stated in *The Souls of Black Folk* that the problem of the twentieth century is the problem of the color line, and race or the racial issue is still fundamental in the construction of African American literature. What is/are the changes(s) of the literary criticism toward race or racial issues in the twentieth century and the twenty-first century?

Ward: Race is an extremely problematic idea, but race or a reasonable facsimile thereof can be located in the construction of many literatures throughout the world. Contemporary mainland Chinese literature has "Han privilege," and racial slurs may circulate in Hong Kong Chinese literature. Edward Said notified us that race is a component of latent Orientalism, and Toni Morrison has spoken of racial aspects of whiteness and the literary imagination.[2] African American literature has no monopoly on race in its construction. Preoccupation with race in the United States ensures the longevity of Du Bois's assertion. Preoccupation is a pathway to a new assertion: "The problem of the twenty-first century is the problem of the color-blind!" Both assertions invite critiques—social and literary critiques—which, as one should expect, are tendentious. What interests me most about Du Bois's statement is the absence of Europe in what he said about the geographical relations of the darker and the lighter in Africa, Asia, America, and the islands of the sea. To be sure, Europe had and has its own problem of a color line.

What has changed with regard to late twentieth-century and early twenty-first-century literary criticism is the choice of seeing or not seeing the importance of race in literary analysis and interpretation. From the vantage of the best modern science, race is a pseudoscientific construct that has no material embodiment; it is not palpable and verifiable. Literary critics who believe in what law calls full disclosure are predisposed to examine race and literature or literature and critical race theory because all habits of the human mind are of interest to them; other literary critics exercise their right to be silent.

Wang: Would you please elaborate briefly on the shifts of "seeing or not seeing" the importance of race in literary analysis and interpretation in different time periods in African American literary history? For instance, in the period of the Harlem Renaissance, in the Black Arts Movement, and in the 1980s and 1990s?

Ward: "The Race for Theory." *Nightmare Begins Responsibility*. Juxtaposing the title of Barbara Christian's famous essay with the title of a 1975 collection of poems by Michael S. Harper is my way of buying time to grasp some of the questions nested within your request. Christian's use of *race* to refer both to ethnicity and a contest triggers ideas about human agency. Harper's title ignites thought about why psychological, even physical, suffering should have any role in how African American literary critical postures shifted from the Harlem Renaissance to the 1990s. The brief explanation you ask for has been elegantly provided by Professor Angelyn Mitchell in "Introduction: Voices within the Circle: A Historical Overview of African American Literary Criticism."[3] She avoids what is incendiary in my wording "choice of seeing or not seeing" by neatly locating choices of analysis, interpretation, and evaluation within an intellectual history of aesthetics, ideologies, theories, and sociopolitical determinants.

Wang: Besides race or racial issues in the study of African American literary criticism, gender issues or gender equality has been foregrounded at least since the 1970s. What do you think of different approaches/aspects in Black feminism and their possible tendencies in the new century?

Ward: Any thinking I do in this area of cultural study is centered on womanism, not feminism, because Alice Walker's making a distinction between the womanist and feminist perspectives was a key moment in intellectual history.[4] Her distinction is a warrant for investigating gender as a thread of concern interwoven with other threads we call class, biology, race, and ethnicity, of seeing the fabric through the lens of American history. Inspecting the nineteenth-century fabric and texture enables us to find similar patterns in the literary criticism that has been manufactured since the 1970s.

Discussions of gender in the North were apparent in abolitionist debates about the evils of enslaving Africans and African Americans, and those debates were enlarged by proposals from the Women's Rights Convention of 1848. In the antebellum South, Black women inscribed their gender issues in the narratives they wrote or dictated, in oral traditions, in successful flights to freedom. After the American Civil War, African American women wrote what Claudia Tate aptly named "domestic allegories of political desire." Those women were exceptionally active in promoting literacy and education and in disputing with white feminists that women's rights pertained to women as a class. In these quarrels we discern how race and economic status made gender equality problematic. Leap to 1920: American women finally got the right to vote, but that political gesture left many gender and racial issues unresolved. Just as abolitionist efforts in the nineteenth century provided models for women's assertive actions, so too did the long struggle of African American women (notably Ida B. Wells, Fannie Lou Hamer, and Ella Baker) and men for civil rights provide a template for political and literary actions among women, the upsurge of women's liberation and feminist theorizing which smashed against the ever-present wall of race, ethnic, and class interests and the immense capability of globalization to reinforce abuses of women.

Cultural critics should use the discipline of history to study the fragmentation and bifurcation of feminism and womanism. We should learn from such twentieth-century writers, scholars, and critics as Trudier Harris, Carolyn Fowler, Frances Smith Foster, Gloria T. Hull, Audre Lorde, Jacqueline Jones Royster, Deborah McDowell, Darlene Clark Hine, Elizabeth McHenry, Claudia Tate, Nell Irvin Painter, Andrée Nicola McLaughlin, Nellie Y. McKay, Joanne V. Gabbin, Brenda Marie Osbey, Sherley Anne Williams, Margaret Walker, Octavia Butler, Toni Cade Bambara, Thadious M. Davis, Hortense Spillers, Maryemma Graham, Barbara Christian, and dozens of other women—all of whom worked assiduously to build foundations for twenty-first-century work.

In a near future, the tendency in African American literary criticism may lean toward androgyny, more exploration of gender's bending and blending without minimizing the need to use literary knowledge in substantive critiques of material conditions perpetuated by the gendered rhetorics of public policy, sex traffic, and religious bondage, of the gap between wealth and poverty in the African diaspora and everywhere else, and of the now permanent threat of amoral terrorism. I would hope that significantly more attention would be given to excellent qualities in women's minds and their contributions to science, sports, statespersonship, and life-affirming literature and culture and less to shameless praise of women's bodies in the transnational neo-slave auctions of "beauty pageants." This new century offers many opportunities to spend our enormous intellectual capital wisely, particularly in efforts to minimize the cruelties human beings inflict upon human beings. Many of our colleagues would argue rigorously that such is not the responsibility of scholars. If they are right and I am wrong, I shall hold fast to my heresy and transgressions.

Wang: Thanks to the significant influences of the 1960s and 1970s civil rights movement, and Black Arts Movement, African American literature has boomed increasingly, especially in the creation of fiction, would you please comment on the development of it?

Ward: Making an assumption that a cause-and-effect relationship exists between the civil rights and Black Arts movements and the creation of African American literature is a matter of common sense, but in the fields of literary and cultural studies, common sense is dreaded. It is good for conversation but not for scholarship. In the common American imagination, the civil rights movement started in 1954–55 and ended in the 1970s; the

Black Arts Movement dates of choice are unstable: 1960–74/75; 1965–75; 1968–80. If we want to speak of literature and other art forms and their temporal connections, we may find our training in literary analysis is insufficient. We may deal awkwardly with historiographical and epistemological issues germane to the making of connections. If we want to earn respect as scholars, we have to retrain ourselves about methods and methodology in the human sciences. Many critics lack genuine interest in such unglamorous work and stern discipline. They flee to ahistorical, trendy arenas of theorizing and its less exacting reading of "texts." If I chose to take flight, I might easily answer your question. I will not take flight. Your question is serious. It would be absurd to give you a trivial response.

The development of ethnic cultural expressions occurs simultaneously with developments in technology and sciences, politics and changes in law designed to make social justice possible, protracted struggles against and for ideological positions, and the dynamics of economy. Making links and then discussing what events have influenced what outcomes demands a breaking of your question into parts and setting limits and negotiated agreement that you and I are using language in the same way. Induction serves our purpose better than deduction. We must examine individual texts before we generalize about traditions and texts.

For example, we can begin with the premise that it is difficult, even in the most exacting sciences, to establish cause-and-effect relationships that are immune to dispute. After examining vast amounts of information from books on (1) the very long history (the 1830s to the 1970s) of African American efforts to secure civil rights, (2) the Black Power and Nation of Islam (Malcolm X) challenges to a specific civil rights movement (Martin Luther King Jr./SCLC/SNCC), and (3) the Black Arts/Black Aesthetic Movement—after all this information gathering, we begin to discover clues and patterns that might justify our saying that Margaret Walker's novel *Jubilee* (1966) has thematic and structural features that correspond to rhetorical and thematic features in African American discourses on civil and human rights prior to 1966, or that Ishmael Reed's narrative strategies in *Yellowback Radio Broke-Down* (1969) provide a sophisticated illustration that the abstract Black Aesthetic considered in the landmark anthology *Black Fire* (1968) was not a totally accurate representation of aesthetic experiences among a most diverse population of African Americans. There are realities of literary politics or publication choices to be considered also. Walker was published by Houghton Mifflin, Reed by Doubleday and Company; *Black Fire* was published by William Morrow. None of these publishing houses were owned by

African Americans. The evidence we need about influence must account for time, music, economics, ideologies, visual arts, political struggles, and both individual and collective manifestations of choices and talents.

We need to consider three basic, classic genres: fiction, poetry, and drama. And we can use three "enabling" texts for reasons that will eventually reveal themselves: *Theory and Practice in the Teaching of Literature by Afro-Americans* (1971) by Darwin T. Turner and Barbara Dodds Stanford, James E. Smethurst's *The Black Arts Movement: Literary Nationalism in the 1960s and 1970s* (2005), and *The Cambridge History of African American Literature* (2011).

Wang: I do agree with you that there is no simple cause-and-effect relationship between the development of literature and the social context; however, it is also true that contemporary African American fiction did show its difference to its readership. I use *contemporary* here to refer to the time after the 1960s. What do you think of the difference(s)?

Ward: In the long history of fiction and narrative practices, the only constant is change. The appearance of audiobooks after 1960 necessitates our considering that readership was complemented by listenership, and our ideas about reading were slightly altered by a recycling of orality and the revival of fiction as storytelling. For centuries, the act of reading texts has been associated to some degree with the act of seeing or "reading" what is visual, including cuneiforms, hieroglyphics, and alphabets. We have long used pictures to encourage children to read. We use pictures to promote literacy. Not needing pictures to navigate texts may be a signal that one has moved from childhood to adulthood. Sound as an element of reading is not new. Before technology encouraged passivity, some readers sounded out the signs they were deciphering.

The older generation of the listenership for audiobooks might have remembered how narratives were dramatized by radio. What was heard could be supplemented by visual memory derived from illustrations, newspaper comic strips, and movies. The increasing popularity of e-books and the graphic novel (nostalgia for the pleasures of the cartoon and the comic book) and the vast possibilities the computer offers for interactive fiction do shape ideas about what readership entails.

You remind me that discussion of what mimetic and other differences are immanent in African American fiction from 1960 to the present is a complicated enterprise. You are interested mainly, I think, in the showing of difference between 1960 and 1980. Most likely the difference is one of content and form. Accounting for differences after 1980 is work for younger scholars.

I admit my limits. I am aware of a few rhetorical differences in African American fiction written after 1960. Given my attraction to Kenneth Burke's ideas about literature as equipment for living, I focus more on content than form. I make a choice of emphasis because I am not free to ignore the indivisibility of form and content, of sound and sense. My reading habits limit what I can say to you about the showing of difference. The word *difference* in relation to your question refers to how a writer might want a reader to think about the gravity of the theme or subject matter.

The scholar who has thought more profoundly than I have about form, content, and differences is Bernard W. Bell, because his studies, *The Afro-American Novel and Its Tradition* (1987) and *The Contemporary African American Novel: Its Folk Roots and Modern Literary Branches* (2004), provide a broad range of clues about the difference. I recommend that you read his books along with more specialized inquiries about fiction.

I am interested in radical views about the function of fiction. Let us say I am interested in polemical, disruptive roots. What does a fiction writer want me to do in addition to buying and reading her or his works? What was Richard Wright proposing about an implied or ideal readership in "Blueprint for Negro Writing" (1937), and is his novel *Native Son* (1940) a touchstone for measuring failure or success in achieving desired ends in African American fiction? *Native Son* is a capital example of engaged social realism. It compelled readers to dwell on possible outcomes of systematic racism and its violations of human rights.

Let us contrast Wright with LeRoi Jones (Amiri Baraka). Jones's essays in *Home* (1966) bespeak his distrust of the insufficiently examined integrationist thought we find in the civil rights movement. His "Myth of a Negro Literature" (1962) indicted literature for not being "serious," for consorting with the bourgeois values of the American middle class, and for not fully exploring the territory of African American culture and lived experiences. In "Black Writing" (1963) and "The Revolutionary Theatre" (1964), Jones argued that literature should be "in-looking" and discredit what white Americans wanted Black Americans to think. African American literature, he reasoned, should incorporate the real existential details implicit in the lives of Black folk (blues people as well as assimilated Negroes). His arguments were not racist. They were racialist. The anthology *Black Fire* (1968), which he edited with Larry Neal, showed us examples in essays, poetry, fiction, and drama of what Black writing might be and might demand. All of the examples dealt with racial inferiority. Some of them, particularly the fiction of Henry Dumas, set high standards for aesthetic craft and productive formation of consciousness. The major difference displayed in the new literature was calculated emancipation from the slavery of racist and racialist white thought about civilization, culture, and art. This difference reaffirmed what Langston Hughes said about "The Negro Artist and the Racial Mountain" back in 1926 even as it anticipated the rejection of intragroup assumptions in Trey Ellis's "The New Black Aesthetic" (1989) and the twenty-first-century invitations for readers to erase history and to absorb the bliss of mindless ahistoricity. Fortunately, our best writers refuse to bring the Trojan horse inside the community no matter how much they use their freedom to be innovative.

As a reader, I sense the difference in African American literature after 1960 is a radical mixture of contradictions. The reinvestment in history championed by Margaret Walker, Toni Cade Bambara, Sherley Anne Williams, and Toni Morrison manages to coexist nicely with Charles Johnson's appropriation of Herman Melville in *Middle Passage* and his incorporation of Buddhist philosophy in other fictions and with John Edgar Wideman's and Ishmael Reed's challenging reimagining of history. Womanist fiction does battle with sexist and homophobic resistance in popular, decidedly uncanonized fiction that may express the allegories of desire possessed by nonacademic women and men. Critical examination of fiction in essays collected in Keith Clark's *Contemporary Black Men's Fiction and Drama* (2001) does inspire hope that weary deconstruction can be eclipsed by bracing "complexification." Professor Wang, differences in contemporary African American fiction inform global readerships that Black writing is a cultural necessity rather than an arbitrary embellishment.

Wang: Do you think that contemporary African American drama develops in the same direction as contemporary African American fiction? What is/are the change(s) of it?

Ward: African American drama has not developed in the same direction as contemporary African American fiction, and the possibility of our seeing a significant change in Black drama as a literary genre is minimal. African American drama has plunged into the commercial, the mediocre.

For the period we are talking about, *The Norton Anthology of African American Literature*, 2nd edition, does offer selections of drama by Amiri Baraka, Ed Bullins, Adrienne Kenney, August Wilson, and Ntozake Shange; *Call and Response: The Riverside Anthology of the African American Literary Tradition* has plays by Amiri Baraka, Ntozake Shange, and Anna Deavere Smith. This loose canonization is minimal. It does not draw attention to Ben Caldwell, Ted Shine, Robert Alexander, Charlie R. Braxton, Pomo Afro

Homos, George C. Wolfe, Shay Youngblood, Elizabeth Brown-Guillory, Val Ferdinand (Kalamu ya Salaam), William Branch, P. J. Gibson, Mari Evans, Sonia Sanchez, N. R. Davidson, Elaine Jackson, Beah Richards, Charles H. Fuller, Herbert Stokes, Chakula cha Jua or Suzan-Lori Parks. One has to search out specialized anthologies—*New Plays from the Black Theatre, Wine in the Wilderness: Plays of African American Women from the Harlem Renaissance to the Present, Black Thunder, Colored Contradictions, Black Theater USA, 9 Plays by Black Women.* The minimal possibility of seeing the difference is compounded by the fact that large numbers of plays are never published and by the low priority drama has in our literary scholarship and criticism. Ishmael Reed's published plays are not discussed very much. The growing interest in performance and the dramatic qualities of spoken-word poetry and rap may encourage more notice of drama as literature. I am not very optimistic, however, about an upsurge of interest.

My skepticism about the late twentieth century and my extreme cynicism about what is occurring in the present century disposed me to offer you an answer that is curt, dismissive, and reductive. My respect, on the other hand, for what you and other Chinese scholars are genuinely serious in wanting to know about African American literature and culture and literary history obligates me to expound. Unfortunately, I cannot at the moment give you a thorough exposition. You would need to talk with playwrights or with scholars who specialize in theater and performance. But here are my views.

From the angles of contemporary globalization, the metaphor "All the world's a stage" as we find it in William Shakespeare's *As You Like It* is quite germane for thinking about world affairs and any relationship those affairs might have with cultural expressions in general. Contemporary women and men are profoundly theatrical. Our penchant for the dramatic is a result of our socialization, of our exposure to a world that is a stage for extreme enactments of universal aspects of the comic and the tragic. World cultures manifest recognizable differences in kind and degrees of theatricality. It is difficult, although not impossible, to segregate what is dramatic in everyday life from what ought to be structurally dramatic in forms of art. Our music, cinema and sport events, our representations of economic dynamics and motives, our politics, ceremonies of state, and common speech acts (locution, perlocution, and illocution), our mass media severely limit our ability to know what is dramatic and what is not. To put the matter in a frustrating tautological utterance, imitation imitates imitation.

In the 1960s and 1970s, such playwrights as Amiri Baraka, Ed Bullins, Ossie Davis, Charles Fuller, Ron Milner, Kalamu ya Salaam, Tom Dent,

Melvin Van Peebles, Sonia Sanchez, and Marvin X wrote dramas that did focus on diverse African American experiences, thereby offering active resistance to received ideas about what ought to be represented in American drama propagated in works by Arthur Miller, Tennessee Williams, Lillian Hellman, and Woody Allen. Efforts by such institutions as the Negro Ensemble Company (New York) to develop viable Black drama and the efforts of the Free Southern Theater (New Orleans) to intensify the use of drama in promoting social change and justice had a short life.

The ascent of film (Spike Lee and other filmmakers) and expansion of cable television (HBO, BET, and so forth), swift changes in audience tastes, and the profitability of "blaxploitation" led younger Black playwrights to be less radical or revolutionary than their Black Arts predecessors, less willing to explore differences. Investing one's energy into creating drama as cultural work to benefit a specific community is an act of love that ensures one will become intimate with poverty. Savvy young playwrights retreat from such thankless sacrifice.

I would claim that works by Ntozake Shange and the much-underappreciated innovations of Adrienne Kennedy are noteworthy exceptions to Black drama's slide into mediocrity until breakthrough moments were created by August Wilson and Suzan-Lori Parks and Anna Deavere Smith. It is the phenomenon of theatricality rather than the art of drama in the old sense that is most used in contemporary movements to encourage social change. Pervasive theatricality in everyday life has only accelerated what I call the slide. The slide has culminated in the overwhelming popularity of satiric minstrelsy churned out by Tyler Perry and other commercially oriented dramatists. If we had drama in the old sense, in the sense that was important for the 1960s, it would address the genocidal implications of nihilism and self-hatred that is so apparent in American society as to be invisible. African American fiction is rising; African American drama is descending.

Wang: It is sad to know that African American drama is descending, Professor Ward. Compared with fiction and drama, how about contemporary African American poetry? And what would you predict the role of race or racial issues plays in African American literature in the twenty-first century?

Ward: So as not to leave you and other Chinese scholars in utter confusion about how African American drama is "descending," we will have to return to the question about drama before we conclude the interview. The question about drama provokes me to think about deep and dirty aspects of the work we seek to do as scholars and critics. So often we are like the James

Brown video of "Living in America," moving with amazing speed from issue to issue, seeking to understand everything in a fairly superficial way and truly understanding nothing.

The question you are asking about race and racial issues would be ill served by my giving you an answer in the form of a prediction. Richard Wright's essay "The Literature of the Negro in the United States," oddly sandwiched among lectures he gave in Europe between 1950 and 1956, appears in *White Man, Listen!* Prediction is one of the intriguing features of the lectures, and what Wright predicted about African American literature convinces me that horror is a consequence if the passage of time proves some portion of a prediction to be accurate. Wright made a conditional prediction in two parts. Part one suggested that if Black writers "should take a sharp turn toward strictly racial themes, then you will know by that token that we are suffering our old and ancient agonies at the hands of our white American neighbors."[5] Part two, equally dependent on an "if/then" proposition, proclaims that when African American "expression broadens, assumes the common themes and burdens of literary expression which are the heritage of all men, then by that token you will know that a humane attitude prevails in America towards us" (109). Wright's rhetorical gesture is grounded in a naive optimism that I do not share with him. From the vantage of global modernisms and world affairs, I find no persuasive evidence that "strictly racial themes" and "common themes" are not truly two sides of a single coin. The demographic character of the United States in 2013 leads me to think multiracial American neighbors (I prefer to say fellow citizens) are more significant than white American neighbors. The use of binary oppositions in literary discussion has historical but not contemporary importance. Ours is the problem of struggling to account for an endless bifurcation of oppositions. In the twenty-first century, binary oppositions tend to be signals of the good (historical memory) and the bad (cantankerous ignorance). Race and racial issues have a presence in all modern nations—consider the use of Black images on Chinese television—and all writers in the world have some stake in reacting to that presence. An opaque wall stands between my consciousness and the dynamics of global changes in literature and other expressive forms. Pre-future wisdom precludes my making any predictions about what African American literature will or will not do. Let us turn back to your question about African American poetry.

In addition to being the best record of how African American poetry developed up to 1975, Eugene B. Redmond's *Drumvoices: The Mission of*

Afro-American Poetry: A Critical History (1976) prompts us to recognize an idea which ought to be at the very center of literary discussions. Literature (fiction, poetry, drama) is not a material object. Literature is an aesthetic transaction. Louise M. Rosenblatt observed some years ago that whether a "text" is visual or audible, it is only a cluster of symbols that a reader can activate. "The reader," in Rosenblatt's opinion, "brings to the text his past experience and present personality. Under the magnetism of the ordered symbols of the text, he marshals his resources and crystallizes out from the stuff of memory, thought, and feeling a new order, a new experience, which he sees as the poem."[6] This view of the reader and the poem allows us to see how instructive the study of reading can be. The mission of African American poetry was not accomplished in isolation from a multilayered readership; it was realized in concert with the diverse readers, including the writers as readers. The immense body of work created by hundreds of poets was brought into being as literature by many thousands of readers.

In the 1960s, the efforts of some poets to address African American readers more directly by evoking the Black Aesthetic (an effective construct) was complemented by critics, both popular and academic, who understood the poverty of ideas assumed by the strictures of formalism. They did not deny the efficacy of careful examination of texts. They denied that formalism was the sole and most correct approach to understanding the function of poetry in the lives of people who were outside the academic cloisters. Reexamination of critical work associated with the Black Arts Movement suggests that Chicago poet Carolyn Rodgers had a more powerful, vernacular understanding of what was happening in the new Black poetry than did Stephen E. Henderson in his admittedly brilliant introduction for the anthology *Understanding the New Black Poetry: Black Speech and Black Music as Poetic References* (1972). In "Literacy and Criticism: The Example of Carolyn Rodgers," I tried to sketch out why Rodgers's categories of transaction served as prototypes for later criticism and theorizing, particularly critical work that concerns itself with performance in hip-hop and spoken-word poetries.[7] We are indebted to the thinking of Carolyn Rodgers as we continue to ask what is significantly different in African American poetry from 1980 to the present. Our research should try to find historical explanations which are located in culturally anchored speech acts and reader/hearer responses. Such inquiry might reveal, in part, the motives of successful African American poets who think the MFA degree is a Roman Catholic communion wafer or a well-paved expressway to artistic freedoms as well as the motives of academic critics who aid and abet their standardized

American behaviors. Meaningful differences in content and stylistic choices are located in desperate acts of erasing differences.

Wang: Thank you, Professor Ward, for your comprehensive answer to contemporary African American literature. What do you think of James Baldwin's remarks about Richard Wright's "Protest Novel," and is there a protest tradition in African American literature? If so, does it develop and how does it develop in the new century?

Ward: James Baldwin's remarks in "Everybody's Protest Novel" about Wright's *Native Son* are excellent examples of how protest functions in world literature. Much intellectual energy has been wasted in suggesting that protest is a unique feature of writing by African Americans. Is protest not a defining feature of the satire and the jeremiad, of ancient genres that were not forged in American experiences?

It would be insane to argue that all literature is protest literature, but it is prudent to argue as W. E. B. Du Bois did that all literary art is propaganda. One can't sever the development of American protest tradition in the works of Herman Melville, Walt Whitman, Nathaniel Hawthorne, Frank Norris, Lillian Smith, and William Faulkner from the evolution of African American protest tradition in the works of Phillis Wheatley, Harriet Jacobs, Sutton Griggs, Nella Larsen, and Alice Walker. People who segregate the two traditions apparently misunderstand the aesthetic properties of Thomas Jefferson's Declaration of Independence. The intensity of protest in African American literature may be stronger than it is in Jewish American or Chinese American writing, but all of these literatures give us evidence of protest. Indeed, globalization ought to prepare us for twenty-first-century expansions of protest in all of world literature, and our guide to what is different about African American protest must be cultural specificity.

James Baldwin turned to Harriet Beecher Stowe's *Uncle Tom's Cabin* to buttress his comments on the character Bigger Thomas and *Native Son*. His remarks arose from the cosmopolitan desires of 1950s New York intellectuals as much as they did from his agony about how the American protest novel as a literary form which entrapped readers in ideological premises of theological terrorism. He saw the protest novel as a cage—an iron cage that limited exploration of our complex humanity. Baldwin's forte was moral criticism of literature and culture. I do not agree with his conclusions, but I do respect his oppositional vision and the role he played in the drama of critical protest. He propagated his values.

Wang: There would be many distinguished writers and scholars in the study of African American literature besides James Baldwin. Would you please list some of the outstanding African American literary critics, briefly describing their contributions to the study of African American literature and culture? And what do you think of the mission of African American literary critics pertaining to African American literature and literary tradition?

Ward: Three anthologies contain the listing of African American literary critics you are requesting:

> Mitchell, Angelyn, ed. *Within the Circle: An Anthology of African American Literary Criticism from the Harlem Renaissance to the Present.* Durham: Duke University Press, 1994.
> Ervin, Hazel Arnett, ed. *African American Literary Criticism 1773 to 2000.* New York: Twayne, 1999
> Napier, Winston, ed. *African American Literary Theory: A Reader.* New York: New York University Press, 2000.

Mitchell, Ervin, and Napier provide editorial material which explains the contributions the critics they selected have made to the study of African American literature and culture. Lawrence P. Jackson's *The Indignant Generation: A Narrative History of African American Writers and Critics, 1934–1960* provides valuable information about some critics who produced foundational work, critics who are not included in the three anthologies. Jackson's meticulous scholarship in this book and in his earlier study *Ralph Ellison: Emergence of Genius* establishes him as a major critical voice in the area of literary biography and literary history; his excellence matches that of Arnold Rampersad, whose literary biographies of Langston Hughes and Ralph Ellison provide insights of special critical value. I mentioned earlier the important critical work of Carolyn Rodgers, George Kent, Stephen E. Henderson, and Alice Walker. The poet and novelist Gayl Jones deserves more attention than she has received for the quality of her critical judgments in *Liberating Voices: Oral Tradition in African American Literature*; likewise, Bernard Bell merits more than casual notice for *The Afro-American Novel and Its Tradition* and *The Contemporary African American Novel: Its Folk Roots and Modern Literary Branches.* The poet Harryette Mullen's *The Cracks between What We Are and What We Are Supposed to Be* demands, as Hank Lazer has remarked, that we listen to what her critical voice says about "issues of central importance to African American poetry and language, women's voices, and the future of poetry." T. J. Anderson III's *Notes to Make the Sound Come Right: Four Innovators of Jazz Poetry* and Tony Bolden's *Afro-Blue: Improvisations in African American Poetry and Culture* are stimulating explorations in cultural poetics just as Howard Rambsy II's *The Black Arts Enterprise and the Production of African American Poetry* is a challenging study of the literary politics of publishing. I would be remiss if I did not mention Gene Andrew Jarrett's *Representing the Race: A New Political History of African American Literature*, Thadious M. Davis's *Southscapes: Geographies of Race, Region, and Literature*, and John Ernest's *Chaotic Justice: Rethinking African American Literary History*. Davis, Ernest, and Jarrett give us new critical configurations for what the ongoing work of African American literary criticism should entail. It would be irresponsible not to suggest that since the late 1970s, Ron Baxter Miller has produced remarkable critical work in editing the collections *Black American Literature and Humanism* and *Black American Poets between Worlds, 1940–1960* and in writing *The Art and Imagination of Langston Hughes* and *On the Ruins of Modernity: New Chicago Renaissance from Wright to Fair*.

These scholars and writers are representative of the large number of people who have given shape to the mission of African American literary criticism. In a nutshell, the mission of our critics is to analyze and evaluate the always-expanding body of Black writing and to prevent our forgetting the diverse ways that African Americans have made contributions to literature and culture.

Wang: African American writers and critics have been actively exposed to the environment in their creative and critical writings. What would you comment on the shifts of African American literary criticism from the social-oriented content to structuralism/poststructuralism and to womanism/queer studies and even to the so-called postracial?

Ward: All of us are exposed to biocultural environments. It might be argued that our relationship to those environments is symbiotic in the sense that our critical, discursive practices alter and are altered by the environments we live in. Regardless of how we mark our practices—structuralist, poststructuralist, womanist, queer, or postracial, the practices are not divorced from social concerns and content.

The structuralist character of Robert Stepto's *From behind the Veil: A Study of Afro-American Narrative* and the poststructuralist inflections of Henry Louis Gates Jr.'s *The Signifying Monkey: A Theory of Afro-American Literary Criticism* manifest ideologies that are social: those works sought to change modes of analysis and reading in higher education, in the academy or profession of English. Feminist and womanist criticisms do not avert our critical eyes from socially constructed behaviors named heteronormativity, racism, sexism, classism, and homophobia. Proofs of discursive immersion in the social and cultural are provided by the range of critical thought in *All the Women Are White, All the Blacks Are Men, but Some of Us Are Brave*, edited by Gloria T. Hull, Patricia Bell Scott, and Barbara Smith; in *This Bridge Called My Back: Writings by Radical Women of Color*, edited by Cherríe Moraga and Gloria Anzaldúa; in *Wild Women in the Whirlwind: Afra-American Culture and the Contemporary Literary Renaissance*, edited by Joanne M. Braxton and Andrée Nicola McLaughlin. These works are prototypes for criticism that focuses more specifically on sexuality, the queer, and the body not as a biological entity but as a commodified object of sexual desires.

We find terms of order for discussions in queer studies in Melvin Dixon's *Ride Out the Wilderness: Geography and Identity in Afro-American Literature* and *A Melvin Dixon Critical Reader*, edited by Justin A. Joyce and Dwight A. McBride; in Keith Clark's *Black Manhood in James Baldwin, Ernest J. Gaines, and August Wilson*; in Robert Reid-Pharr's *Once You Go Black: Choice, Desire, and the Black American Intellectual* and Audre Lorde's *Zami: A New Spelling of My Name*. There may be a tincture of the postracial in the *African American Review* 41.4 (2007), which was devoted to theorizing the postsoul aesthetic, Kenneth Warren's *What Was African American Literature?* and Charles Henry Rowell's introduction for *Angles of Ascent: A Norton Anthology of Contemporary African American Poetry*. But Michelle Alexander's *The New Jim Crow: Mass Incarceration in the Age of Colorblindness* and the surplus of reports about ethnic and racial retrogression in the United States that we find in the daily news cancel the legitimacy of postracial concepts as anything other than vacations in fantasy. I assure you that African American literary and cultural criticisms are not forms of thought which can be disassociated from our social lives.

Wang: Looking back to the past century, we can see that the constant change has always been with the African American literature and literary criticism, which has been propelled by arguments or debates between Blacks and whites or among Black writers or scholars. How can you evaluate these arguments or debates?

Ward: When we consider that literature has always served to confirm preexisting ideas or to challenge those ideas by modifying them or replacing them, our sense of wonderment becomes quite minimal. We recognize that William Faulkner, Paule Marshall, Robert Penn Warren, John Oliver Killens, Eudora Welty, Norman Mailer, Ann Petry, and James T. Farrell did not share identical ideas about what a good novel should be and that Sherman Alexie and Joyce Carol Oates have very different ideas about what kind of short stories American audiences should read. It is irrational to think that Elizabeth Bishop, Wendy Rose, Brenda Marie Osbey, Sylvia Plath, Wanda Coleman, and Sonia Sanchez should write about the same historical themes in poetry or that Gish Jen, Octavia Butler, Toni Morrison, N. Scott Momaday, Colson Whitehead, Leslie Marmon Silko, Ishmael Reed, Richard Ford, and Amy Tan should use similar ways of representing life in fiction.

If we think of African American literature and criticism as a closed system of discussion, we limit ourselves to thinking of identifiable arguments or debates as instances of "family resemblance" as described by Ludwig Wittgenstein in *Philosophical Investigations*. We encounter another kind of "family resemblance" that is located in the literary history of the United States when we talk about "arguments or debates between Blacks and whites." The critical perspectives on literature and literary values are stuck in the swamp of race. Our American preoccupation with race keeps the arguments within a dreadful prison or cave of binary thinking about literature, culture, and everyday life. When I evaluate the arguments within the walls of this cognitive prison, I find that their principal value seems to be an exposing both to the imprisoned and to the rest of the world how the United States has historically nurtured intellectual poverty and maximized the possibilities of vicious disagreement because it is impossible to wash the scientifically bogus concept of race out of American thought.

I must reiterate that African American literary and cultural criticisms are not forms of thought which can be disassociated from our political and social lives. Gene Andrew Jarrett recognizes the possibility of making future debates more progressive than they have been in *Representing the Race: A New Political History of African American Literature*. John Ernest gives us parameters for truly civilized literary argument and debate in *Chaotic Justice: Rethinking African American Literary History*. These two scholars do inspire me to believe that African American literature has a viable future.

Wang: The practice of literary criticism is almost always late compared with the literary creation. There are new directions in the creation of African American literature. They may try either to ignore the role race played in the past or to cater to the imagined stereotypes that many people assume to be true. I'm just wondering how African American literary criticism can reflect, represent, or even lead this direction in the nature of literature, socially and aesthetically.

Ward: Literary criticism is only late in the sense that it can only address specific works of literature after they are published or performed. Some literary critics will attempt, usually by way of book reviews or blogs, to render early judgments about new literary works; then those critics have the option of making more detailed, nuanced, and trenchant evaluations after the specific work manifests itself as a singular occurrence or as part of a trend among writers. Other literary critics, especially those of my generation, may prefer to withhold judgment for the sake of having critical distance between themselves and the new works. The rate of reflection on new directions and representation of what the new directions may possibly mean varies according to the sensibilities and practices of individual critics.

The only instance I can imagine of literary criticism leading a new direction in the social and aesthetic development of literature would be one where the creative writer and the literary critic are the same person. I sense that such a phenomenon is present in some critical essays by Harryette Mullen which stand in a witty relationship to her poetry or in such works as *The Great Negro Plot* and *PYM* by Mat Johnson. I would hazard that Mullen and Johnson succeed in destroying African American stereotypes both in critical production and in poetry and narrative because of the unusual demands they make on their audiences. Nevertheless, older models of aesthetic engagement with new works will remain entrenched; they will be in creative tension with new directions.

Wang: [. . .] Since Barack Obama's 2008 presidential election, the so-called postracial has been raised in many subjects: What do you think of the viable future of African American literature in the new context?

Ward: There is perfect timing in your asking this final question. Yesterday, I watched the new film *Twelve Years a Slave*. The day before I watched the video of a most noteworthy discussion of Black feminism between Melissa Harris Perry and bell hooks. Just this afternoon, the scholar and writer Keenan Norris, whose first novel *Brother and the Dancer* was published the first week in November, sent me links to interviews that refocus thinking about the postracial nonsense in American culture since 2008. The first link leads to an interview Norris and Omar Tyree did for their forthcoming anthology *Street Lit: Representing the Urban Landscape*, and the second link has to do with Norris's poetics of fiction and the clarity of his understanding that twenty-first-century African American fiction must incorporate nuanced, historically informed representations of the multilayered complexities of African American experiences—race, class, impact of new technologies on cognitive functions, socioeconomic circumstances, gender, and sexuality.

The postracial has created an enormous amount of work for American scholarship and criticism in all disciplines. It has signaled the swift descent of world cultures into the pathos of the irrational. It has marked, to be specific, the transparent hypocrisy of the American democratic experiment and the impasse of the American dream in the context of globalization. Obviously, new kinds of writing are needed to address our contemporary human condition. By default, a viable African American literature will be a measuring rod for inadequacies in non–African American literatures.

The ideology that drives the postracial is as deadly as the typhoon that caused massive loss of life and property in the Philippines earlier this week. That ideology is as deadly as reckless urbanization and environmental destruction are for mainland China. The postracial concept is being used by ultraconservatives, neo-Nazis, the obscenely wealthy, fascists, white supremacists, racists of every shade of human skin, agents of state apparatus, and neoliberal thinkers to do one of several things: (1) cultivating seventeenth-, eighteenth-, and nineteenth-century plantation mentalities in the twenty-first-century American mindscape, (2) transforming the precious metal of American ideals into dross, or (3) preparing us for such chaos as will probably create the absurd horrors of World War III.

Your perfect timing allows me to repeat that critics and scholars ought to retreat from sophisticated but childlike play and take up the dirty work of intellectual responsibility. We ought to assume the human wisdom in imperatives from the great poet Gwendolyn Brooks: "Win war. Rise bloody, maybe not too late / For having first to civilize a space / Wherein to play your violin with grace."[8]

Wang: Would you please elaborate briefly on the impact of Donald Trump's triumph in the 2016 presidential election over the ethnic groups and the ethnic literatures. Will Trump's presidential triumph produce a dramatic difference for African American literature and literary criticism?

Ward: Now you have asked the most challenging final question. What you call Trump's triumph is one part of a dramatic change in what many American citizens believe and think about the political ecology of our democratic experiment, our identity as a nation in the world order. One of the reasons for Trump's debatable "triumph" is the resurgence of ethnic hatred, a probable backlash against President Barack Obama's eight years of trying to promote the audacity of hope. President Trump and those American citizens who love him unconditionally are creating an environment in which nonsense is normal and despair is necessary. Thus it is logical to speculate that the new American politics, a slow drifting from democratic ideologies into palpable neofascism, will have some impact on the topics writers deal with in African American literature and on the assumptions literary critics make about the function of their discourses.

Consider the topics some writers have addressed recently. Colson Whitehead's novel *The Underground Railroad* (2016) expands the genre of slave narrative (narrative of the enslaved). He transforms the metaphor of the underground railroad as we have used it since the nineteenth century into a material description of rails and tunnels that might be operative in movement from slavery to freedom. The transformation of metaphor is crucial. *Counting Descent*, Clint Smith's powerful, accessible, and beautiful collection of poems, inspired the poet Gregory Pardlo to write that the book immerses "us in the America that America so often forgets." In my mind, Smith's book alerts us to how President Trump is tweeting America into oblivion as he invites us to make a compact with insanity. *Hunger: A Memoir of (My) Body* by Roxane Gay is a poignant meditation on why she will always be "fat, first and foremost." Her book anatomizes the innate cruelty of stereotypes. In the arena of literary and cultural criticism, Lawrence P. Jackson's excellent *Chester B. Himes: A Biography* explores the role of literary politics in Himes's life and works.

I do not claim these books are representative of dramatic difference; they suggest directions the difference may take. They provide clues about the environment wherein African American literature and literary criticism shall continue to grow, although it is impossible to say what shapes the plants shall assume. All American ethnic groups feel the heat of Trump's eccentricity in some degree. All of them must choose between remaining silent about the "triumph" or resisting its impact bravely and relentlessly. Much of the resistance might involve a calculated use of aesthetics. And literary critics who have some expertise with digital humanities will use a new array of methods and methodologies. It is probable that writers and critics will express more concern with the interrelatedness of American morality, ethics, and politics.

Notes

1. George E. Kent, "Ethnic Import in American Literature (Reflections on a Course)," in *Black Voices: An Anthology of Afro-American Literature*, ed. Abraham Chapman (New York: New American Library, 1968), 691.

2. See Kwai-Cheung Lo, "Invisible Neighbors: Racial Minorities and the Hong Kong Chinese Community" in *Critical Zone 3: A Forum of Chinese and Western Knowledge*, ed. Douglas Kerr, Q. S. Tong, and Wang Shouren (Hong Kong: Hong Kong University Press, 2008), 59–74; Edward Said, *Orientalism*. (New York: Vintage, 1978); Toni Morrison, *Playing in the Dark: Whiteness and the Literary Imagination* (Cambridge: Harvard University Press, 1992).

3. Angelyn Mitchell, ed., "Introduction: Voices within the Circle: A Historical Overview of African American Literary Criticism," in *Within the Circle: An Anthology of African American Literary Criticism from the Harlem Renaissance to the Present* (Durham: Duke University Press, 1994), 1–18.

4. See Alice Walker, *In Search of Our Mothers' Gardens* (New York: Harcourt Brace Jovanovich, 1983).

5. Richard Wright, "The Literature of the Negro in the United States," in *White Man, Listen!* (1957; New York: HarperPerennial, 1995), 109.

6. Louise M. Rosenblatt, *The Reader, the Text, the Poem: The Transactional Theory of the Literary Work* (Carbondale: Southern Illinois University Press, 1978), 12.

7. Jerry W. Ward Jr., "Literacy and Criticism: The Example of Carolyn Rodgers," *Drumvoices Revue* 4.1/2 (Fall–Winter 1994–95): 62–65.

8. Gwendolyn Brooks, "First Fight Then Fiddle," in *African American Literature*, ed. Al Young (New York: Addison-Wesley, 1996), 407–8.

The Septuagenarians' Sankofa Dialogue

Kalamu ya Salaam / 2018

From *Kalfou: A Journal of Comparative and Relational Ethnic Studies* 5.1 (2018): 112–41. Reprinted by permission of Kalamu ya Salaam.

Kalamu ya Salaam: We might call this the Sankofa Dialogue because we are looking back in order to orient ourselves as we move forward. Approximately eight years or so ago in 2008, there was a great brouhaha and hope because of the upcoming election for the US presidency. For the first time in the history of the United States, a Black man—and it's befitting that he was truly an African American—

Jerry W. Ward Jr.: —a Kenyan American—

Salaam: —was running for office. Our exclusion from the national electoral process had been the case from the founding of this country in 1776 all the way up until that Obama election moment. We don't generally have such pivotal moments in history either as individuals or as a people.

Ward: But I would suggest that in the closing months of the second term of President Obama, we had a devastatingly pivotal moment. Perhaps we can recognize it in the complete circus that American politics has become—an embarrassing circus. As we scrutinize the behavior of Donald Trump, we ought also to be concerned about what is driving people who, under other circumstances, might have hesitated to elect a clown. Those voters were so full of disgust, disappointment, and dismay that they saw Trump as the Great White Hope. "Make America Great Again" was a smokescreen. Many of the voters wanted a president who might restore the bogus privileges of white superiority.

Salaam: As they say down at city hall, I concur, but I would broaden the dialogue a bit. I think this historic moment, this turning point, comes at a critical moment in what defines what it means to be American. Obama's ascendancy caused us—all of us—to think about what it means to be an American in ways we previously had not fully considered—the positives and the negatives thereof; both the deep-titude and the shallowness of it. It can be sometimes very shallow to be an American.

All of which is to say I don't think there's a post-Obama era as such. I think Obama was just part of this era where we are grappling with what it means to be an American now that it no longer means what it has meant from the beginning of the United States up until Obama. We're still struggling with that. It's interesting to me that what we see right now is a repetition of what happened at the closing of and in the immediate follow-up to the Civil War in terms of the identity questions that were being raised.

At that moment, there were two major political forces: (1) the question of citizenship for those of us who were previously noncitizens, which for the most part was the discussion of what to do with Black people, newly emancipated and having access to suffrage, and (2) the women's movement, which was very strong at that point. One of the questions was whether women would be given the right to vote. I think it is absolutely a repeat of history that following the ascendancy of a Black man, the complex and sometimes intertwining issues of race and gender would become the focus of attention. We've seen this before.

I think this society was able to suppress that question after the Civil War. They found ways to adjust to having Blacks have the right to vote and ways to hold off women having the right to vote. We forget—indeed many of us never knew—that the vote (i.e., suffrage) was offered to Black men at the end of the Civil War, but that suffrage did not happen for white women until 1920. You go from 1865—or, factually, depending on where you were located in the United States, the ending of slavery could have been as early as 1863 or as late as '66 (hence the Juneteenth celebrations).

We go from that Civil War period all the way to 1920, and women still didn't have the right to vote. The gender question was a major issue, but at the same time it's a relatively overlooked condition when American history is discussed by the mainstream. In 2016 the two main candidates were Donald Trump and Hillary Clinton. Donald Trump represents the embodiment of the popular white male psyche—i.e., the belief that life is all about securing wealth. It's all about owning things and that when "we came here, we didn't have to explain that to anybody." *We* being the white males who were in charge. Thomas Jefferson, who is often credited as the primary architect, the intellectual architect, of the Constitution, didn't feel he had to explain his relationship with Sally Hemings to anybody.

Ward: His refusal to explain proved to be a political liability. In parts of the popular press of the time, it was promoted that he did have a relationship with Hemings, an intimacy that contradicted his sentiments, for example, in *Notes on Virginia*.[1] Nevertheless, I think what you pointed out about a pivotal moment is important. I suggest that if we're going to deal with pivotal moments, we have to deal with the vexed, scientifically bogus issue of race. In terms of social relations, especially in terms of gender, race is a powerful issue.

Salaam: But it's not highly publicized nor widely acknowledged.

Ward: We are socialized to think race is "normal." When we ask, "What does it mean to be an American?," the question has to be dealt with from angles of thinking or not thinking about Indigenous peoples. We need to somehow account for our being in this space in relation to that decimated population. Why is it so easy for us to forget, unless we live in certain states, that there are still descendants of these people with whom we have not engaged the question of reparations while we have had reparations for a number of other groups that are elements of the American mix? Indigenous people are also a part of what it means to be American.

When we begin at early American history, colonial history, the political situation becomes complex in strange ways. I've recently read Robert G. Parkinson's book about the "common cause" and the American Revolution, a moment in the development of capitalism.[2] The common cause was as much about the desire to assert dominance and white superiority as it was about liberty or freedom.

I say this because when we go back to the American Revolution, what is now becoming better known is that through the newspapers and broadsides and other printed materials, a special case was being made for the rights of those European people who lived in the colonies and who were not prepared to be loyal to the British Crown. Those were the people who wanted to be independent in a very special way. No matter what beautiful words were written in the second draft of the Declaration of Independence, confirming their independence meant that they had to diminish and demean other peoples, particularly Native Americans and Africans. And they had to insist that those two populations did not and would not deserve to be fully invested in the enterprise of liberation from what was called the tyranny of the king or the tyranny of the monarchy, the tyranny of Britain.

Indeed, using various arguments, especially those from what was known as natural history at the time, those two populations were completely set outside the pale. This is very important, especially in terms of ourselves as

African American peoples who have criticized the American democratic experiment without totally rejecting some of its premises. One of our oversights—I think *shortcomings* might be too strong a word—one of the things that we overlook is our relationship to Indigenous peoples and how that "common cause" is a major part of our changing locations within capitalism.

We should recall that in the years before 1776, it was an obligation for European settlers to minimize the presence of Indigenous peoples in the North American geography they wanted to own. We begin with colonial history and remember how that history is still operative. Our mass media has not thoroughly examined why a considerable number of Indigenous people and their allies gathered a few months ago to protest an oil pipeline. This Indigenous assertion of historical claims, moral issues, and ecological fears has not been accorded sufficient attention.

Let us begin with remembering colonies, plantations, and common causes. [. . .] I am trying to learn something from Parkinson's book, *The Common Cause*. The master narrative of the American Revolution has to be rewritten with greater accuracy. Research by Parkinson and others informs us how a species of literature—newspapers, broadsides, and other printed materials—was used to promote a specialized rather than a universal idea about independence. In 2017, digital media are used to promote a similar objective: that independence, no matter what beautiful words were written in the second draft of the Declaration of Independence, required white colonists to diminish and demean other people, particularly Native Americans and Africans. The twenty-first-century heirs of white colonists have not abandoned that enterprise.

Salaam: Again, to use the city hall phrase—

Ward: —you concur?

Salaam: Yes, I concur. However, there are points of emphasis that I think we need to consider. The first of which is what it means to be an American: up until the twenty-first century, and really roughly up to the ascendancy of Obama on through what we're now seeing, what it means to be an American is an assumption of male privilege. The American identity, the American character as defined by Constance Rourke's definitive characterization—I say definitive in the sense that that was the mainstream accepted identity. By accepted identity, I don't necessarily mean that everybody agreed with it; there were many who disagreed with her. That became the generally accepted definition of the American character. Rourke pointed to what she called "American humor."[3]

As a study of national character, it's very interesting. This is written by a female author, but it's adopted in general. Because she is a woman, her point of view of what it means to be an American is genderized, but at the same time, genderization is hidden. Here was a woman who codified, let's put it that way, what it meant to be an American. It's adopted by males in the academy and in the political establishment. You can't read serious histories of America without somebody referring to that.

That's one element. It's very important to understand that just in that process of defining what it means to be an American, the patriarchy set the standard even when a man didn't set the standard. They took over what a woman wrote. Now, the work of a woman becomes the standard, but we don't see the gender aspect. Her work is simply presented as the American thing.

Ward: It is necessary to put the American thing into a category of predation. Globally, patriarchy is assumed to be the right path. In most societies, males are dominant. They are determined to remain so, even in the progressive societies that have elected women to positions of leadership. The overwhelming number of nations, especially those included in the United Nations, are dominated by males. Males cause an overwhelming number of problems throughout the world, particularly in irrational terms of masculinity. Women are overwhelmingly the victims of male arrogance.

I think when we ask what it means to be an American, I would agree with you that the discussion has always been predicated on a notion of male dominance or male superiority or the right of the male among various genders to always take positions of power and leadership. This is not limited to being an American. It may be something that has to be considered on Planet Earth whether one is male or female.

When we look back and try to make a discussion manageable about what it means to be an American, the pivotal moment is 2016. It is then that we cannot ignore any longer the difficulty of speaking about gender, because the candidates belong to two different genders.

Salaam: Yes, that is the case, but I am simply saying that this is the first time in the long history of what is called the American experiment that gender is now at the forefront of discussion. Even if people don't want to talk about it, it's implicitly talked about because there is a woman who for the first time was a major candidate to be the president. The issue of the nature of power in global terms, in hemispheric terms, and whether patriarchy is dominant or not dominant is an interesting question, and one that I'm willing to engage. At this particular moment, when we look at the so-called

American society, this is an issue that up until this moment has not been fully engaged in our society. In other modern societies, they've had questions of "Will we have a woman as leader?" You can go from Britain to the Caribbean, to Africa, to India—

Ward: —to the Philippines and South Korea.

Salaam: Yes, all over. People have grappled with the question of whether there can be a woman as a leader of the national identity. This is the first time that the United States has had to seriously grapple with that issue. I'm saying that I think that that's a defining moment. That's all I'm saying. I'm not saying that gender in and of itself is now the defining moment worldwide. I think other people have crossed that bridge before. The United States is about to set foot on that bridge. It's an interesting moment because throughout the history of the United States, not only have women not been in power, but their lack of power has been hidden. Even when women assert their power, as Constance Rourke did in writing as an intellectual, it is just assumed into their general worldview, and men take it over and run with it.

Ward: I think we should note the full title of Rourke's book—*American Humor: A Study of the National Character*. I want to emphasize the word *humor*. Just listening to that word, we think, "Oh, this is comedy or something comic."

Salaam: It's not serious.

Ward: Right, but I mean much more than not serious. If we go back three or four hundred years, *humor* refers to certain theories about the composition of people as well as the passions, traits, and instincts that they possess. For example, you can talk about being of a sanguine humor. Perhaps her book on national character takes advantage of this ambiguity in the use of the word *humor*. What is the character of what she calls the American character? What are those qualities? Why is it that in part, to be an American is to be funny, is to be humorous; humorous in a sense that's almost nonsensical?

Salaam: Without seriousness.

Ward: Yes, without seriousness. That's crucial for the path you want to follow about the lack of discussion of women's position in the American mix. Let us go back to our childhoods in the 1950s. Although our mothers were—

Salaam: When you say "our," are you speaking about our generation (i.e., our age group) or—

Ward: No, I'm speaking of your biological mother and my biological mother. They were not projected on television screens, but the women who were projected on television screens, unless we point to one or two rather daring films in the cinema, were docile, domestic. Domesticity was very much promoted, including domesticity in terms of the development of household items: how to make the kitchen better, how to free up the women from a certain kind of labor so they could labor in a different way.

Salaam: I think it's important that you talk about the domestic thing. It occurs to me that when we look at American labor, the image of the woman, particularly in the fifties, is as a housekeeper. The fact of the matter is that women have been at the forefront of actual productive labor in this society but not at the forefront of the consciousness about that productive labor. The image that was put forth of the ideal woman was not the laborer, which most of them were, but rather the housewife, which most were not. The majority of women in America were not housewives, even though that is the image that is projected. When you say "my mother and your mother," they were housewives in the sense that they were married, had families, and had household duties that they assumed, but they were also laborers. They were also workers.

Ward: Because they came out of a rather difficult history of women who worked in the United States of America.

Salaam: I'm saying precisely this point that even the majority of white women were not simply housewives, even though that is what is projected.

Ward: Right, but it's still important that we note this fiction that got widely broadcast because it created a climate of belief about what domesticity is. You brought to the foreground the companionship if I might put it that way, of the abolitionist movement and the women's suffrage movement. In modern America, the notion of women's liberation goes back to Mary Wollstonecraft: women's liberation from the dominance of patriarchy and women's desire to have the ability to be educated and to be productive in ways that were at that time reserved almost exclusively for males. African American women—we will not speak of African women because I wouldn't know what I'm talking about—African American women were always compromised because they were not considered female enough. They were not ladylike enough in the dominant discourses to be included as proper Americans, proper female Americans.

What was pushed on them was this image or set of images of how you must behave and how you must look if you wish to be acceptable. Of course, you have to give over to—to use a rather vernacular phrasing—give over to the male, whether that male is African American, Caucasian, whatever. In America, women were supposed to always be subservient and submissive. This issue is attached to experiences that we have been talking about within the past months after the conference at Dillard University on the Black Arts

Movement and its southern influences.[4] There the representation of women was quite remarkable. I'd guess there were more women attending the conference than men.

Salaam: It is important to point out that it was a woman who initiated and led that conference: Kim McMillon.

Ward: Yes, Kim McMillon was the force behind the project. She conceptualized this particular iteration of remembering the Black Arts Movement. She had organized a previous conference, I think in California.[5] The Dillard conference was a great effort, which she prevailed in carrying off with the help of many, many people but certainly through her own determination to have this particular moment.

It's very important because as we study what is happening now in America, we look back to what happened in the period 1960 to 1975, which is called the Black Arts/Black Aesthetic Movement. I really always want to use that slash, Black Arts *slash* Black Aesthetic, because if you simply say the Black Arts Movement, the problem of the aesthetic—not aesthetics in the sense of philosophy of art but aesthetic in the sense that I favor, of perception, borrowing from a very ancient meaning of the word *aesthetic*—gets lost.

Salaam: Truth from beauty.

Ward: No, not truth from beauty. Perception. The word *aesthetic* in Greek may have had something to do with truth and beauty, but primarily it had to do with the consciousness of those things which probably we could say were external to human beings as well as those things we now call internal—

Salaam: You're talking about aesthetics as awareness of self and the environment?

Ward: Yes. I think this is so very important because this has been played and played and played throughout a long period of what we would call American history. It has been played for much of the twentieth century and continues in ways that are assisted by emerging technologies in the twenty-first century to suggest a disconnection in some degree between our lives as human beings who work or don't work or just exist and some special activity called the arts, which is supposed to be separated from the conduct of everyday life and of course from whatever heritage we have, particularly if it's African or if it comes from Indigenous people.

We do not necessarily at our deepest level imitate this dissociation of sensibility that comes out of the seventeenth or eighteenth century in European aesthetic theory about what art is. Prior to that time, if you just go to any ordinary church on the continent of Europe—and I do mean ordinary church—there is adornment. Art was a part of the architecture of a place of worship. Art had a function. It isn't an accident that blond-haired, blue-eyed or green-eyed saints adorn Roman Catholic places of worship.

Salaam: Yes, this great question of adornment in combination with the African American identity and that identity as being enshrined with but at the same time separate from the general American identity. Here is the critical historic moment. Up until now, to be Black—to be African American, if we speak precisely, but to be viewed as Black—was to be viewed as part of the United States but at the same time sociologically separate, an entity unto itself.

In the era—just to use a convenient phrase, in the post-Obama era—suddenly (although it's not really sudden, it seems sudden) to be Black, to be African American, is to be American. For instance, Jesse Owens was not considered just a great American athlete. He was considered a Black American athlete. The separation of Black Americans from Americans in the global context is not quite the same now.

Colin Kaepernick is very interesting in the context of our particular discussion because his mother was white and his father was Black. On top of that, he was a foster child, so his biological mother was white and the mother with whom he was reared was also white, but he is being presented as an exemplar of this new Black attitude among athletes. It's really interesting because we're no longer talking about someone whom you could just consider Black in the sense of someone who grew up in the ghetto.

That racial dimension is still there, except now it's part of what we call the American identity. It causes us to question what it means to be American. Just take the name *Jesse Owens*: we recognize that as an American name, and for most of us, we would think, "Okay, he's probably Black." With Colin Kaepernick, you cannot tell by the name of *Colin Kaepernick*, depending on how you want to pronounce it. You cannot tell by the name what he is. If you ask, "Who were his parents?" someone would say, "Well, he was mixed," but you don't get immediately that Black identity. When you look at him, that's a different story, but, I mean, just considering the name, you don't automatically get a Black identity.

I'm suggesting that what America has become is a mixed society rather than a strictly segregated society. We talked about it in previous eras of the United States, but previously, even though mixed was the social reality, mixed was not the intellectual reality and certainly was not the generally accepted political reality. Mixed was not the symbolic presentation of what it meant to be an American. Previously, we had this legal segregation that separated races, even intellectually. There was a real separation. That separation is not predominant now.

You brought up this interesting discussion about the Indigenous people. Indigenous people now must be considered part of the American story. I'm saying it's not an accident that this happens now. Nor is it an accident that gender issues are at the forefront. All of this is, I think, a result of a major change in both the perception and the social reality of what it means to be an American.

One of the things it means to be an American today is that the racial binary is no longer the dominant discourse. I'm not saying it's been erased; I'm not saying there's no such thing. I'm saying it is not the dominant assumption, it is not the establishment any longer. The gendered binary is no longer simply the status quo to be assumed and in the American case not even discussed. What we have now is that all of these issues are suddenly on the table. The Indigenous/not Indigenous, the Black/non-Black, ethnicity, gender: all of these issues are now very much on the table to be discussed. This, it seems to me, is a remarkable shift in terms of how one looks at being American.

Ward: I agree with you about the shift. I want to point out, however, that we have an important and problematic phrase that is used now as a part of this shift. To preserve the semblance of the binary, one talks about "people of color." Often those who are assumed to be people of color are the very people who use the phrase. More often, however, the people who use the phrase automatically assume they have no color. They call themselves white, as if white is not a color. This is extremely troubling to me because I realize that *people of color* is a code that is being used. *People of color* is a basket. You can throw into *people of color* a person from India, a person from Thailand, a person from Uganda, a person from Mississippi or Louisiana, a person from Colombia. These are all people of color. You're not making any intelligent differentiations about those people.

Along with this fiction of postracial whateverness, I think it is reprehensible that in the discourse about what it means to be an American, we still have to contend with people saying or thinking, "Well, if we don't talk about people of color, what are we to say?" I have a very perverse response to that. If you are not a person of color, you should be annihilated.

Salaam: You're calling for annihilation. I'll let that stand as a rhetorical flourish, but I do want to address the question. Actually, it seems to me there are two questions that intellectually the United States has not grappled with and needs to grapple with. One is the question of ethnicity, as you rightly point out. The other is the question of economics, which includes observing the social groups and social classes of the people asking that question. When we look at those two questions, ethnicity and economics, then we see the issues that the United States, the American character, has avoided dealing with for a long time.

Just thinking about television, when you and I came up, you had a lot of Westerns on there. The Westerns were implicitly about the major population moving west of the Mississippi River during the post–Civil War period and toward the Pacific Ocean as well as the industry and social constructs that came out of that movement of people. I thought some of those television programs were interesting. Most of us think of the West simply in terms of going from Texas to New Mexico, Arizona, on into California on the southern edge of the western United States. If you do the Midwest, you think of from Chicago and St. Louis across to the West Coast. Of course, you had the Lewis and Clark expedition and all of that, that whole geopolitical area.

If that is indeed the Western, we need to look more closely at the ethnicity and the economics because then we will get a handle on what is really the American experience. I submit that the American experience has been presented solely as the views of the ruling class—i.e., those who had power in terms of money and military might in this society and heritage. The two forces were ethnically white and economically rich. When I say ethnically white, I'm being very precise. I'm using *whiteness* as a precise term. It was a catch-all that enabled those who had power to frame what it meant to be an American. If you were European, your ethnicity was wiped out. You were no longer Swedish or Polish or French or Spanish or anything else like that. You were American, and hence you were white.

That ethnic identity of what it meant to be American became the basket, but if you look at it from a Black standpoint, you'll say, "Well, we were excluded from that definition." The sociopolitical reality of what it meant to be an American excluded Blackness from the basket. If you look at it from an ethnic standpoint, there was an erasure.

I remember being in Minnesota in 1964. I graduated from high school, and there was a scholarship I had to Carleton College in Northfield, Minnesota, fifty-seven miles below the Twin Cities, Minneapolis–St. Paul. I had an accident at the school, and my front tooth was knocked out. A dental bridge was put in. The dentist was of Swedish heritage. I remember two things about talking to him during the course of the treatment. I was struck by his accent and also struck by his attitude. At that point, I had never met a white person who didn't immediately treat me like a Negro. I didn't get any racist vibes from him. That really struck me.

I realize now, over fifty years later, that part of what I was seeing was someone who had not yet been fully Americanized. He was probably first- or second-generation Swedish American, and he hadn't been fully Americanized yet. There was not a bunch of Negroes in Northfield, so he didn't see me in a twisted way. Television was not yet the dominant cultural map of what it meant to be an American.

Ward: No, in 1964, we had radio as the dominant map or sound map of that time. I think of how I had to coordinate radio with film in my growing up when I listened to some of my favorite stories on the radio in the 1940s and 1950s. There was a ritual in my house on Saturday night of listening to certain stories, which my parents and I shared and enjoyed. My imagination was working feverishly to supply the images. The images I could supply were those that I had picked up from film, magazines, mail-order catalogs. Even in the science fiction stories, of which I was very fond, I could never imagine the characters as Negroes.

Salaam: *Twilight Zone?*

Ward: *Twilight Zone* was television, not radio. I was not watching television before the late 1950s. There were probably a handful of Black characters in *The Twilight Zone*, but my visual imagination had to be retooled to deal with them.

Salaam: I mean that sarcastically. We were in a twilight zone in the sense of being there and at the same time not being there, not politically important. Then as television came in—

Ward: On television, some things seemed to be African American, but generally they were caricatures and absurd versions of dialect—for example, *Amos 'n' Andy*. I processed them without critical consciousness. Even in our imagination, we didn't see ourselves as equally a part of the American identity. I remember the comic strip *Mandrake the Magician*.[6] I had a vision of the Black male sidekick to go along with the Indigenous-person sidekick Tonto from *The Lone Ranger*. Always, the hero in the narrative is Caucasian. When you tell me about this, I think we had to consider such images much more than people who were, let's say, born after 1990. We're dealing with younger people who have never known the job, the chore, of constructing a self-identity from sound and grappling with the conundrum of disentangling our self-identities from the caricature identities popularized on television. Basically, we're talking about radio: about constructing visual images from sound or reaching into one's consciousness to pull forth visual images.

Salaam: We are talking about people who have now had their imaginations polluted by the images that are presented by the American status quo. Whereas before, in our generation, our imaginations might have been informed by the mainstream, but they were not visually polluted by the mainstream because we were not allowed in the mainstream and did not think of ourselves as an integral part of the mainstream. We recognized that there was a difference between who we were and how the mainstream saw us.

I remember when *to bogart* meant to take over something, just by the force of your own personality. The person who did the bogarting was implicitly male. It came from Humphrey Bogart. That image was presented in a nonracialized sense. In the Black community, we said, "Oh, you going to bogart that?" "Yeah, I'm just going to take it." That became the dominant thing, but there was no visual image with bogarting something.

Young people today don't have that same experience because they have visual imagery with all of their ideas. There's a certain—I started to say richness, but I would be probably more accurate to say a certain agency that goes with thinking of your own image for whatever is your received or imagined idea. If you grow up and don't have that ability to put your own image on because your imagination has been polluted by what's being presented, then it's rough. I imagine you cannot make certain steps. You cannot even see yourself as a potential agent of change. As we used to say, "I know that you think you can do whatever you want to do, but can you really want to think anything?"

Ward: Although you used the word *polluted*, perhaps we should say it was a matter of saturation.

Salaam: Stephen E. Henderson.

Ward: Yes, the scholar Stephen E. Henderson, because he uses the term *saturation* so very well in *Understanding the New Black Poetry*.[7] But in 2017 how we think of saturation is enormously different. We now have a disabling surplus of saturation.

What saturation can mean in 2017 is not what saturation meant when you and I were growing up. We were saturated, certainly, with a sense of differentness based as much on notions of race and ethnicity as on ideas that had to do with economics and class, especially when we're talking about segregated community structures, where class is a real limitation affecting everyone. The Afro-Saxons, for example.

Salaam: E. Franklin Frazier.

Ward: Yes, Frazier, *Black Bourgeoisie*, where class is demonstrated in terms of both the acquisition of some wealth—not a great deal of wealth but, within our own communities, some degree of wealth in terms of entrepreneurship—and also a variety of social activities, organizations, performances that are richly endowed with attitudes of being better or worse.[8]

The cheap way of talking about this, the very reductive way of talking about this, is to make a distinction between house Negroes and field n------.

The old house/field separation as a racist and racialized dichotomy is as bad as the contemporary binary that is now, as you suggest, a matter of something that is vanishing. You can't have that kind of division and truly understand it unless we also account for why it was (and still is) a part of the effort for upward mobility. In the 1950s, I admired Dr. So-and-So, who had a degree from Morehouse or was a dentist or a medical doctor or a government employee, or Ms. So-and-So, who was a schoolteacher or someone who owned a mom-and-pop store, a funeral home, a barbershop or beauty parlor, or a restaurant. These people were unlike the common laborers in my family, who betrayed the dreams of my great-grandparents and grandparents. I saw that a person was doing fairly well by the measures of those days, so I was determined to be somewhat like that person. That aspiration was also fed by sports heroes.

If you were very athletic, you wanted to be like Jesse Owens or Joe Louis or Sugar Ray Robinson or someone who had made it, according to our then-limited notion of what "making it" was about. Rarely were you encouraged to want to be other than that or more than that. Social restrictions ordained by segregation were vicious. Few of us had the dubious advantage of resembling [longtime NAACP leader] Walter White. On the other hand, few of us knew much about W. E. B. Du Bois or [entrepreneur and activist] Madam C. J. Walker or some of the brilliant women coming out of the nineteenth century, like Anna Julia Cooper. Knowledge about those figures was not easily available to the boys and girls of my generation except during Negro History Week. Of course, they were always there, but we were less aware of them than I'd like to think young people are today. Young people have greater opportunities to be aware. The dreadful question is: Do they elect to be aware, or is the pollution or negative saturation of misleading "integration" in the United States too strong for them to embrace a critical, historical consciousness?

Salaam: I don't think that many young people want to be separate from the American norm. I don't think they want to expand beyond the American dream. I think they want to be part of American society as it is presented to them. Whereas with our generation, we wanted to see something different from what was presented to us. How much we wanted and whether that was really different from the status quo, that's a whole other story. What did we really want, that's again another story, but what we wanted was different from what has been presented to this generation—I'm referring to people born after the 1990s. They want access to what is now the norm, and they're not thinking about expanding that into something different, something else. They want to be part of that, whereas we came up wanting to challenge if not expand what was the dominant discourse. Today's young people are just part of the dominant discourse and do not see themselves in opposition to the dominant discourse.

Ward: We were in opposition to dominant discourses. I admit my opposition involved ambivalence. To a great extent, the Black Arts/Black Aesthetic Movement helped me to reduce my ambivalence, particularly as I became more aware of hard-core politics, conservative and liberal hypocrisies, and the ambiguity of legal systems. I had a deep resentment of how I was compelled to exist with the experiment of American democracy. I tried to deal with that subject in my essay "Abrasion: Aesthetic Challenges in African American Poetry."[9] According to the letters of the law, we are American citizens, but on a day-to-day basis, well, we know there's an asterisk on our citizenship.

Indeed, both the legal systems and the illegal systems ran the machinery of segregation and racial discrimination. Deep racism and the whole nine yards were always a barrier for us, always a thing against which we had to operate, either actively in defiance or with some kind of resentment when we could not be overtly defiant.

Salaam: We were forced to be submissive, on one hand, but we also felt resentful.

Ward: Right, a deep resentment of the fact that you existed within the American experiment. By the law, you were an American citizen. There were various constitutional amendments that were supposed to guarantee your entitlements and rights and privileges, but those were only guaranteed on the page. Depending on what part of the country you lived in, the conduct of everyday life and your rights therein were constantly—deeply or shallowly—violated.

Salaam: We grew up under segregation. The '64 Civil Rights Act and '65 Voting Rights Act were enacted after we became adults. There were momentous changes that happened as a result of those two pieces of legislation. The Civil Rights Act was significant, but the Voting Rights Act seems to still have contentious repercussions that are under discussion right now. There's no discussion about civil rights per se. Civil rights are nominally branded as part of the American fabric, but there's some deep discussion about how one determines who has the right to vote and to economically be in a position to make decisions about this society. That battle is ongoing.

I think you're absolutely correct when you bring up that there's a difference between de jure and de facto. The de jure issue, which many of us thought was settled, is still lurking, and its legal and social implications have to be confronted. De facto, I think everybody has accepted that in fact "all men are created equally," with all of the gender blindness notwithstanding. People accept political equality in principle, but our legal and day-to-day reality vis-à-vis the criminal justice system is both complicated and racist. Because equality is de jure—the law—does that mean that we no longer need to have laws to mandate and enforce political and social equality? That's what all the questions about voter suppression and convoluted voting qualifications are about. In principle everything is cool, but on a mass social level, we still have a lot of problems. I think this twilight zone of free in principle and victimized by racism in practice is where we are today.

Part of what I wanted to revisit was not just the de jure/de facto split, which is I think very real, but also the whole question of resistance. The Black Lives Matter movement does not have, from my perception and evaluation, the same force the civil rights movement had, precisely because of two things: (1) it does not have a defined enemy that you can point to immediately; (2) not only is there not a defined enemy, there's no organized and centralized leadership.

A person wants to be part of the Black Lives Matter movement—for example, a student at McDonogh 35 or any other public high school in New Orleans: and except for marching in a demonstration, what do they do? Generally speaking, there is no perceived national organization that they can become part of. At the same time, they have in their hands a smartphone, which gives them access to a lot of the discourse nationally and internationally. It's a very interesting dilemma to have more than you need as far as information and not have anything you really need as far as organization.

While we did not have as much information as is commonly available to a young person today, we did have organizations. If you think back during that period, you could become part of CORE [Congress of Racial Equality], NAACP, the Urban League, or the Student Nonviolent Coordinating Committee [SNCC]. You also had various regional and local organizations and chapters.

Then on top of that, on the self-determined and militant end of the spectrum, we had the Republic of New Africa. Also, above all, we had the Nation of Islam. There were organizational movements that you could join on your local level that were part of the overall civil rights era. The Black Lives Matter movement, however, is in a vacuum because there are no organizations that, off the top of one's head, one can reach out and touch. You've got all this information but, broadly speaking, no organized way to use that information.

Ward: Let's consider something else quickly. You and I come from a generation of people born in the 1940s. In terms of organizations that were important for civil rights, these organizations go all the way back to colonial days in this country. There is organization after organization coming through the abolitionist movement, coming through the women's liberation movement of the nineteenth century, where there was a particular kind of racialized struggle. When you mention the Nation of Islam, let us also recall [Marcus] Garvey's UNIA [Universal Negro Improvement Association] movement predating that. You had the typical, nonviolent NAACP and Urban League, but nineteenth-century literature, particularly political literature, suggests to us an alternative.

Salaam: What do you mean, "political literature"?

Ward: I mean what we call creative writing today. Political literature can be creative literature. However, I think we can make a useful distinction between literature that overtly denies its political implications and literature that is at once aesthetic and covertly political so that we know to a better degree what we're talking about. I don't even know if our history of so-called literary struggle has any popularity or credibility anymore. Contradictions abound.

We are heirs, even in our denial, to a long history of struggles: struggles to be liberated from shackles of enslavement, struggles to be recognized as legitimate citizens, struggles to have better pay for the same work and to have access, which is often denied, to trade unions, to avenues for advancement. Some doors are still locked. Some glass ceilings still retard our growth.

This is why some sense of history as narrative and as a process is so very important for the pivotal moment of 2016. The cliché that if you do not have a sense of history, you are bound to repeat it is exactly that—a cliché—and is very quickly challenged by what has happened now as people look into their iPhones and are preoccupied with that socialization, which does not allow many people—I won't say all, but many people—to even reflect on the fact that we have something called history that does, whether we want it to or not, inform our choices of action.

It is very interesting that a friend of ours whom I will not name asked the question: Why is it that so much literature of today seems to quake before the possibility of speaking of cultural or political nationalism? It's almost as if cultural awareness is anathema. It's anathema for reasons that you have described. You are an American. You are not going to cut your own throat by suggesting that you are a country within a country. No, you're not going to do that. You're not going to raise your fist, as was done in 1968 at the Olympics, or refuse to appropriately cover your heart with your hand when they play the national anthem—only stanza 1 of the national anthem, because stanzas 2, 3, and 4 are not played. When you examine all the stanzas, you find some great surprises there about what Francis Scott Key actually wrote.

Salaam: What the national anthem actually meant.

Ward: And still means. Yes. I must say that between us (that is, you and me) and younger people there may be a very, very deep divide. I am not thinking only of teenagers. I think, from the perspective of seven decades, of people in their fifties and younger. The divide is partly a result of processes of socialization, of different regard for the nature of struggle. Struggle goes beyond talking about politics and social action.

I think struggle also has to be spoken of in terms of ordinary things in our lives. Our generation had struggles that we would not even today call a struggle, and vice versa: this generation has struggles that our older generation would not consider a struggle. What were our struggles while growing up? Did we have a common experience of growing up and being bullied or not bullied or being the bully? Growing up with people having expectations about your success, for example, which now we find is a big issue in our educational systems, was special. I contrast that fact with the current situation. To have expectations today for a young person's success is to fall into the trap of being microaggressive because you insult the tender little brain by suggesting that the tender little brain did not achieve something.

Our tender little brains were certainly assaulted by people who said, "You ain't done shit, and you are going to do shit." I used the vulgarity here to suggest how deeply I feel about this. People who cared told us, "No, you did not achieve an A. You made a D or an F or a C and you can do better." People who were responsible primarily for our educations outside of our home spaces, people who were not our parents, really cared. I'm not going to accuse teachers of yesteryear of not caring. I am going to suggest that the situation involving all parties is such that perhaps how to care effectively is now a major problem.

Salaam: Here you have two issues, but let me just look at one: education. Educationally, we came up with teachers who might be epitomized by the saying that one of my teachers put forth: "You little knuckleheads are going to learn." There was no assumption whatsoever that we couldn't learn. They started from the standpoint that it was a given that you could learn. They were there to instruct you: "I'm going to teach you, and I'm not going to put up with no mess about 'You're not going to learn' or 'You cannot learn.'"

What we need to recognize is those teachers came from a group of people who had extraordinary character. When I said "extraordinary character," I don't mean that they were all heroes or anything, but the crucible within which they had to acquire their education—just to acquire a college education required a certain amount of character. Can you imagine trying to get a college education in the 1940s and '50s so that you could teach school? That in and of itself was a struggle. That's what I mean by, "They had a character."

The larger environment that shaped them and through which they had to pass was a different environment than teachers today face—a vastly different environment. The makeup of those who become teachers today is different. I refer to my friend Ellis Marsalis.

In the 1980s, I did a lot of work as a music producer both here and throughout the Caribbean. Sometimes we'd be on these long trips, like if we went to Barbados, Trinidad. We'd have time to talk during the travel time. One time he was talking about how it's a different story nowadays. When he came up—and, by extension, when you and I came up—if you were a smart Negro, there were only so many avenues open to you. He told me about his son, Wynton Marsalis. He said Wynton had in his band a young man whose name was Todd Williams, playing tenor saxophone. Todd was an excellent saxophonist, but he also had gone to a school, I think in St. Louis, and had a college degree. He had other opportunities, so he decided to pursue some of those other opportunities rather than pursue music.

Ellis was making the point that when we came up, if you could rise to that level in music, there were very few other areas open to you outside of music that would let you rise to a commensurate level. If you got to a nationally recognized professional level in your music, I don't care how smart you were, you probably could not get to that same level if you decided to be a teacher or an administrator or whatever. That's not the case today. Today, you have opportunities in a lot of different fields.

The deeper point Ellis made was that our music was so strong because many of our smartest people went into music. Today, our smartest people have a choice of areas that they can go into. When we start talking about the aesthetic thing, there's a smaller group of artists precisely because there are more opportunities for a smart person other than art and entertainment.

Ward: You just forced me to think about why there is a preoccupation with prizes—the preoccupation with winning this prize or that prize. Every time a person's short or long bio is presented to us, the prizes have to be all listed. Maybe it's a fact that once you are part of the total American mix, you lose a particular kind of specialness that was enhanced by segregation. Once the laws of segregation were removed, we entered a transitional period within which we were now compared with and competing against the whole population and not just our own people. I am not taken in by prizes. In my opinion, many people who do the most good in helping us to become more tolerant, generous, and humane will never be awarded a prize of any kind.

Let's say, post-1954, if we might use the year arbitrarily, what was happening with arts then? You still had a specialness, a sort of specialness accorded to arts by Negroes. Let's use Langston Hughes as an example. We looked at him with a great deal of admiration. He had his enemies, of course, but I think most people really liked Langston Hughes and were so pleased that Langston Hughes published books. He was in the newspapers, and he had these funny "Simple" stories, etc. So we admired his achievements.

In a similar way, we liked many of our musicians because they were heroic figures. You wanted to dress like Duke Ellington. You wanted to be able to play like Armstrong or Coltrane or like Lionel Hampton because these were the great people. If you were male, you wanted a voice like Billy Eckstine's. Billy Eckstine's artistry, by the way, was continued through doo-wop. When we listen to the sound quality of many of those singers and compare it with the sound qualities that are now par for the course, there's a remarkable difference.

I'm suggesting, however, that one of the burning issues for us this year and in the future is indeed to more fully examine the matter of Americanness in light of what we tried to produce in the name of Black Power. The Black Arts/Black Aesthetic Movement had some success, but consider how gains can be taken away very quickly unless one is exceptionally vigilant. We need to ask: What is the possibility of a future? We need to remember the wonderful title of a collection of writings by Larry Neal and question whether we have "visions of a liberated future" and how we would define what it means to be liberated.[10]

I'm not at all sure that any of us can have visions of a liberated future. And I mean anybody. I don't care what ethnicity you belong to because I do not see the future as a period when human beings can be liberated from anything. I think out of necessity and by default, we're all going to be more and more enslaved to something—not by our volition, but just by the fact that you are a living human being and by how capitalism is acting out its drama throughout the world, you are going to be enslaved to something.

Salaam: Is it possible to be human and to be free or are we saying implicitly that to be human means to be attached to some social order? When I say "attached to," I mean that you identify with some social order and at the same time that you are opposed to and if not opposed at least circumscribed by some social order. Are we saying that there's a tendency for there to be two different social orders? For all human beings, regardless of who they may be, there's a social grouping that you see yourself as part of. Even if you want to be a hermit, you see yourself as part of those people who went off on their own to live, to be a lighthouse master or whatever they wanted to do to live a solitary lifestyle. At the same time, you are part of a society, and there is no way to be human and to be totally an individual. Indeed, humanity itself is ipso facto a social definition. To be human is to be social, and that sociality has two aspects: (1) that which you identify with, and (2) that which circumscribes you. They may in fact be one and the same, but in general, they are not the same, especially in terms of their purpose or intent.

Ward: We are complex. Let me suggest that to be human is first and primarily a matter of biology. Among other animals, we are differentiated by what we call our humanity. Perhaps that has to do with the evolution of our brains and the ability to manipulate sounds, which we call language, differently from how other animals manipulate sound. They have languages too, but they are not as highly evolved as our own. You are absolutely right to bring again to mind that no man is an island. Nor is any woman or any transgender person an island. We are all part of the whole whether we accept or reject our links with other people we call human beings. And there are many reasons that we accept or reject linkages.

The very notion of being linked, attached, associated with can be described in various ways when we look at the total context—the matrix, if you will—within which human beings find themselves operating along with other animals, along with inanimate things, or along with the total environments, none of which are pristine anymore. The humanity that we are capable of does not allow us—except by way of extreme fantasies, and we had many of those thrown at us—to believe that we are free. Yes, in a material way, we're not all enslaved. We're not chattel slaves. That's not what I wish to suggest. But there are things that you are obligated to do or that you suffer certain kinds of punishments if you do not do, particularly in terms of paying your taxes. If you're very smart, like somebody reminded us a couple of days ago, you find ways not to pay them.

The bulk of Americans are going to pay taxes of one kind or another, large or small. The bulk of people in America, as we drive down the highways and try to drive cautiously, are preoccupied with their devices. I don't mean the vehicles that they are driving. I dread hearing, "Within thirty or forty years, you won't have to drive vehicles because they will drive themselves." Many people are enslaved by devices: smartphones, iPads, mainly smartphones, and text messaging or sex messaging or conducting business or gossiping and not always being as attentive to the nature of traffic on the road. This makes those of us who look at people attached to their devices very uncomfortable. I want to get away from you if you're driving and texting. I want to be as far away from you as possible to maximize my chances of not having an accident. Therefore, although people are free, they're also enslaved.

Salaam: I resist calling it enslaved because I think to use your term, there's a complexity. We are not necessarily enslaved as much as we are tethered—that is, connected. A tethering may be involuntary, but it's not the same as being forced to do certain things and disallowed from doing other things. Enslavement is different from being a part of something. It seems to me that the condition of being human is ipso facto, in and of itself, one of being connected to other humans. The most distinctive part of being human is not our biology. As you rightly point out, other animals have language. The most distinctive part of being human is that we are social creatures who do more with language than other creatures do. We do not merely exist as individuals. We self-identify on a social level.

Ward: I will overstate the matter of enslavement because the major narrative of the United States of America involves the peculiar institution that is known as slavery. You make a fine distinction between being enslaved and being tethered or connected. I do not. I would suggest that in understanding the peculiar institution, we should not be ignorant of the fact that all involved in that institution were deeply affected by it—whether you were an overseer, a so-called slave, a minor slave owner, or one of the masters who had the privilege of large acreage and a large population of enslaved people.

I will admit that I overused the term *enslavement*, but I did not use it to produce shock or humor. I just gave it more emphasis than some people think it probably deserves. I don't want us to embrace the notion that slavery is over, particularly when there are some efforts now to talk about the continuing presence of slavery in the world from ancient times to 2017. Now, when some people talk about slavery, they think we have the privilege of talking as if it doesn't exist in our nation. Our Thirteenth Amendment has an exception, a clause, that allows enslavement as a punishment for crime to thrive in the United States. Let us not forget that.

My good brother, let us remember that several decades ago, there were a number of programs focusing on the question of slavery, but even today, gathering information on the topic is dangerous. There were a number of programs constructed to inform us about what migrant labor was, particularly migrant labor in Florida, which seemed to be a little different from migrant labor in California, and that there were certain places that were like plantations or being run very much along with the principles of plantations in the eighteenth century and the nineteenth century. It was something rather different from the system of oppression that came along with tenant farming and sharecropping. It was a little worse than that because many of these people were not necessarily US citizens. They were dependent on seasonal work. They were also forbidden to do a lot of things, and they were under heavy surveillance. If they did certain kinds of things to assert their dignity as human beings, I think many of them were killed.

Part of this redefining or this new recognition that you're talking about, of what it is to be an American, is an increased sense that to be an American is also *not to have the privilege* of being something other than a world citizen. We are world citizens, although that particular line of discussion or rhetoric is not encouraged by political conservatism, by people who want to be patriotic. If you recognize some of the world's citizens, obviously you are cheating in some way on being patriotic.

That is part of the problem that we're going to have to deal with more and more as the twenty-first century progresses. In terms of quality of life and opportunities, whatever happens or doesn't happen outside the so-called boundaries of the United States very much affects what happens within those boundaries. Again, we go back to economics. We go back to the behavior and misbehavior of major financial institutions and major financial organizations that are global. I am thinking of how politics and commercial enterprises sleep in the same bed. I'm thinking about those which have obvious political meaning: the Group of Twenty, the International Monetary Fund, the World Bank, an entity named ALEC [American Legislative Exchange Council].

I was really quite enlightened to read a little bit more about the kinds of decisions and opportunities and/or mandates that are passed out by the International Monetary Fund and the World Bank to nations: "You are going to do this in order to receive certain kinds of aid. You are going to have this percentage of production or that percentage of import/export activity for a particular period of time." I'm saying, "Ah, I don't hear this in the news." I don't read the *Wall Street Journal* faithfully, either, but I don't hear this in the news. This is not what comes through to me at 4:00 or 5:00 or 6:00 in the afternoon when I'm supposed to be informed about what's happening in the world.

Salaam: Well, as I said in one of my short stories, when this guy questions this woman and she says something and he says, "You didn't tell me about that," her reply, very simply, is, "A woman would be a fool to tell a man everything she knows."

Ward: You were saying: Who is the fool to tell me everything that she or he knows?

Salaam: Right.

Ward: Fair enough.

Salaam: These people, the [International Monetary Fund], and all of these other folks, they're in the business of running the world, not of informing the world of how they run the world. Those are two different things. To be informed about how the world is run is one thing. To actually run the world is another. The people who are running the world are not interested in telling us how they actually run the world.

Ward: I think this is the reason not that we have failures in education but that we have inadequacies in American systems of education. What can we reasonably expect the so-called best school systems to produce in terms of presenting people with information and helping them to develop the critical ability to process all of this information? To give them a maximum sense of literacies is not enough. It's always going to have to be supplemented by the recognition that there are other forms of learning that take place outside of classrooms. A great deal of nonclassroom learning is not organized. The more of it that can be organized is all to the good if you can have receptive people, young people, and teachers, to deal with it.

Perhaps the organizations, like wise women, are not going to tell us everything they know. However, I think it is to my benefit—also to my agony, but particularly to my benefit—to know more about some of the things that are in motion in terms of how the world is organized, how the world is run. If I don't know these things, I'm going to become complacent. I'm going to become comfortable with my state and suggest that God is in heaven and all is right with the world, which is a very foolish position to have.

Salaam: It hearkens to what you said earlier: whether you want to or not, whether you are aware of the fact or not, you're going to become a slave. We become slaves by our own perception of reality, which is limited. Unless we recognize that our perception is limited and attempt to find out more than we know, then we are enslaved.

Ward: Was not the finding out of more than we know one of the parts of [the Black Arts Movement]? It was not the most pronounced part, but it was very important that one would find out what one did not know so that if you started off with the goal of eradicating ignorance, well, that's what the Black aesthetic was really about.

Salaam: *A* Black aesthetic, not *the* Black aesthetic.

Ward: *A* or *the* Black aesthetic, regardless, what you were really getting at is that you believe we have the right to create our own standards of judgment, of evaluation, and of appreciation. When you started doing that kind of work, you began to ask—or rather, some of us began to ask—some other questions about things we found offensive. Why is ballet highly valued but not the South African boot dance? Why is so-called classical music the thing? Why are you supposed, in some scheme, to listen to Mozart and Beethoven, but you don't necessarily have to listen to Monk, and you don't have to listen to Muddy Waters? I think these questions, initially without a great deal of system, began to come out, to emerge as vernacular theory. Perhaps this was one of the contributions that we have to look at.

I just completed—no, I haven't completed it; I'm still revising—a piece on Carolyn Rodgers and vernacular theorizing based on those four remarkable essays that she published in *Negro Digest/Black World*.[11] I haven't got past the first one yet, with her tense categories of describing how poems operate. I'm totally fascinated by it, and as Tony Bolden points out, her categories are very problematic because they're slipping and sliding and overlapping and whatnot.

For me, the great thing is that she came up with the categories to begin with as a way of saying, "Well, you're told by new critical scholarship that you are to deal with the poem itself. You are to deal with it in terms of structure. You're not supposed to give too much attention to biographical information, to subjectivity, and to all those other messy things."

Salaam: What they call the New Criticism.

Ward: That's the infamous New Criticism. It was still influential when Rodgers was writing in the late 1960s. Although post-whatever stuff is rising, the procedure of close reading is still based very much on New Critical principles. I think now our most publicized discussions of literature and of other forms of cultural expression have become—I don't know if it's pasteurized or homogenized—have become acceptable within what is called the academy. I'm not even sure that we're raising the right questions.

I'm going to bring this down to something very current. There's something circulating now as a result of the video that Beyoncé Knowles released or dropped on HBO in the spring: *Lemonade*.[12] It's called the Lemonade Syllabus.[13] It's about how to study the phenomenon—the video and everything that's behind it. It has achieved a great deal of popularity. I got several email messages about the fact that *Vogue* magazine came out with a very interesting story about a new course that was based upon *Lemonade*.[14] My first response was: Who reads *Vogue*? How much money do they have? Where do they shop? Why is *Vogue* doing this? I suspect that some of the people Beyoncé was trying to address in her work could not afford to buy anything in some of those stores where *Vogue* readers shop.

Salaam: That may be the case, but I think that circles back to my assumption that much of what we consider Black culture and Black cultural production today is totally entwined with American culture, the economics of which is capitalism, pure and simple. Make a buck. I don't think people see Beyoncé as being purely and simply about making a buck, but the system that she is part of—the whole enterprise that is Beyoncé, not just the image that is Beyoncé—is capitalist-driven. It seems to me that's what it's about. If one is to talk about what it means to be American, in a very, very, very, very reductive sense, one of the things, one of the foundational things it means is to make a buck.

Today, there is no prohibition on Negroes making a buck. In fact, I think that the people who are responsible for the society in the sense of running the society—the establishment: not the figures, but the owners and managers—they see it as to their advantage to have a Beyoncé. Whereas fifty years ago, a Beyoncé would have been frozen out. You would have someone like, for instance, an Eartha Kitt or a Pearl Bailey.

They were immediately reduced to their sexuality and not seen as part of the establishment figures in terms of economics. Today, Beyoncé is seen, is talked about, in terms of driving the economics: "When her album drops, she makes X amount of money, blah, blah, blah." That's what I mean by that becoming a foundational part of the identity of being American. Moreover, the identity of being Black is now subsumed into the identity of being American. Whereas before, no matter how much money you made, you were still Black.

Ward: A footnote to something you're saying when you mentioned Pearl Bailey and Eartha Kitt. Consider their contemporaries in two different fields, Lena Horne and Dorothy Dandridge.

Salaam: Yes.

Ward: I mention those two because of color consciousness. Beyoncé fits very well and comfortably into the color-consciousness slot because she is not Lupita [Nyong'o]. No way. You can market, unfortunately, the very talented Lupita. I say "unfortunately" because I don't think she's a commodity. I think of her as a gifted human being. She can be marketed in a certain way, but she could not be marketed or market herself the same way Beyoncé can.

Salaam: No. First of all, Lupita's hair is too short.

Ward: She could get a weave.

Salaam: No, not Lupita. She wouldn't be Lupita. She would not be the self, the image, she has projected of who Lupita is.

Ward: I think our unfinished dialogue is a follow-up, Kalamu, to previous efforts you and I have made, as individuals and as collaborators, to account for our coming of age during a particular period in American cultural and social history. The Dillard University conference was an opportune moment for your book *The Magic of Juju: An Appreciation of the Black Arts Movement* to come out.[15] To follow through on that with this dialogue about a number of interrelated issues may be significant to a few people.

I'm not going to say much more about where we have been, what we have thought, what we are thinking now, and how we can or cannot think about a future. I'm making a kind of joke, which is a very serious joke for me, that I am always, always politically incorrect and pre-future. I am post-nothing. I mean this very seriously. To be pre-future is to engage in a significant amount of thinking about what that thing we call a future might become. To be pre-future is to be certain that I am incapable of any certitude about a future. I cannot know what the future is. There are hundreds of variables I cannot account for.

Salaam: I think obviously you're a part of what I would call the jazz aesthetic. What's interesting to me is in terms of the jazz aesthetic being different from the hip-hop aesthetic. The hip-hop aesthetic has two elements in it, one that is shared with the jazz aesthetic and one that the jazz aesthetic doesn't have. The two elements that, to me, make hip-hop are the combining of the past and putting it into [. . .] one of these blenders. Just throw it all in there, all the ingredients. Throw them all in there, blend it up. Then we come up with this drink. That's part of the hip-hop aesthetic. Jazz has that also. In fact, whatever was happening, whatever music you like to support, you could put part of that into jazz.

Where hip-hop and jazz diverge, however, is in terms of technology. Jazz was primarily analog and human. Hip-hop at its basis is digital and computerized and not human. When you talk about how hip-hop is produced, how it is made, and so forth and so on, you cannot have hip-hop without a computer. People can argue if they want. They can give an example of people doing a capella hip-hop and so forth and so on. All of that may be fine, but as someone pointed out, hip-hop itself, the way it's presented, requires the digital, a microphone, and a computer: two things that you need in order to achieve the hip-hop sound. The drumbeat. The *boom-bap*.

In jazz, the drum is acoustic. In hip-hop the drum is digital. There are a number of aspects and inferences contained in that difference. I'm not going into that at the moment; I want to simply note the difference in terms of drums and drumbeat. What I am more interested in is the element of human agency. However, I do not deny the power of the computer.

Or to put it another way: We can do a second line on our way to the block party. At the line we will have a brass band with both a bass drummer and a snare drummer. The band is totally acoustic. We will get down and dance our asses off. When we get to where the party is stationary, usually where the food is, the *boom-bap* will take over, the beats will drop. The music will be digital, and we will dance our asses off. The common element is the pulse of the beat, even when we have two different approaches, acoustic versus digital, for producing the beat. It's all good. In this context, the human element remains located in *who* produces the beat, the music, rather than an emphasis on *how* the beat, the music, is produced.

A jazz artist is identified with the instrument and with the sound. You don't immediately think of a computer. You do think of an instrument, whether it's a saxophone or a trumpet, piano, or what have you, and the sound of the voice, the sound of the jazz performer him or herself so that you immediately know. You hear and immediately can ascertain, "Oh, that's Coltrane. That's not Coleman Hawkins." "Oh, that's Nancy Wilson." You understand what I'm saying? "That's not somebody else," or, for instance, "That is somebody trying to sound like Nancy Wilson. That's not Nancy Wilson." You know that from the sound, just from the sound. You don't have to see it. You know it from the sound.

Ward: Those people had their own signatures in the same way we speak of writers having signature poems.

Salaam: Yes, but I'm going a step further. I'm saying their signatures partially had to do with the way they used their instruments—the individual sound of the voice or the saxophone or whatever—but also, inherent in the sound was the era within which they lived as well as how their sound was presented. The signature sounds today with hip-hop are different. You have a lot of hip-hop artists that have their own sound, so you recognize a Common from a Kanye, for instance, to use two Chicago references, but overall, the hip-hop thing is so computerized that it could almost be anyone sounding like anyone or everyone else. The individuality is subsumed within the overall sound.

But there is also another dynamic at work beyond the individual sound—for example, the microphone. The amplification of sound—i.e., simply making the sound louder—is an acoustic process. Digital technology takes the microphone into a whole other category. It's no longer simply amplification: it's now also alteration. The mic is about more than just an acoustic sound made louder. In fact, using digital technology, you can now create sounds and use microphones in ways that you can't do acoustically.

Moreover, from my perspective, the deepest element of hip-hop is the elevation of what is said—the content. Yes, much of it is an advertisement for hedonism and outright decadence, but even in that regard, the main point is that the individual is given a voice and a platform for the dissemination of specific content.

Beyond amplification and alteration, there is a third characteristic. When it comes to the human voice and vocalists, the jazz aesthetic was more about interpretation than about original statements—or it might better be said that the jazz aesthetic was about either an original/authentic statement or a unique interpretation of a preexisting composition. In jazz, while there certainly was an appreciation for the composer, far more appreciation was given to the expert interpreter. Hip-hop, with its emphasis on authenticity, placed a premium on composing, and that premium was so rigid that, generally speaking, you weren't considered a good rapper if you presented other people's words and ideas. But in jazz, on the other hand, it was more about *how* you said what you said rather than mainly or solely about the authenticity of *what* you said.

In fact, a valuation given to expert interpretation is true of the arts in general. Whether it is mimesis—the art of replicating what exists mainly through imitation—or whether it is an interpretation of style, of content, or of both style and content, most art is not about creating something new as much as it is about creating something new out of something old. I don't want to minimize or downgrade the art of interpretation because, as with anything else, there are levels of achievement, and a great interpretation can even—and often does—exceed the original.

Two pieces of music in the contemporary jazz context that are associated with John Coltrane illustrate the point. *A Love Supreme* is an original.[16] On the other hand, Coltrane's soprano saxophone version of "My Favorite Things" is an interpretation that fundamentally altered the sound of jazz.[17] Coltrane made the use of the soprano saxophone a standard after it had virtually disappeared in the context of modern jazz. Plus, Coltrane's approach—to both how to play the song itself and how to play the instrument—fundamentally changed the music. In Coltrane's case, interpretation was far more than imitation. Even if the material itself was not original, his interpretation was so radical that he established new standards.

I believe that this is inherent in the Black American ethos. It is not inaccurate to say that a Black ethos was about turning a segregated reality into a liberated dream. Transformation was the focus and force of our artmaking. Black interpretations elevated non-Black originals. That was the case whether we are considering social relations or material production. We were not about mimesis but rather about interpretation as well as original statements. Moreover, we strove to make the interpretation better than the original. For us, the original was a starting place and not a destination, and as such—because times, contexts, and conditions change—ultimately, even though we may start off from the same point, we can end up moving in different directions.

Within a Eurocentric context, the original is viewed as sacred, as authentic. Both jazz and hip-hop are based on a different aesthetic. Whereas jazz validated individual interpretation rather than composition (or authenticity in the sense of originality), ultimately hip-hop elevates not only authenticity but also point of view—for example, coming of age, which is really a matter of self-awareness coupled with maturity. The hip-hop approach also is an elevation of analysis, which necessarily implies inspection and introspection. We can explore all of these elements in greater depth at another time. In summation, I merely wanted to lay out some of the concerns and aspects of the two dominant forms of discourse in our communities today: the hip-hop aesthetic and the jazz aesthetic.

That's the self-defining aspect of our being, a being that exists within the social context of the larger capitalist environment. Ultimately, capitalism is the dominant force overall, even though there may be pockets of resistance and alternatives. Back in the day, the popular saying was, "People make the world go round." That was contrasted with the other saying: "Ain't a damn thing funny, it's all about money."

The question confronting us is whether our activities will be people-centered or finance-centered—i.e., relationships or ownership. I don't see these two elements as necessarily at odds, nor do I think it has to be exclusively one or the other. I'm not for the either/or dichotomy. I believe in the both/and dialectic. Whether relationships or ownership should be in the forefront is not a static question or an unchangeable equation. As far as I'm concerned, it's all relative. Sometimes I do. Sometimes I don't. Sometimes it's one. Sometimes it's the other. It all depends on the time, place, conditions, and where I am in my own state of development, dreams, and desires.

Ward: And I believe the Black Arts/Black Aesthetic Movement illuminated options for collectivity and individuality that have to do with the totality of living. We need to use the options that were most beneficial in our dialogues and material struggles in 2017 and beyond.

Notes

1. Thomas Jefferson, *Notes on the State of Virginia* (London: Stockdale, 1787).
2. Robert G. Parkinson, *The Common Cause: Creating Race and Nation in the American Revolution* (Chapel Hill: University of North Carolina Press, 2016).
3. Constance Rourke, *American Humor: A Study of the National Character* (New York: Harcourt, 1931).
4. Black Arts Movement: Southern Influences Conference, Dillard University, New Orleans, September 9–11, 2016.
5. The Black Arts Movement and Its Influences: Fifty Years On Conference, University of California, Merced, February 28–March 2, 2014.
6. Created by Lee Falk, *Mandrake the Magician* was a newspaper comic strip launched in 1934. The titular character had an African friend and sidekick, Lothar.
7. Stephen E. Henderson, *Understanding the New Black Poetry: Black Speech and Black Music as Poetic References* (New York: Morrow, 1973).
8. E. Franklin Frazier, *Black Bourgeoisie* (New York: Free Press, 1957).
9. Jerry W. Ward Jr., "Abrasion: Aesthetic Challenges in African American Poetry," *Journal of Ethnic American Literature* 5 (2015): 1–16.
10. Larry Neal, *Visions of a Liberated Future: Black Arts Movement Writings* (New York: Basic Books, 1989).
11. Carolyn Rodgers, "Black Poetry: Where It's At," *Negro Digest* 18 (September 1969): 7–16; Carolyn Rodgers, "Feelings Are Sense," *Black World* 19 (June 1970): 5–11; Carolyn Rodgers, "Break Forth in Deed," *Black World* 19 (September 1970): 13–22; Carolyn Rodgers, "Uh Nat'chal Thang—The Whole Truth," *Black World* 20 (September 1971): 6–17.
12. Beyoncé Knowles, *Lemonade* (New York: Parkwood Entertainment and Columbia Records, 2016). The full visual album premiered on HBO on April 23, 2016.
13. Candice Marie Benbow, "Lemonade Syllabus," May 6, 2016, https://issuu.com/candicebenbow/docs/lemonade_syllabus_2016.
14. Michelle Ruiz, "Beyoncé's *Lemonade* Has Now Inspired an Awesome College Class," *Vogue*, September 29, 2016, https://www.vogue.com/article/beyonce-lemonade-texas-college-course.
15. Kalamu ya Salaam, *The Magic of Juju: An Appreciation of the Black Arts Movement* (Chicago: Third World Press, 2016).
16. John Coltrane, *A Love Supreme* (Englewood Cliffs, NJ: Van Gelder Studio, 1964).
17. John Coltrane, "My Favorite Things," on *My Favorite Things* (New York: Atlantic Records, 1961). Based on Oscar Hammerstein II and Richard Rogers, "My Favorite Things," from *The Sound of Music* (New York: Columbia Broadway Masterworks, 1959).

A Scholar Born to Write Poetry: Interview with Jerry W. Ward Jr.

John Zheng / 2019

From *Mississippi Quarterly: The Journal of Southern Cultures* 73.2 (2020): 247–65. Published by Johns Hopkins University Press. Reprinted by permission of John Zheng.

John Zheng: When did you begin writing poetry?
Jerry W. Ward Jr.: In 1958.
JZ: What prompted your attempts to write poems at the age of fifteen?
JWW: In my high school English classes we had to memorize and recite such poems as "The Creation" and "Lift Every Voice and Sing" by James Weldon Johnson, "The Chambered Nautilus" by Oliver Wendell Holmes, and "Thanatopsis" by William Cullen Bryant. I discovered the poems of Carl Sandburg in the tenth grade and began to write imitations of what I thought was robust and expressive in his verse. I read a few poems by Sterling A. Brown and T. S. Eliot in an anthology I borrowed from one of my great-aunts, and I sampled work by Paul Laurence Dunbar. I thought it was easier to write poetry than to write a prose essay, and I'm sure I wrote dozens of horrible poems. I was prompted to write poems by my fascination with words and my yearning to develop my skills in the arena of art.

JZ: Who are your favorite poets? How did they influence your poetry writing?

JWW: For me, the words *favorite* and *influence* are jail cells when we talk about literature and the act of writing. They incarcerate writers. I do not have favorite poets. I have a limited number of favorite poems, including Matthew Arnold's "Dover Beach" and Howard Nemerov's "Political Reflections" (which I habitually misname "The Sparrow in the Zoo"). I have read many poets ancient and modern, and from all of them I have gained insights about meter, imagery, diction, form, and ways of using words to communicate ideas differently. Yes, Dante, Langston Hughes, Shakespeare, Amiri

Baraka, Walt Whitman, Robert Hayden, Emily Dickinson, Federico García Lorca, Margaret Walker, T. S. Eliot, Lance Jeffers, Bob Kaufman, Gwendolyn Brooks, and dozens of other poets have been my mentors. But music—blues and jazz—have taught me essential lessons about sound and historical consciousness of being in the world. Music has had a major role in shaping my frequent use of allusions to articulate motions of history, to give voice to the chaos, entanglement, and contradictions of being human. Indeed, I am indebted to poets who may be cleverer and more gifted than I am, but I do not suffer the anxiety of influence from recognizing that fact.

JZ: I like your metaphor of *favorite* and *influence* as jail cells. You have lived in Mississippi and New Orleans. Could you use examples from *Fractal Song* to illustrate how music helped you give attention to the sound of your poetry and shape your use of allusions?

JWW: Although it is common to associate the blues with Mississippi and jazz with New Orleans, I cultivated a sense of musical aesthetics from both traditions quite early in life. Perhaps I inherited a fondness for jazz from my mother; my father, an excellent dancer, a man very conversant with Black musical traditions, listened to music infrequently. He had little impact on my musical tastes. Music definitely has a strong impact on how I remember things. I associate the singing of civil rights activists with many of the soul-shattering events of the long civil rights movement. I did not, however, fully incorporate specific references to music in my poetry until I wrote "Jazz to Jackson to John" in 1981. It is my signature poem, a touchstone for subsequent experiments with poetry and music.

That poem in *Fractal Song* illuminates my attention to sound and the use of allusions to provoke and challenge the memories and cultural literacy of those who read my poems. When I perform that poem, I use vocal techniques from spirituals, blues, and jazz. In "movement one: genesis" I associate an unidentified occasion with "sheets of sound wrinkled / with riffs and scats," with the blues flying out into jazz. I refer to sounds one might have heard in Jackson, Mississippi, on Farish Street—the voice of Billie Holiday, the playing of Monk and Parker; here also are fragments of album titles, song titles, and lyrics—"these foolish things," "angel eyes," and "around midnight." Near the end of this movement are the crucial lines "who dug whether race records were / lamentations or lynchings: jazz."

The form and content of "movement two: blues people in the corn" draws attention to African American spiritual codes—"steal away," the enslaved stealing away; to the Middle Passage—"coffers packed / with golden music and time" in "sardine ships" (tightly packed human beings as cargo); the adaptation of Christianity to the contours of Black needs and Miles Davis running "down the voodoo avenue" to bring what is quintessentially West African to the United States. The first stanza of the movement has a short catalog of musicians and compositions which is prefaced by the line "is the foundation with my brothers" (a slantwise allusion to a book by Walter Rodney).

"Movement three: and this, John, is our new day" instructs John Reese to never forget the blues, the jazz, the spirituals, and the repeated phrase "hot peanuts, hot peanuts" is appropriated from Dizzy Gillespie. "Jazz to Jackson to John" is the best gumbo I ever cooked.

A very different example of how I write in jazz is "REPARATIONS: a process poem" in *Fractal Song*, which is more a direction score to be performed than a poem to be read in solitude. Some readers will detect an allusion to the US Constitution in "⅗ person" and to Frederick Douglass's Fourth of July Oration in

(for us/them
for them July 4th
for us 4th of July)

in the use of variant dating for marking historical discord. Once when I performed this poem with two jazz musicians, I forgot that I can't sing and managed to transform the score into a radical song.

The long poem "Pregnant Memories of Your Live-in Boyfriend and Your Baby's Baby-Daddy: Notes on an Everyday Affair" borrows its structure and allusions from the gospel song "Precious Memories." And "4 & 5 Remix for 3 & 8/Bday Jazz for Dave/Three Hours in 1967" is a performance poem, very dependent on the sounds/traces of jazz in my head. The sacred and the secular clash and complement by way of Aretha Franklin, Wayne Shorter, Miles Davis, Eddie "Lockjaw" Davis, Ed Blackwell, Eric Dolphy, and Tony Williams. A treat for lovers of jazz.

JZ: What was the genesis of "REPARATIONS: a process poem"?

JWW: The genesis existed in my penchant for experimenting with language and my interest in how speech acts either fail or succeed. The beginnings include thinking about reparations in the context of US history and all the pros and cons about reparations that are often passionately argued; doubting that any compensation for still enduring psychological injuries produced by slavery is ever adequate; exploring ways of distributing words and parts of words in order to make a design which invites curiosity, a design as a puzzle; reading the poetry of Harryette Mullen and examining her attention in *The Cracks between What We Are and What We Are Supposed to Be* to "words hidden within other words"[1] and Hank Lazar's writing poems in circular shapes; and capturing readers in a net of implications, thereby forcing or encouraging them to think about reparations from unusual angles. I wrote the poem before Ta-Nehisi Coates's essay on reparations made the word famous.

JZ: What were your views about cultural discourse on reparations?

JWW: I am convinced that cultural discourse on reparations is a necessary exercise in remembering how impossible it is to have compensation for the psychological wounds African Americans suffered from the institution of slavery in the United States. The wounds have never healed. They are opened again and again by the permanence of what Charles Mills has named "the racial contract," and we shall never have a genuine eradication of racism in American society. We shall not have any relief from suffering that is systemic. Two decades ago I wrote a poem entitled "I Did Not Ask to Be a Palestinian," which ends

> Once my tongue confessed
> that dispossession is rancid wine in an open wound.
>
> They asked:
> *Why not request reparations?*
>
> And I replied:
> *How can I,*
> *blessed by Allah,*
> *ask for money*
> *kissed by Yahweh?*
>
> But they still don't understand.
> I did not ask to become Palestinian.

Those lines reflect my ultimate views on reparations.

JZ: What was your intention to use symbols, slashes, and parentheses in the poem? I feel you wanted to emphasize words inside words, like *rap* in *re(rap)ation* and *rat* in *repair/rat/ions*.

JWW: Your hunch is correct. I did want to highlight words inside of words, to reverse to some degree what James Joyce did in smashing words together in *Finnegan's Wake*. The symbols, arrows pointing up and down, direct us to possible connections or the process of joining fragments or single alphabets to other fragments. The slashes and parentheses have a dual function: (1) they divide words into segments, and (2) indicate where and how one should pause in reading aloud.

The parentheses are private notes for how I want to manage starts and stops and pauses in a live performance. "REPARATIONS" commands more attention when it is heard than when it is read in silence. It is akin to spoken-word poetry, but by reason of its design in print, it is not a spoken-word poem. Let us be clear about that.

JZ: Are there any distinctions between performance and spoken-word poetry?

JWW: I think there are distinctions which are quite difficult to describe because *performance* is a slippery word. Spoken-word poetry maximizes oral qualities and a poet's ability to perform out of her or his memory without a written text. To be sure, some spoken-word poets do write texts, but one can only get the full impact of what they attempt to do from listening to their oral performances. All poets perform in greater and lesser degrees during live readings. I find many gifted poets read poorly—that is to say, they expend little energy in exposing the implicit drama that may exist in the words of a text. When I perform my own poems or poems by others, I try to give voice to emotion or to what may be musical in the structure of a poem. Indeed, I have specific ideas about how my poems should sound, and the sound I have in mind often emerges as I write a poem. The matter of distinctions between performance and spoken-word poetry is vexed; it is doubtful that consensus about distinctions is possible.

JZ: What was the creative process that led to the poem?

JWW: The process involved thinking about reparations for many days and deciding that I didn't want to write a more-or-less traditional poem about the topic. Too much clutter in that. After settling on the Fourth of July rather than Thanksgiving or Christmas as the proper holiday to associate with reparations, I sketched the basic design on paper and then adjusted and readjusted the design as I typed on my computer, using the Microsoft Word symbol feature for special signs. Ultimately, the process was a matter of selecting among dozens of associations.

JZ: Can you talk about the language and form of this poem?

JWW: Yes, very briefly. Overmuch talk would give the impression that readers can negotiate the poem with minimal effort. As far as form goes, the poem is divided into eight stanzas or meaning clusters. The primary references in the language have to do with repair, rats, ions, rape, the measuring of things as in economics and commerce; a reader has also to have commerce with the letters *C* and *S* and to account for what occurs when those single letters are pronounced. These hints and clues are sufficient to help readers do the work that can be done.

JZ: What led you to publish *Fractal Song*?

JWW: For many years, I alarmed poets and writers by announcing that I had little interest in publishing a book of poems. I vowed not to publish a book. I was content with having my poems published in magazines and anthologies. There are so many books of poetry in the world. The world is saturated with them. Most of them are read once and then put on a shelf to gather cobwebs. My friend Hank Lazar figuratively twisted my arm in 2014, insisting that I collect some of my poems. He must have pushed the right button because I broke my vow, compiled *Fractal Song*, and sent it to him. He liked the book but wasn't in a position to get it published by the University of Alabama Press. He sent a copy of the typescript to Dave Brinks, who in turn sent it to Joseph Phillips, the publisher of Black Widow Press. Phillips offered me a good contract, and the book was in print by mid-2016. The postscript by Kalamu ya Salaam is dated July 2015; it first appeared in what I call the outlaw edition of *Fractal Song*, the edition published by the Project on the History of Black Writing as a surprise gift for my seventy-second birthday. It is fair to say the urging of friends led to the publication of the book. I do not dismiss the possibility of my publishing a larger book of poems from 1970 to 2019, but I assure you I feel no urgency to undertake that chore.

JZ: As a poet, how did you play with imagination in *Fractal Song*?

JWW: The play with imagination pertains most to my dividing the book into STARTS, MIDDLES, ENDS and using the refrain "Complete incompletes/Imperatives conspire" to suggest how one might read *Fractal Song*.

JZ: That's interesting. Is your poetic imagination shaped by the landscape, cultures, and history of Mississippi?

JWW: Yes, it is partially shaped by Mississippi's geography, cultures, and history, but it is more accurate to say that my terms of engagement with the world continue to shape my poetic sensibility and imagination. In *Fractal Song*, the poems "Black Boy," "Mississippi John," "Don't Be Fourteen (in Mississippi)," "Jazz to Jackson to John," "Kwansaba 61907," "A Peapicking Prayer (1979)," and its companion, "Transition," suggest the impact Mississippi has had upon my poems and other writing.

To be more specific about Mississippi and my imagination, I quote from the first paragraph and the final paragraph of the essay I wrote for *Coming Home to Mississippi*:

> I am an outsider/insider Mississippian, the subject of other people's observations and the object of my reflections. Born in Washington, D.C., in 1943, I was repatriated in the late fall of 1949 to Moss Point, my father's hometown. My six-year-old self changed rapidly from being happy, carefree, and urban to being town-trapped, sullen, and confused. I could not understand why having an ice cream cone in the local drugstore was forbidden. So, this was Mississippi. A land of do-not-say-that and do-not-do-this. I was too young to sense the invisible segregation of the nation's capital and unprepared for the racism of the South and the permanent scar it would leave in my sensibility. [. . .]
>
> Like the tree, my life has been a process. The tree does not control changes in climate; it endures them even as it is changed by them, and so too have I been changed by the historical events that have reshaped Mississippi from 1949 to 2012. The concentric circles of my life are forever attached to Moss Point and Tougaloo College and the profound affinity I feel with the life and works of Richard Wright [. . .]. And there is also the rootedness in the soil of Mississippi. In my life, long teaching career, and writings, I have sought and still seek to fulfill a moral obligation: facing naked truths squarely and articulating them for a future.[2]

As a citizen, writer, and critical thinker, I have an existential love/hate relationship with the state of Mississippi, but what is more important in my life are the relationships I have with people from many lands and cultures, the relationships which engender profound ideas and the necessity of endlessly struggling with the limits and problems of the human condition, with humanity. You have written poignantly of that struggling in your recent collection of poems, *Enforced Rustication in the Chinese Cultural Revolution*.[3]

JZ: I agree with you about the existential love/hate relationship with a place and that what's more important are the relationships with people and cultures. When I refresh my memory of rustication, images of peasants and their dialect are still fresh, like the newly plowed fields. In your poems about Mississippi mentioned previously, could you be more specific about "A Peapicking Prayer (1979)"? Readers would be curious about the use of *Mississippi* as a verb and the use of metonymies; they might also be case-sensitive to the place-names. Also, how to paraphrase "made him New York / in German to California"?

JWW: Let us start with the case-sensitive and move forward to other features. I'll follow some modes of explaining used by C. Liegh McInnis and Kalamu ya Salaam, two poet-critics whom I hold in high esteem. Written for my friend Ahmos Zu-Bolton (born October 21, 1948; died March 8, 2005) before his death, the poem is an ironic mapping of the trajectory of his life and career as a poet and publisher. There is no discernible logic in how I used upper- and lowercase in the naming of towns, cities, and states. I was just playing with the possibility that place-names are rather special (uppercase) and from time to time rather ordinary (lowercase). Certainly the use of *mississippied* as a verb denies the state of Mississippi what I'd call the "normal" status of New York, California, and Louisiana. The metonymic uses of place-names signify on our regard for geography, the qualities of place which may push back against easy, conventional assumptions we often make about place without making any thorough examination of the histories of places. I sought to maximize instability and eclectic applications of place-names. One paraphrase of "made him New York / in German to California" would be Ahmos's experiences in the North made him a bit foreign (German) as he moved from the North to the West. It is a very private joke I had with Ahmos about how his trajectory was akin to Ishmael Reed's move from New York to California. The phrasing catches a reader in a conundrum that is open to multiple interpretations. I wrote "Transition" after Ahmos's death as my meditation on a friend's dying and what he accomplished in his life; I formulated the accomplishments in the italicized stanzas two and three.

JZ: Does the crystal stair image in "A Peapicking Prayer (1979)" echo what Langston Hughes suggested in "Mother to Son"?

JWW: It does.

JZ: Do your poems reveal an examination of the mind or the society?

JWW: In discussions of poetry or writing in general, we must be cautious about using such definite phrases as *the mind* and *the society*. *Mind* refers to an array of cognitive faculties—perception, imagination, judgment, recognition, ways of thinking. *Mind* governs behaviors and actions. *Society* designates groups of individuals who build habitats and institutions, political bodies, cultures; the groups live in harmony or discord with one another. All of my poems deal with society and the mind in varying degrees.

"Footnote 666" is overtly political, mixing words that belong to the categories of sacred and the profane to suggest that in contemporary American society, racial profiling is an operative feature of our nation's decidedly race-marked social contract. Agents of the law ensure that *injustice is all*. That is one reason people in the United States who advocate social justice must constantly identify imperfections in the rule of law. The poem invites readers to examine a small portion of how our society works.

The two erotic poems in *Fractal Song*, "Opening Night" and "Serious," deal with states of mind, desire, and lust as they manifest themselves in talk and consensual copulation. There's a sliver of lust and masculine social habits also in "Mississippi John: Southern Comfort Toast." I don't write poems with any conscious aim of making examinations. If you discover examinations, you are finding what emerges from my subconscious intentions.

JZ: What spurs your cultural sensibility in your poetry?

JWW: John, I'll give you a bullet list of the spurs that come to mind:

- my mixed ancestry—African, Asian (by way of Indigenous people in North America), European
- my heritage as an African American male
- my American citizenship
- my broad reading across disciplines and belief that disciplines are necessary inconveniences; we do not experience life in compartments
- my sense of history as an ongoing process and of history as an always incomplete record of process
- world affairs
- the information, misinformation, and disinformation that assaults me each day
- my interest in the blues and jazz
- my conversations with relatives, friends, scholars, and fellow writers
- my interest in aesthetics (as perception rather than philosophy of art) and visual art (painting and photography, film)

JZ: My question after reading your poem "To Those Who Grieve the Death of a Poet" is: What do you think the role a poet should be?

JWW: That poem warns how irrational it is to have a grand expectation of poets and poetry, to expect them to accomplish much beyond sharpening awareness of our multiple everyday experiences. I am not omniscient enough to say what the role of a poet—or any artist, for that matter—should be. Any role a poet has is to be negotiated within the bounds of the culture or society to which the poet has an allegiance. It is possible for a poet to participate, as does the magnificent Nigerian poet Niyi Osundare, in several cultures, but I doubt Osundare confuses the role he has chosen to play in his native land with the role he plays as a professor at the University of New Orleans. You are yourself an accomplished poet who has a scholarly interest in haiku, so I think you understand my point of view about the matter of role.

JZ: "Son to Father, with Love/Graveside Prayer" is a poignant poem about a fourteen-year-old son who lost his father. It threads through the absence of paternal love. Could you talk about how you choose to tell the truth through the description of existence?

JWW: I choose to tell not *the* truth but merely *a* truth, because truth is relative, not absolute. What we think is a truth in the morning may be less than a truth in the afternoon. When I describe existence in terms of its truth, I am bound by my own historicity, my being-in-the-present. I do take the risk of imaging truth from time past or time future, but that risk is colored by the uncertainty principle associated with a kind of physics. My description of my father sixty-three years ago is autobiographical, an admission of how I think traits are transmitted from a father to a son.

JZ: The poem also suggests the cultural influence of a father or the "like father, like son" traces through the repetition of "And I don't know why I am as like you as I am." What are the "fading traces" you cherish in life?

JWW: The fading traces I yet cherish are my father's remarkable intelligence, his impatience with people who were slow to grasp things, his love of chemistry and his being fluent in Latin, his exceptionally beautiful handwriting, his confidence in himself, his steadfast refusal to be a cowardly Black man in a rigidly segregated American social scheme.

JZ: "Don't Be Fourteen (in Mississippi)" refers to the murder of Emmett Till, but on a large scale, it emphasizes the hard times Black males face in the South. When did you write the poem, and how did you choose the tone to reveal the poignant feeling?

JWW: Some of the thinking which informs the poem was born sixty-four years ago when I first saw the iconic photograph of Till's bloated, brutalized face in *Jet* magazine. As I matured, the subject of lynching from the end of the Civil War to the present in the United States became more thematic in my writing, even when it was disguised and not overtly expressed. I wrote some shorter versions of "Don't Be Fourteen (in Mississippi)" in the 1970s and 1980s, but the version you are reading was written in 1994. Its current shape was much influenced by reading the article "48-Year Sentence May Have Saved 14-Year-Old Felon Bubba May,"[4] I juxtaposed the obvious reference to Till in lines 1–16 with an abbreviated comment on the incarceration of Robert Earl "Bubba" May in lines 17–24. The asymmetry of lynching and incarceration whet my appetite to tell about the South. Thus, the imperatives of the speaker in the poem are cold. Images must carry the burden of tone or emotion. The despair of any ultimate reconciliation and the permanence of enmity suggest the potential for acts of violence. In a few cases, silence is more powerful than protest.

JZ: "Don't Be Fourteen (in Mississippi)" is also one of your poems that present social critique. How did you explore identity around the subject?

JWW: I'd argue that exploration of identity is less important in "Don't Be Fourteen (in Mississippi)" than presentation of a problematic attitude. Color-coded stereotypes abound in southern practices of daily life, in what we generalize about the so-called southern imagination, which is nothing more than a historically angled American imagination. My effort to depict the seldom examined power of silence is of greater importance than generalizations regarding identity.

JZ: How did the Mississippi Delta provide the original impetus for your poetry?

JWW: Given the location of Till's murder, I could not avoid thinking about plantation economies and poverty, morbidity, and the social and cultural mores of the Mississippi Delta which systemically demeaned the dignity of Black folk. I could not ignore the spaces of struggles for civil and human rights among those the historian John Dittmer identified as local people as well as the production of the blues among characters in the fictions of William Faulkner and Richard Wright, the lives of blues people. Nevertheless, the original impetus for my poetry is the Mississippi Gulf Coast, where I grew up.

JZ: Could you be more specific about growing up on the Mississippi Gulf Coast and your connection with the place through poetry?

JWW: Poems about place written by Sterling D. Plumpp (Clinton) and C. Liegh McInnis (Clarksdale) cast light on geographical and cultural differences between the Delta region and the Gulf Coast region where Natasha Trethewey (Gulfport) and I (Moss Point) grew up. I never saw a cotton plant until I was in my late teens.

At first, I hated my father's hometown, its animal life (hogs, chickens, cattle), its mosquitoes and sand bugs, and people who chewed tobacco and talked strangely. Gradually I began to accept what I didn't have a name for—*exile*. The longer I associated with my father's aunts and uncles and cousins and his childhood friends, the more I sensed that we were people of some importance, Black middle-class importance, a family who got more than ordinary respect in the community. My father had a degree in pharmacy. We were not sharecroppers. I was better and smarter than many of my playmates on Barnett Street. I was Roman Catholic in a largely Protestant family, and upward mobility secured my sense of being somebody. I got teased a lot for not being athletic. To hide my shame, I retreated into the world of books, where my mind could do what my awkward body couldn't. And I got respect from my peers for being smart, for being very good in mathematics and science.

The air of Moss Point was filled with smells from the paper mill (acid) and the veneer mill (cheesy); we did not have the smell of burning crosses, and certainly not the stench of chitterlings in our house. The sounds of L&N trains were so accurate one could tell time by them. Our house sat on two acres of land. I took it for granted that people should have large lawns and space for growing corn, butter beans, okra, string beans, tomatoes, figs, cabbage, sand pears, mulberries, pecans, and persimmons. We always had fresh fish on Fridays and freshly caught shrimp and crabs for gumbo. My parents were both excellent cooks, and I was raised on Creole cuisine—my mother was from Louisiana—rather than a typical Mississippi diet of greens, fatback, buttermilk, and cornbread. Most of the radio stations we listened to were in New Orleans, and trips with my parents to visit relatives in the Crescent City were a special treat, as were less frequent trips to Convent, Louisiana (St. James Parish).

The Mississippi Gulf Coast did have an impact on my poetry, on my regard for speech. The drawl of the South did not appeal to me. I kept, as much as I could, my vowels, consonants, and distinct word endings. I was teased for sounding "white." I indulged my passion for reading because I wanted to be as intelligent as my father and as wise as my mother, who insisted that *she* was not Negro but Creole. And made sure I would not become food for the appetites of white folk. The nightmare I had in 1955 about the lynching of Emmett Till assured me she did not insist too much.

We did not have as much money as some of our relatives. We were working class, poor in pocket but rich in aspiration, sense of self-worth, dignity. I truly did not know I was poor until I enrolled at Tougaloo College in 1960. In my childhood imagination, I was an aristocrat exiled in Mississippi. I resented the ethics of living Jim Crow, the evil, absurd low expectations most non-Black Mississippians had for Black Mississippians. I used my intellectual gifts to become the person and writer I am, a person for whom liking or hating Mississippi is a relatively free choice. All of that recurs in my poetry.

JZ: Do you think writing poetry will improve and expand literary taste?

JWW: Yes, writing poetry probably improves and expands the literary tastes of individual writers. Nevertheless, the conversations I have with people who *read* but do not *write* poetry lead me to suspect their tastes are informed by forces or needs which are not necessarily literary. The French sociologist Pierre Bourdieu made a major contribution to thinking about taste in *Distinction: A Social Critique of the Judgment of Taste* (1986). Although Stephen E. Henderson's objective in *Understanding the New Black Poetry* (1973) was not an examination of taste, his theoretical points regarding saturation are germane to the subject.

JZ: Is there a favorite poet you read more for aesthetic pleasure?

JWW: There are a number of poets whose works give me two related forms of aesthetic pleasure. First, when I consider the aesthetic as a matter of sensual or emotional pleasure or satisfaction, I am focusing most on how words trigger associations. For example, the opening lines of Lenard D. Moore's poem "Mesmerized"—"She struts riveting beats / down sidewalk slopes"—conjure a pleasant image of a woman walking seductively.[5] But when I read the opening lines of Moore's poem "Thursday Night":

> Needle on vinyl,
> miles in the groove,
> & ghosts hover
> over the warped wooden shelf.

It is the pleasure of recognizing how the use of technology in reproducing sound that interests me.[6] That's a different use of aesthetic.

I think I return most frequently to poems by Lance Jeffers to experience the two forms of aesthetic pleasure.

JZ: Any new poems written recently? Can you share some with us?

JWW: Certainly. These are a few recent ones—

THE POEM UNDONE
(*for Julia Wright*)

To be addressed at a beach
she thought most square.
To be called to a window to see
what ought to be heard.
What might sting like a mosquito
infecting one with knowledge.
She thought of Yeats, of Leda, of time,

the coming of a terrifying swan.
Did he say the sea's calm, tamed by moonbeams,
when sound visualized is turbulent?
Is music's allegory of war
no more than conceits of violence
gathering to clash in the death of light?
How violated can a body be?
What's put in pain
by a mosquito's ignorant gift,
by its eternal tweet of sadness,
by retarded misery's ebb and flow
and slow torture of climate changing?
Such faith, such hope, such charity
did Antigone, imitating Isis, sprinkle on a corpse.
Honi soit qui mal y pense
and *mea culpa* invades the heart.
Tragedy has gone with the breeze
somewhere to fall apart in another country,
to alarm with lack of joy, love, light,
certitude, peace impossible for bloody jewels to restore.
She thought he murmured a snatch of fatal allegory:
". . . let us be true/to one another!"
She thought she was a dream, a dissonance
arising from a mosquito's donation.
She thought of her mind and his
sinking in the quicksand of a beach
as poetic armies clashed that night.

THE LAST EPIPHANY
"They had guaranteed our happiness forever.
. . .
And in a way such promises may come true
In spite of all our evil day and ways."
—Robert Penn Warren, "If Snakes Were Blue"

Guarantees cut from imperial cloth
and tailored with hope-violent threads
just ain't worth much. Much to our sorrow

we wore starch-bloody shirts for centuries,
aliens lusting for happiness in a stolen land
until prophetic tatters became real
and fit only for a pauper's funeral.

Such is the way your new world gives birth
to funky cognition and devil dust
forecast in confession,
in visitations from fetid spirits,
in agony of butts soaking in swamps.

Not much to say now, not much
as our blind eyes gawk and lament
that promises of vicious irony did come true.

ALAS, POOR ERNEST

He reformed,
so said his last wife,
Milton's Paradise,
hammered into Eliot's tradition
his rich anxiety, his guilt
regarding the whiteness of supremacy.

So enlightened, in 1961,
or perhaps aggrieved
by insatiable arrogance,
he penetrated his mouth
with a shotgun,
pulled the trigger.

TRANSPARENT PERFECTION/T AND Z PRESIDENTS
(an unfound poem)

You did terrific, boy, terrific.
(*Yes, I used your skills*).

You exceeded presidential regress.
(*Yes, I used your knowledge*).
You want to drain your swamp.
(*Yes, I am glad you failed to fill it in*).

Don't trust nasty woman Merkel, boy, or nasty man Macron;
buy Javelins from us. And mission possible playlists.
(*Yes, I am willing perhaps, willing perhaps to sign, seal, and signify*).

And do me a favor, boy. Instigate Biden and son.
I really mean post-vegetate the Bullstrike
and bitch-brewed aux-news. And unholy ghosts. They re-danger me. Do me
    a favor.
(*Yes, you think me an incompetent performer?*)

I'll send Rudy to sniff you out, boy, and send no aid
if you don't dark-damn the witches well.
(*Yes, did you think I have no morals, no integrity? Do you think?*)

I have glad water for your stay at Tower T, boy.
(*Yes, I'll take your plane which is better than mine
because I have a better mind*).

This has been perfect for 7/25/19, boy.
(*Yes, the perfect incredibility of a you-trained-me dog*).

IMITATION OF DEATH

Swear. Take the knee
on rural prayer rugs
and bets that deliverance
will not come as genteel rain
from a head that wears
violent-colored yarn for hair
or fingers decked out
with the not-beauty
of paste-on black/yellow/red claws

or hands calculating
efficiency and actuality's last resort
with guns, drones, dread drums,
bombs bursting in acid air,
mushrooms that blind and burn
earth with ashes and embers.
Beware what you curse.
Beware when your ancient eye
does see bodies and blood
in Jesuit joints of immortality.

Notes

1. Harryette Mullen, *The Cracks between What We Are and What We Are Supposed to Be* (Tuscaloosa: University of Alabama Press, 2012), 7.

2. "Jerry W. Ward Jr.," in *Coming Home to Mississippi*, edited by Charline McCord and Judy Tucker (Jackson: University Press of Mississippi, 2013), 215, 219.

3. Jianqing Zheng, *Enforced Rustication in the Chinese Cultural Revolution* (Huntsville: Texas Review Press, 2019).

4. *Jackson Clarion-Ledger*, April 10, 1994.

5. Lenard D. Moore, "Mesmerized," in *The Geography of Jazz* (Eugene, OR: Mountains and Rivers Press, 2018), 23.

6. Lenard D. Moore, "Thursday Night," in *Geography of Jazz*, 22.

Cultural Exchanges: An Interview with Jerry W. Ward Jr.

Tian Zhang / 2021

From *Journal of Ethnic American Literature* 11 (2021): 111–20. Reprinted by permission of *Journal of Ethnic American Literature* and Tian Zhang.

Tian Zhang: Please allow me to start our conversation with your first visit to China. Can you tell us what brought you here?

Jerry W. Ward Jr.: I first visited China in December 2009. Jianqing Zheng, who was then on a Fulbright grant at Central China Normal University, invited me to participate in a conference. I am very grateful for his doing so because his invitation initiated my yearly visits to China from 2009 to 2016. Zheng opened a new chapter in my life. My participation in the CCNU conference and meeting Chinese colleagues and students who extended to me such hospitality I had not previously experienced persuaded me to volunteer to return in 2010. Despite the growing animosity between China and the USA, I will continue efforts to build cultural bridges.

Zhang: I am extremely touched by your words, which have reminded me of the happy days that you stayed with us at CCNU. I am also appreciative of what you did in building the cultural bridges. As for your visits, how many times have you been to China? Have you experienced any culture shock?

Ward: I visited China seven times between 2009 and 2016. During these visits, no culture shock was involved. I did, however, experience many instances of cultural surprise. For example, the differences between Chinese academic practices and American academic cultures did surprise me. I am not sure I will ever understand the assumptions that undergird the Chinese grading system. I was told several times that the grades I assigned were too high. The graduate students at CCNU were exceptionally polite and reluctant to disagree with my opinions. They took copious notes and remained silent. That was surprising. I was accustomed to having civil disagreements with undergraduate and graduate students because American students tend to be more aggressive. In several of my special classes, I made it mandatory for students to express their ideas. My pedagogy may have produced culture shock for many of the students. We can't make unwarranted generalizations about students because I did notice slight differences among students in Wuhan, Enshi, Nanjing, Chengdu, and Beijing. A quite different matter that surprised me was the flow of traffic in Wuhan. I told a few of my American friends that to cross the street, one had to know how to dance with death. I quickly learned how to dance with traffic.

Zhang: Wow, seven times. You've almost been to China once a year between 2009 and 2016. I am glad to know you are quite accustomed to Chinese culture. Now the traffic rules have been amended, and the traffic has been changed tremendously. If you come to Wuhan again, you will have a refreshed idea. What was your first impression of China? Was there any change in your impression since you visited this country several times?

Ward: It is difficult to talk about a single first impression. One has multiple impressions that are predicated on what one has read about a country or seen in films or bits of information from the Internet. My first impressions were focused on the size of China, the density of the population, and the variety of old and new architecture. China is the third-largest country in the world; its land area (3.7 million square miles) reminded me that I was visiting a former empire peopled by many ethnicities. It is larger than the United States. When I traveled by train from Wuhan to other cities, I was quite taken with size and scenery. I once thought that New York was very large, but I was overwhelmed by the population density both of Wuhan and Beijing, especially Beijing. How do so many people live in proximity to one another? During my first visit (2009), I became very fond of the Yellow Crane Tower. That edifice is more aesthetically pleasing than the hundreds of tall apartment buildings that symbolize the rapid modernization and urbanization of China since 1949.

Yes, my impressions changed greatly during my subsequent visits because I had opportunities to see what exists beyond Wuhan and to learn a great deal about the strength, ingenuity, and determination of Chinese people, whether they are Han or not Han. The Great Wall, the fabulous Qin Dynasty terra cotta warriors in Xi'an, the Forbidden City, the Mausoleum of Sun Yat-sen, and other monuments are etched in my memory. The excellence of the tea, cuisine, and hospitality reminds me of the antiquity of Chinese civilization and why devoted preservation of much from the past is crucial for a nation's future. Finally, I think Ai Qing's poem "Dayanhe—My Wet-Nurse" is a very fine articulation of the spirit of modern China.

Zhang: Do you have any unforgettable experience you would like to share about your stay in China?

Ward: My visit to the Memorial Hall of the Victims in Nanjing Massacre by Japanese in the Jiangdongmen section of Nanjing was unforgettable and devastating. I was moved to tears. I felt a very strong, very spiritual relationship with the victims. I am still haunted by it. Suffering is universal. On May 31, 2021, we will be remembering the massacre of African Americans in Tulsa, Oklahoma, in 1921. From time to time, what happened in Nanjing forces me to meditate on the most brutal aspects of the human condition.

Zhang: So did I when I went there with my family. Can you tell a bit more about your visiting professorship and scholarships in China? Anything exciting to know?

Ward: It *is* exciting to know that CCNU gave me two very high honors. On October 30, 2014, I received a Credential of Honor for my service as Chinese Ministry of Education–sponsored Distinguished Overseas Professors Project professor from 2011 to 2014. The same day, I received a letter of appointment as Honorary Professor of Central China Normal University China, from 2015 to 2017, a reward for my academic achievements. On December 2, 2016, I received a third honor: an appointment as special professor at Hangzhou Electronic and Technology University. These honors made me humble and grateful. My book *The China Lectures: African American Literary and Cultural Issues* (2014) was my gift to the Chinese people. I concluded the introduction with these words: "Effective exchange of ideas from one culture to another depends on installing clean panes of glass in spaces where bricks once existed. Clarity must be primary. These revised lectures are not transparent, but I do hope they are accessible and clear. They are my modest gifts to people who have given me moments of happiness and enlightenment. And I am grateful to Luo Lianggong for urging me to publish them." The book was the culmination of my visiting professorship and teaching in China.

Zhang: [. . .] As a visiting professor in Wuhan, what courses did you teach there? How long did you stay in Wuhan each time you were there?

Ward: During most of my visits, I stayed at CCNU for three or four weeks. My longest stint was eight weeks. Most of my courses were lectures on topics in American and African American literatures. I did teach one formal course on American literature using a textbook written by Professor

Luo. The course I enjoyed teaching most was a seminar on research methods for graduate students. I gave special attention to students who were preparing to write dissertations. The next favorite seminar was one on four African American texts: Frederick Douglass's 1845 autobiography, W. E. B. Du Bois's *The Souls of Black Folk*, Jean Toomer's *Cane*, and Ralph Ellison's *Invisible Man*. One objective of that seminar was an effort to discover how the rhetorical successes and failures of genres enable writers and their readers (immediate or remote) to become aware of spatial and temporal locations, of complicated historicity. My visiting professorship enabled me to give lectures at Nanjing University, Zhejiang University, Taizhou University, Beijing International University, and several other institutions. And I either lectured or chaired panels for many conferences at CCNU.

Zhang: [. . .] Since you have lectured around China, what's your idea about African American studies in China?

Ward: From the generally positive response to my lectures, I concluded that there was a strong interest in African American literature at the universities where I gave talks. As you know, African American studies goes beyond analyses and assessments of works designated as literature and devotes substantial attention to a broader range of cultural categories—ideology, history, education, class, gender, race, economy, and so forth. The most thorough description of its paradigm is contained in *Introduction to Afro-American Studies: A Peoples College Primer* (1973), edited by Abdul Alkalimat. Many Chinese scholars and students I had conversations with between 2009 and 2016 were still in the first stages of becoming familiar with the breadth of African American literature. Many of the senior scholars who had studied in the USA were better informed about established and emerging Black writers. Lack of easy access to texts and evolving critical resources slowed the process for the younger scholars; even the full texts of works canonized in *The Norton Anthology of African American Literature* (1997) and *The Riverside Anthology of the African American Literary Tradition* (1998) were not easy to obtain. It was not surprising to me that progress in acquiring knowledge was slow. However strong the interest in African American literature was, the library resources were limited, and many factors limited the development of necessary curricula. After the national reform of Chinese universities that began in 2016 was completed, the opportunities for specialized study of foreign literature and culture may have improved.

In 2014, I urged my Chinese and American colleagues to establish the African American Research Network (AARN). I wanted CCNU to become the principal center for the robust study of African American literature and to have stronger connections with the Project on the History of Black Writing (University of Kansas) and a spectrum of American scholars. AARN did flourish for a brief period, and the exchanges that I and other American scholars had with our Chinese colleagues were productive. I hope the AARN can be resuscitated.

Both Chinese and American scholars might consider the implications of Zhenzhao Nie's influential writings about ethical literary criticism for studies of African American literature because ethical issues are pervasive in Black writing. Lili Wang's "Critical Reception of African American Women Writers in Mainland China" suggests to me that critical reception of African American men writers is still underdeveloped.[1] When I sampled the China Academic Journal database recently, I found zero articles on Jeffery R. Allen and Sterling D. Plumpp and only one article on Edward P. Jones and eight on John Oliver Killens. The number of articles on Richard Wright, Amiri Baraka, and James Baldwin is relatively impressive, but the work of such writers as Keenan Norris, Ernest Gaines, John Edgar Wideman, August Wilson, and Randall Kenan also merit attention.

Zhang: [. . .] What's the importance of African American literature that you think Chinese scholars and students need to know?

Ward: It is important for Chinese scholars and students to understand that like the very long evolving of Chinese literature, African American literature is an individual and collective historical process that occurs in contact and combat zones. I provided some hints in the "Tradition and Acknowledgement in Combat Zones" chapter of *The China Lectures*. I am convinced that wise use of Marxist analysis permits us to identify key elements in the process. I recommend that students and scholars read *Critical Zone: A Forum of Chinese and Western Knowledge*, vols. 1–3 (2006–8), which contains a remarkable range of argument and counterargument. I don't know if *Critical Zone* continued publication after 2008, but it is a good place to start figuring out what might be the most productive uses of Chinese scholarship in the study of African American literature.

Zhang: While teaching in Wuhan, did you ever learn about Chinese culture or philosophy?

Ward: I learned much about Chinese culture and philosophy from 2009 to 2016. It became apparent to me why Chinese people treasure pandas. Pandas seem to be the most stress-free animals on Earth. I suspect pandas, who have been around for more than eight million years, have absorbed more genuinely than have human beings the importance of yin and yang, the importance of balance. It was a treat to tour one of the giant panda sanctuaries. I only made one visit to the Forbidden City, but that visit was sufficient for me to determine, at least from a foreign perspective, what is exquisite and labor-intensive. The work ethic of Chinese people is utterly amazing, and I saw it displayed fully in the streets of Wuhan and Nanjing. I learned a similar lesson from watching textile workers manipulate looms. I was fascinated by the dramatic histories of the thirteen dynasties and the extensive range of foods. It was quite instructive to learn how the Italian Jesuit priest Matteo Ricci initiated cross-fertilization of Chinese and Western science and technology. I have a vivid memory of going to Shaolin Temple to inform myself about Buddhist rites and physical exercise. Between visits, I read many books on ancient and contemporary literature, including Gao Xingjian's *Aesthetics and Creation*, two volumes on sources of Chinese tradition, and books on Chinese political history. I learned a lot, but I still have much to learn.

Zhang: [. . .] Did you ever write any poems about Wuhan?

Ward: Yes, I wrote a few poems. Only one refers specifically to Wuhan. I will share two of them with you.

CHINA KWANSABA

Should alien light with furious love smash
against the ancient Great Wall and time
become pixels to float in frantic design
down upon the face of worded Earth,
could vision make wiser speech of physics
or parse better, for you, for us
a bolder meaning of tragic magic beauty?

WUHAN 2020 / a kwansaba
(*for my Chinese colleagues besieged by coronavirus*)

Quiet. A yellow crane ascends to sing
songs of new years old in spring,
to make normal unknowns, deep viral fears,
red dragon words turned now to stone.
What ancient poet dared write the river?

Dao, a sacred shroud, grips this city,
and love is life's only primal virtue.

The first was written in 2016; the second, last year. A longer poem, "Winter Solitude," was included in *The China Lectures* and in my poetry collection *Fractal Song*. The kwansaba, a poetic form that has strict rules, was created by the poet Eugene B. Redmond in the late 1990s. The form is demanding.

Zhang: What inspired you to write these poems?

Ward: Visual memories of my many adventures in China.

Zhang: [. . .] Can you explain why you choose this kind of form? Among many other poetic forms, which is your favorite?

Ward: I chose the kwansaba because the form is concise and difficult. It demands that a poet must be very disciplined in using the rules that define the form. [. . .] I think [my article "The Discipline of the Kwansaba"] is more widely known in China and Korea than it is in the USA.[2] Kwansabas do not limit the range of subject matter, but they limit lexical choices in much the way fidelity to classical haiku limits syllable count. Given my tendency to be rather wildly experimental, I need the discipline. The poet Charlie R. Braxton and I undertook a yearlong project of writing one kwansaba and one haiku on alternate days. That project culminated in Braxton's book *Embers among the Ashes: Poems in a Haiku Manner* (2018). Braxton was kind enough to describe the origin of his book in the afterword. He dedicated the book to me. Obviously, discipline matters.

The sonnet is one of my favorite forms, although I rarely write a sonnet. During my senior year in college, I wrote twenty-four sonnets for my creative writing class. Horrible attempts to be literary. I never destroyed them; they just disappeared.

Zhang: Are there any poetic forms invented by the Africans? What do they mean to African Americans today?

Ward: The seminal works on the poetic forms invented by African peoples are Ruth Finnegan's *Oral Literature in Africa* (1970), Isidore Okpewho's *African Oral Literature* (1992), and *The Cambridge History of African and Caribbean Literature*, vol. 1 (2004), edited by F. Abiola Irele and Simon Gikandi. Enslaved African people retained some of their vernacular poetic forms and traditions despite the horrors of Middle Passage and slave trade. It was possible to retain traces, however faint, of the forms in what Europeans called the New World.

I cannot honestly tell you what the forms mean to African Americans today because African Americans live in diverse communities and have no unified agreement about the meaning and values of literary forms. If I gave you the question, "What do poetic forms mean to Chinese peoples in 2021?," you would understand immediately why it is impossible to formulate a persuasive answer without conducting quantitative and qualitative research and writing a book about the findings.

I can tell you that since the early years of the twentieth century, some African American writers and artists have sought to reclaim African forms and identity, focusing on expressive elements of African cultures. In the United States, our poets have been adept in creating innovations derived from oral literature, from music—spirituals, seculars, blues, gospel, jazz, funk, hip-hop. There are noteworthy divisions among poets and audiences; some poets strive for prize-winning performances in print, while others devote their energies and creativity to highly acclaimed spoken-word poetry. And some poets navigate print and orality with skill and ease. There is a mountain of work to do in studying the expansive tradition of African American poetry. I believe the print forms that stand out as original in terms of structure are the kwansaba, the bop form created by Afaa Michael Weaver, and the eintou, which has rules as strict as those for kwansaba—it can only have seven lines with a total of thirty-two syllables or words.

Zhang: Did you do poetry readings in China?

Ward: I did not give formal readings at CCNU, but I did talk with many students about poetry, and occasionally I would read a couple of my poems in a class. Once at Nanjing University of Posts and Telecommunications, I had a wonderful exchange with a student. He read my signature poem, "Jazz to Jackson to John." I then performed the poem for him. He followed by reading the poem again and did an excellent job of imitating my performance.

Zhang: What a wonderful experience! Did you ever meet with any Chinese poets there? Are there any differences between poetry creation in China and that in America?

Ward: I didn't have any special meetings with Chinese poets aside from talking with some of them at various conferences.

The major differences between poetry creation in China and America would be matters of language, aesthetic choices, ideological input, the long history of poetry in China and the much shorter history of verse in America, and the contexts and venues for poetry in the two nations. In terms of themes, I think modern American and Chinese poets share similar interests.

Zhang: Thank you, Jerry.

Notes

1. Lili Wang, "Critical Reception of African American Women Writers in Mainland China," *Journal of Ethnic American Literature* 9 (2019): 62–79.
2. Jerry W. Ward, "The Discipline of the Kwansaba," *Journal of English Language and Literature* 63.1 (2017): 115–28.

Index

Ahern, Rosemary, 93
Alexander, Elizabeth, 78
Alexie, Sherman, 147
Allred, Jeff, 125
Anaya, Rudolfo, 114
Anderson, T. J., III, 145
Anthony, Susan, 115
Aubert, Alvin, 15

Bacon, Francis, 90
Baker, Ella, 134
Bakhtin, Mikhail, 84, 118
Baldwin, James, xii, 38, 54–55, 70, 83, 104, 108, 111–12, 114, 118, 144, 147, 205
Bambara, Toni Cade, 83, 115–16, 135, 139
Baraka, Amiri (LeRoi Jones), 14, 108, 112, 118, 138–40, 185, 205
Barnett, Etta Moten, 107
Bell, Bernard W., 138, 145
Benjamin, Walter, 14
Bishop, Elizabeth, 107, 148
Bloom, Harold, 55
Book of the Month Club, 56
Boyers, Robert, 110
Bradstreet, Anne, 96, 114
Brees, Drew, 98
Brinkley, Douglas, 40
Brinks, Dave, 40, 189
Brocks-Shedd, Virgia, 13
Brooks, Gwendolyn, 56, 78, 92, 107, 115, 152, 185

Brown, Sterling A., 57–58, 184
Brown, Wesley, 11
Bullins, Ed, 139–40
Burke, Kenneth, 118, 138
Butler, Octavia, 148
Butler, Robert, ix, xix, 61, 85–86, 123

Catlett, Elizabeth, 107
Cayette, McNeal (Chakula cha Jua), 34, 140
Cayton, Horace, 70
Cherry, James E., 86
Chesnutt, Charles, 57
Christian, Barbara, 133, 135
Clark, Colia Lafayette, 60, 67
Clark, Harold, 86
Cocteau, Jean, 53
Cohen, Hettie, 112
Cooper, Anna Julia, 115, 166
Cooper, Kevin, 67
Cortez, Jayne, 78
Cruse, Harold, 123

Darwish, Mahmoud, 102–3
Davis, Angela, 115–16
Davis, Charles T., 123
Davis, Ossie, 115, 140
Davis, Thadious M., 123, 146
de Certeau, Michel, 127
Dee, Ruby, 115
Dent, Tom, 15, 86, 108–9, 118, 140

Dickinson, Emily, 96, 114, 185
Douglass, Frederick, 96, 186, 204
Dove, Rita, 70, 131
Du Bois, W. E. B., 12, 20, 55, 74, 83, 98, 118, 132–33, 144, 166, 204
Dumas, Henry, 93, 138
Dunbar, Paul Laurence, 57, 93–94, 184

Eliot, T. S., 95, 98, 118, 184–85, 198
Ellison, Ralph, 12–13, 55, 111, 114, 118, 145, 204
Emerson, Ralph Waldo, 95
Ernest, John, 146, 148
Ervin, Hazel Arnett, 145

Fabre, Michel, 84, 123, 128
Fanon, Franz, 63, 113
Faulkner, William, 83, 118, 127, 144, 147, 194
Fauset, Jesse, 115
Ferber, Edna, 115
Ferris, William, 60
Ford, Richard, 40, 148
Forrest, Leon, 5–6
Foucault, Michel, 12, 127
Foulcher, Keith, 104, 125
Fowler, Carolyn, 11, 135
Freud, Sigmund, 122
Fuller, Hoyt, 107

Gabbin, Joanne V., 135
Garvey, Marcus, 115, 169
Gates, Henry Louis, Jr., 77, 79–80, 146
Gay, Roxane, 151
Giovanni, Nikki, 116
Gomez, Michael, 80
Graham, Maryemma, ix, xvii, xix, 9, 61, 76–77, 80, 83, 123, 129, 135
Green, Paul, 60
Green, Tara, 60
Grisham, John, 102, 106

Hakutani, Yoshinobu, 128
Hamer, Fannie Lou, 134
Hansberry, Lorraine, 115
Hardison, Ayesha K., 125
Harper, Frances Ellen Watkins, 114–15
Harper, Michael, 108, 133
Harrington, Ollie, 112
Hawthorne, Nathaniel, 96, 102, 144
Hayden, Robert, 108, 184
Hemingway, Ernest, 102, 112
Henderson, Stephen E., 143, 145, 165, 196
hooks, bell, 149
Howells, William Dean, 94
Hughes, Langston, 57, 61, 129, 139, 145–46, 172, 184
Hunter, Clarence, 82
Hurston, Zora Neale, 57–58, 67, 90, 115

Jackson, Candice Love, 80
Jackson, Lawrence P., 145, 151
Jacobs, Harriet, 144
James, C. L. R., 105
James, Henry, 98
Jarrett, Gene Andrew, 146, 148
Jay-Z, 98
Jeffers, Honorée Fanonne, 88
Jeffers, Lance, 9, 13, 86–87, 185, 196
Johnson, James Weldon, 93, 184
Johnson, Mat, 149
Jones, Gayl, 145
Jordan, June, 83
Jordan, Lawrence, 92
Joyce, James, 119, 187–88
Joyce, Joyce Ann, 61

Kaepernick, Colin, 161
Kent, George, 123, 132, 145
Killens, John Oliver, 87, 92, 102, 107, 147, 205
King, Martin Luther, Jr., xviii, 136
King, Stephen, 102

Kingston, Maxine Hong, 19
Kinnamon, Keneth, 86, 129
Kwansaba, 189, 206–7, 208

Landow, George P., 123
Landrieu, Mitch, 25
Lavender, Bill, 41
Lazer, Hank, 110, 145
Lee, Spike, 110, 141
Lefebvre, Henri, 127
Lincoln, Abraham, 132
Louis, Joe, 54, 166
Luo, Lianggong, 203

Mailer, Norman, 54–55
Malcolm X, 136
Marsalis, Ellis, 171
Martin, Reginald, ix, 61, 86, 129
Maxwell, William J., 114
McDowell, Deborah, 60, 135
McInnis, C. Leigh, 75, 191, 194
McKay, Nellie, 77, 79, 135
McLaughlin, Andrée Nicola, 135, 147
McMillon, Kim, 160
Melville, Herman, 139, 144
Michener, James, 97
Miller, Eugene E., 119
Miller, James A., 129
Miller, May, 115
Miller, Ron Baxter, 146
Mitchell, Angelyn, 134, 145
Moody, Anne, 20
Morial, Marc, 44
Morrison, Toni, 5, 12, 77, 80, 97, 129, 133, 139, 148
Mullen, Harryette, 145, 149, 186

Nagin, Ray, 21, 25
Napier, Winston, 145
Neal, Larry, 138, 172
New Orleans, xi, xiii, 21, 26, 29–36, 38, 41–50, 66, 90, 93, 185, 195

Nie, Zhenzhao, 205
Nielsen, Aldon, 108
Nietzsche, Friedrich, 126
Nkrumah, Kwame, 62, 69, 105, 113
Norris, Keenan, 149, 205

Oates, Joyce Carol, 147–48
Obama, Barack, 78, 149–50, 153–54, 156, 161
Osbey, Brenda Marie, 88, 135, 148

Padmore, George, 63, 105
Painter, Nell Irvin, 9
Pardlo, Gregory, 151
Parsons, Joe, 41
Perry, Melissa Harris, 149
Perry, Tyler, 110, 141
Petry, Ann, 115, 147
Plumpp, Sterling D., 15, 86, 194, 205
Polite, Allen, 112
Pound, Ezra, 112
Powell, Colin, 117
Powell, Kevin, 87

Rambsy, Howard, 61, 87, 146
Rampersad, Arnold, 55, 145
Rawls, John, 126
Redmond, Eugene, 86, 142–43, 207
Reed, Ishmael, 14–15, 86–87, 109, 135, 139–40, 148, 191
Roberts, Brian Russell, 104, 125
Rodgers, Carolyn, 143, 145, 177, 183
Rosenblatt, Louise M., 143
Rowell, Charles, 109, 147
Rowley, Hazel, 113
Rukeyser, Muriel, 107
Ruoff, A. LaVonne Brown, xvii, 10

Said, Edward, 133
Salaam, Kalamu ya, 189, 191
Sanchez, Sonia, 61, 116, 140–41, 148
Sandburg, Carl, 118, 184

Sartre, Jean-Paul, 87
Shakespeare, William, 140, 184
Shange, Ntozake, 139, 141
Shaq, 98
Smith, Anna Deavere, 139, 141
Smith, Clint, 151
Smith, Virginia Whatley, 126
Spender, Stephen, 114
Spiller, Robert, 96
Stein, Gertrude, 112
Stepto, Robert, 146
Stowe, Harriet Beecher, 132, 144

Tan, Amy, 148
Tate, Claudia, 134–35
Taulbert, Clifton, 20
Thomas, Lorenzo, 108–9
Thompson, Julius, 15, 57, 60, 86
Till, Emmett, 52, 73, 193, 195
Touré, Askia Muhammad (Rolland Snellings), 14, 109
Trethewey, Natasha, 78, 88, 194
Trump, Donald, 150–51, 153–54
Turner, Darwin T., 90, 137

Vendler, Helen, 131

Walker, Alice, 134, 144–45
Walker, Margaret, 135–37, 139, 185
Ward, Jerry W., Jr.: on abrasion, 108, 115, 163, 183; on affinity, 52, 65, 84–85, 104, 119–20, 190; on African American studies, 90–91, 204; on alienation, 121; on authenticity, 181–82; on autobiography, 9, 15, 17, 19–20, 38, 85, 87, 112, 120–21; on Black aesthetic, 11–12, 14–15, 87, 108, 136, 143, 160, 167, 172, 177, 183; on Black Catholics, 5–6; on Black community, 59, 107, 165; on Black preaching, 119; *Black Southern Voices*, 92, 102; on blues music, 11, 14, 45, 73–74, 94, 122, 138, 185–86, 192, 194, 208; *The Cambridge History of African American Literature*, 66, 76–81; on Catholicism, 3, 5, 62, 105, 126; *The China Lectures*, 127, 203, 205, 207; on class, 31, 44, 46, 53, 57, 73, 84, 96, 107, 121, 134–35, 138, 149, 162–65, 194–95; on common sense, 129, 135; on confluences in literature, 132; on criticism, 10–13, 55, 79–81, 125–26, 132–35, 143–51, 177–78, 206; on culture, 11–15, 24, 44–45, 48, 79–80, 94–98, 122, 127–29, 140, 149–50, 189–92, 201–3, 205–6; on dialect, 57, 94–95, 164, 182; on digital humanities, 89; on dignity, 4, 175, 194; on Dillard University, 29–39, 42–43, 90, 159–60; on diversity, 67, 86, 110; on drama, 108, 139–44; on education, 28, 43–44, 47, 96–101, 170–71, 176; on exile, 48, 62, 66, 71, 111–12, 194–95; on expatriation, 111–12; on family, 3–5, 27, 52, 74–75, 104–6, 148, 166, 194–95; on film, 9, 52–53, 141, 164; on gender, 11, 45, 96, 134–35, 154–55, 157; on honesty, 44–45, 88; on horror, 121, 142, 207; on hunger, 17, 83, 120–21; on Hurricane Katrina, 21–26, 29–50; on identity, 43, 103, 106, 121, 150, 164, 194, 208; on integration, 4–5, 28, 166; on introduction to *Black Boy*, 20; on jazz, xiv, 24, 45, 74, 87, 179–82, 185–86, 189, 192, 208; *The Katrina Papers*, 22, 26, 41, 66, 87, 99, 110–11; on limits, 19, 52, 121, 136; on literary canons, 76–79, 89, 101–2, 132, 139, 204; on literary history, 56, 77–78, 80, 87–89, 92, 95–96, 116, 124, 140; on literature, 7–13, 56, 77–81, 89, 95, 97, 102, 114–15, 124, 132–51, 156, 169, 204–6, 208; on Marxism, 57, 84, 96, 113, 123; on minorities, 5–6, 46, 131–32; on minstrelsy, 46, 124, 141;

mission of, 29, 68, 101, 143, 146; on Moss Point, 6, 27, 51, 190, 195; on New Orleans, 21–26, 29–30, 33, 42–49, 66, 95, 185, 195; on "outsideness," 121; on pan-Africanism, 62, 69, 105, 113; on poverty, 84, 106, 135, 141, 143, 148, 194; on race, 6, 20, 45, 112, 122, 124, 133–35, 142, 148–49, 154–55, 165, 192–93; on reading, 7, 17, 20, 34, 51, 80–81, 84–85, 104, 132, 137–38, 177, 188; *The Richard Wright Encyclopedia*, 61, 66, 86, 123; on roots, 4, 138; on sensitivity, 37; on "situatedness," 11; on society, 72, 154, 191–92; on surrealism, 53, 122; on the African American male, xi, 52, 192; on the African American Research Network (AARN), 204–5; on the civil rights movement, 27–28, 82, 115, 135–38, 168, 185; on the Richard Wright Circle, 16, 86, 129; on the *Richard Wright Newsletter*, 9, 123, 129; on the South, 54, 58, 60, 71, 75, 92, 95, 105–6, 120–21, 127, 134, 193–94; on Tougaloo College, 27, 29–30, 51, 65–66, 82, 90, 99, 118, 123, 190, 195; *Trouble the Water*, 15, 92, 101–2; on truth, 121, 160, 193; on values, 3, 79; on womanism, 134–35; on women writers, 96, 107, 115–16; on young people, 5, 25, 44, 47, 165–67

Ward, Theodore, 123
Warhol, Andy, 109
Warren, Kenneth, 132, 147
Watkins, Hollis, 9, 15
Webb, Constance, 122
Wells, Ida B., 115, 134
Welty, Eudora, 68, 73, 147
Wheatley, Phillis, 18, 94, 114–16, 144
White, Charles, 107
Whitman, Walt, 83, 144, 185
Wideman, John Edgar, 61, 139, 205
Williams, Sherley Anne, 135, 139
Wilson, August, 139, 141, 205
Winfrey, Oprah, 110
Wittgenstein, Ludwig, 148
Wright, Ellen, 19
Wright, Julia, 60–61, 67, 196
Wright, Richard, 9, 15, 16–20, 37–38, 49, 51–64, 65–75, 83–86, 90, 103–5, 110–14, 118–30, 138, 142, 190, 194, 205

Young, Andy, 109

Zheng, Jianqing, 75, 201

About the Editor

Photo courtesy of the author

John Zheng is professor of English at Mississippi Valley State University, author of *A Way of Looking*, which won the Gerald Cable Book Award, and editor of scholarly books including *African American Haiku: Cultural Visions, The Other World of Richard Wright: Perspectives on His Haiku*, and *Conversations with Dana Gioia* (University Press of Mississippi).

www.ingramcontent.com/pod-product-compliance
Lightning Source LLC
Chambersburg PA
CBHW022011220426
43663CB00007B/1043